Truman

Thank you for taking your grandparents on a tour of Washington, D.C. including getting tours. Keep standing for the Constitution. God bless you.

Sharron Angle
9-29-11

RIGHT ANGLE

One Woman's Journey to Reclaim the Constitution

Sharron Angle

authorHOUSE®

AuthorHouse™
1663 Liberty Drive
Bloomington, IN 47403
www.authorhouse.com
Phone: 1-800-839-8640

First published by AuthorHouse 5/18/2011

ISBN: 978-1-4567-5425-9 (sc)
ISBN: 978-1-4567-5424-2 (hc)
ISBN: 978-1-4567-5428-0 (e)

Library of Congress Control Number: 2011904475

Printed in the United States of America

Front cover photo by Victor "Snakemann" Wolder, © Sharron Angle.

Any people depicted in stock imagery provided by Thinkstock are models,
and such images are being used for illustrative purposes only.
Certain stock imagery © Thinkstock.

This book is printed on acid-free paper.

The Federalist Papers signed "PUBLIUS" consist of eighty-five essays generally attributed to Alexander Hamilton, James Madison, and John Jay. The Federalist Papers are the reference for understanding the U.S. Constitution and the Founders' intent. Today a new generation of federalists responds to a movement's hunger for constitutional comprehension from articles, books, talk radio, websites, and the blogosphere. They are in turns educators and protectors of the grail of freedom from the elite ruling class that forces socialism into American governance. Two representatives of the "new federalists" have honored me with introductions to this book.

Introduction by Mark Levin

I wrote *Liberty and Tyranny,* a bugle call warning to mainstream America that the conservatism of Ronald Reagan and Barry Goldwater requires emergency resuscitation. Sharron Angle answered that call by courageously stepping in front of Statist Obama's henchman Harry Reid's train bound for the soft-core socialism that is destroying Western Europe. She is the epitome of the new conservative movement that swept this land in the 2010 election.

Sharron Angle's new book *Right Angle* is an autobiographical look at the values that shaped the baby boomer generation stepping into leadership. Some boomers refused to leave the 1960's spoiled child "if it feels good, do it" philosophy becoming the elite of academia, Hollywood, and politics and the recipients of big government entitlements. They served up large doses of globalism, force-feeding the rest of us unrestrained debt and out of control big government. Sharron Angle represents the majority who matured, repented of their misspent youth, went to work living the American Dream, and learned from history. With the zeal of the Founding Fathers, they are determined to take this country back to constitutional principles or die trying.

Right Angle introduces the real Sharron Angle's opinions on the issues, confronting the Left's hatchet job under Harry Reid's ruthless direction using their press clones, A.C.O.R.N. machinery, and perversion of the truth. It covers the 2010 campaign against the Senate Majority Leader, and much more. It is a thoughtful, factual discussion of today's issues (economic failure, green energy, *Obamacare*, political seduction, guns, and religion) based on the underpinnings of conservatism from the Founders to Reagan. She candidly shares her childhood, family, and faith. Sharron Angle, like other conservative women, offers a bold fresh voice, fearless and relentless. As Sharron Angle steps onto the stage of the twenty-first century, her book becomes a battle cry of a movement that inspired a nation in TEA party protests and struck like a knife into the very heart of the Statists.

I endorsed Sharron Angle for U.S. Senate in 2010, for U.S. Congress in 2012, and I endorse her book.

Mark R. Levin

(Mark Levin is a nationally syndicated talk radio host and president of Landmark Legal Foundation. Levin is author of bestselling books, has worked as an attorney in the private sector and as a top adviser and administrator to several members of President Reagan's cabinet.)

Introduction by Dr. Lee D. Cary

Sharron Angle wrote this book with her own hand; she did not use a ghostwriter. It received only the attention of a light editing, something that any responsible writer would do and most of us would welcome for our autobiography. Consequently, through the words that follow you will hear Sharron Angle's true and genuine voice. Hers is a voice that you will like and respect. It speaks a citizen's language, not politico-speak; a voice of which Nevada can be proud.

By the time you have finished reading, you will perceive Sharron as an authentic candidate who would have represented Nevada well, had she been elected to U.S. Senate in 2010. She is an experienced legislator, having served four terms in the Nevada Assembly. There she accumulated a record for fidelity to conservative principles and personal integrity that is beyond reproach. In an era where skepticism abounds about the honesty and character of many of our elected politicians, Sharron Angle is a breath of fresh air. In a national field crowded with politicians who do not instill confidence in the American voter, she does. She is the real deal.

In a November 10, 2009, article in the *Las Vegas Review-Journal,* John L. Smith wrote, "There's a way Republicans can prove they really want a conservative revolution. They can support U.S. Senate candidate and certified conservative true-believer Sharron Angle." Smith added, "One conversation with Angle, the four-term state assemblywoman who has served on education, election, ethics, health and judiciary committees, is enough to convince you she's the real deal and isn't just parroting the latest from the Rightwing radio dial."[1] Although this may come across as a left-handed compliment by some conservatives, given the reference to "Rightwing radio," we hear Mr. Smith's words as unbiased certification of Sharron Angle's credibility. With Sharron Angle, what you see is what you get.

She is a proven, tireless campaigner. She is thoroughly educated and informed on the issues that matter most to the citizens of Nevada, regardless of their political alignment. Sharron is a woman of integrity and character.

Like many of us fortunate enough to have them, her concern for the future of America centers most heavily on her children and grandchildren. Also like many of us, her roots are traceable to hard-working, loving parents who struggled to sustain a small business and support a family.

In the narrative of her personal story that follows, you will get much more than a cursory glimpse into just who Sharron Angle is. When you do, you will conclude that she is the kind of person that Nevada would have been proud to call its newest United States Senator.

Dr. Lee D. Cary
(Writer for the *American Thinker* website)

PEOPLE ARE PRAISING *RIGHT ANGLE*

"The press calls Sharron Angle the TEA Party Darling, but I know her as a strong representative for an American Main Street Movement. Within the pages of *Right Angle* is an invitation to all Americans to join our movement to take our country back to constitutional principles. She is a tireless defender of the Constitution and we need more true constitutional conservatives like her. I give *Right Angle* loud applause for liberty." *Amy Kremer—Chairman Tea Party Express*

"Sharron Angle and I have worked side-by-side as Nevada State Legislators through several sessions voting against tax and spend policies, increased government regulation, and unconstitutional laws. Sharron stands strong with her unquestionable honesty and integrity and *Right Angle* tells the inside story of a true stateswoman." *Don Gustavson—Nevada State Senator*

"As a social conservative I am grateful to Sharron Angle for speaking out on the issues. *Right Angle* tells Sharron's personal story about how her values were formed. When I ran against Harry Reid in 2004, the movement was just beginning and coalitions of conservatives were forming. Sharron is a tried and true conservative patriot. It is an honor to work with Sharron on behalf of families, the unborn and marriage." *Richard Ziser—Director, Nevada Concerned Citizens Former Chairman, Coalition for the Protection of Marriage, Republican Nominee for U.S. Senate 2004*

"Sharron Angle's fighting spirit and simple, straight-forward eloquence in a plain language shines through in *Right Angle* as she shares her courageous no-holds-barred battle for the truth and the welfare of the American people. Sharron Angle recognizes and appreciates the value of the friendship between the United States and Israel. She is committed to the First Amendment right to religious freedom and the Judeo-Christian ethics that have made this nation great." *Rabbi Nachum Shifren*

"Like most Americans, my friend Sharron Angle is a descendant of immigrants and her daughter-in-law is a Latina immigrant. Within the pages of *Right Angle* I found the personal story of Sharron's quest for the American Dream; Sharron Angle articulates that same simple message of freedom we all cherish." *Didi Lima—President Integra Multilingual International Business Services*

"Sharron Angle is an accidental politician. *Right Angle* is the story of her journey from government intrusion into her family, to home school freedom fighter, private school teacher, public school board member, state legislator, and a nationally recognized conservative voice. Sharron and I worked with other Nevada home school parents to pass one of the most freeing home school laws in America. She is passionate about preserving our nation's constitutional principles for our children and grandchildren." *Barbara K. Dragon—Co-author "The Nevada Home School Freedom Bill" in 2007. Barbara currently serves as an Officer for Nevada Homeschool Network*

"Veterans have sacrificed (and will continue to sacrifice) for liberty. Sharron Angle recognizes, appreciates, and shares this commitment. Within the pages of *Right Angle*, she tells about her father, a veteran of World War II and Korea. As a physician, I am grateful for the stand she has taken against the socialization of medicine in this country. I found an understandable treatment of the pathologies and the cures for America. In *Right Angle*, we see the soul of Sharron Angle a true philosophical conservative." *Dr. Scott Magill—Founder/Executive Director, Veterans in Defense of Liberty; SAEPE EXPERTUS, SEMPER FIDELIS, FRATRES AETERNI "Often Tested, Always Faithful, Brothers Forever"*

Foreword

Today's federal government is in crisis. Corruption is rampant. Congress represents special interests instead of the wishes of the people that elected them. At both the state and federal level, there is ignorance, disregard and, even more threatening, a desire to rewrite the Constitution and Bill of Rights. Can America recover from the downward spiral of debt, immorality and "good-old-boy" power-for-paybacks corruption?

Drastic measures must be taken to stop these politicians in their tracks. Does this mean a revolution is in order? No. I am simply saying the American people can replace corrupt, weak, and self-interested politicians by raising the standard to that which proclaimed liberty in 1776. The "Silent Majority" can be silent no longer. We do not have the option or the luxury to sit on the sidelines. Transition means a grassroots movement with grassroots leadership.

I became involved in politics nearly fifteen years ago, as an outsider to the "Old Boys Club" political machinery in Nevada and shocked the political establishment with my victories. These elections earned me the reputation as the best grassroots campaigner in the state. Even my political detractors, like Senate Majority Leader Harry Reid, have said, "She's quite a campaigner."[2] I am prepared to help lead a movement of citizens dedicated to the principles of the Constitution. Are you ready to go with me all the way and take our country back to those constitutional principles?

I write this book with the intent that my answers to the "Why" questions be easily understood by all. Herein, I will state political beliefs and values formed by my life experiences. I will also point out the spread between the lessons we learned in civics class and the current world of real politics. I believe that the truth will set us free and keep us free. It is my aim to offer facts with grace, mete out truth with mercy, and inspire you, the reader, to help me reclaim our constitutionally guaranteed freedoms.

"Begin at the beginning," Garry wrote to me. "How did you get started in politics? At the Legislature, what did you expect and what did you find? What was the high point of your time there? What have you done since your time in the Legislature? What brought you to the decision to challenge Harry Reid? How are you different from other challengers?"

Another friend, David, responded to my first attempts, "Okay, you said I could be a nasty English teacher. The content is fine, but the writing style is not narrative. The most grievous flaw is you have not yet personalized the material."

I realize that to be truly personal, I cannot protect myself. I must write from my heart. I must give a full and accurate account of my values, beliefs, and experiences to expose my opponents' spin when they try to use my words and actions out of context against me. U.S. Senator Chuck Schumer (D-NY) revealed (to top Democrats in what he thought was a private conversation) that the simple but effective Democrat campaign strategy against Tea Party GOP is to use the word "extreme."[3] That certainly has a familiar ring.

William said, "Have courage, Sharron. If you do not write the book, people do not know who you really are. They need to see you."

Garry also advised, "Go big or go home. Either tell the truth without flinching, or do not write the book at all. Do not write another fluffy political piece. Expose the machinery behind the political doors from which the consequences often fall on the average person like a bomb or curse."

I asked David and my friends to hold me accountable in the writing of this book and be brutally honest. To my benefit, and I hope yours, they have done what I have asked.

I know this Proverb to be true, "A friend means well, even when he hurts you. But when an enemy puts his arm around your shoulder—watch out!"[4] Politics is full of those arms around your shoulder—the kisses on the cheek.

I asked myself, *Is my skin thick enough? Do I have the courage to write the good, the bad and the ugly of politics?*

In this book, I examine the issues, give personal insights, quote the heroes of the conservative movement, and offer solutions with plans for implementation.

Acknowledgements

Special appreciation must go to Lee Cary, David Elliott, Jeanette Ward, Garry Duff, Rosemary DiGrazia, Greg Hudson, Alan Hall, Jeanette Hanscome, Linda Massey, and my faithful "Lick & Stick" gang of volunteers—my heartfelt gratitude to all. I could not even dream of this challenge without the support of the "constituent" I admire most and the love of my life, my husband Ted Angle.

CONTENTS

Chapter One

ABOVE THE FOLD

I was not casting votes in the Legislature with my eye on the next election. I was voting for Will, for his generation, for my children and grandchildren, and for all those who cherish our American Dream.

IT WAS THE FIFTY-FIRST day of the 2005 Nevada Legislative session, and I felt miserable. I sat at my desk trying to focus on the list of bills for the morning's floor vote, but I could not get my mind off the Legislature's unconstitutional vote on property taxes the previous night. My arguments had failed to prevail in the face of clamorous opposition.

Just then, Will, my legislative intern, burst into the office and exclaimed, "You did it! You did it! You're my hero! You're above the fold!"

Will was nineteen years old and just beginning to grow into his genius. With youthful enthusiasm, he jumped up and down, waving a copy of the *Nevada Appeal*, slapping the headline. Will was a political science major at the University of Nevada, Reno, and an intern in my legislative office. He was one of three students who volunteered to do work to enrich his studies. Without knowing it, he displayed one of the traditional virtues of an effective aide: help keep your boss's name on the front page "above the fold" of the newspaper in order to build name recognition to enhance a politician's career.

I smiled, losing my self-pity to his exuberance. He fluffed the paper and began to read aloud, "Property tax plan goes to the Senate on a 41 to 1 vote," then he skipped to the body of the article.

"AB 489 was approved 41 to 1 by the Assembly Tuesday evening. Only Sharron Angle, R-Reno, voted 'no.' She announced that instead, she will push for a California-style Proposition-13 amendment slashing property taxes…"

He continued reading on full-auto, eagerly turning pages. Then he thrust the front page toward me. "This is what every politician wants! Your picture and name on the front page, *above the fold!*"

I took the paper and sighed, "It is not all good news, Will. Here's the spin." I pointed out the caption below the colored legislative picture of me. It read:

"Assemblywoman Sharron Angle was the sole hold-out vote on the tax plan."

"So?" he challenged. "That's why *The Club for Growth* called you. This is why the people want *you* to be their Congresswoman," he pressed on. "Do you think you voted wrong?" His implied doubt of my convictions stung.

"No," I said, "the vote was correct. I just wish it was easier to stand alone and take the heat knowing that it may give both Democrats and Republicans the ammunition to characterize me as just a *no-voter.*"

At that time in the Nevada Legislature, conservatism seemed alive only in my office and in the hearts of the voting public. I felt I had a target on my back by being a practicing Christian. Being both conservative and Christian made me a favorite whipping girl for my liberal opponents in the Legislature and in the media.

Will's joy drowned out my plaintive explanation, and without missing a beat, he said, "I'm going to frame this." The next day he gave me the framed article. On it, he had written "Always above the fold!" Vintage Will.

Since my priorities never included being above the fold, I knew then that I did not fit the typical "politician" profile. I was not casting votes in the Legislature with my eye on the next election. I was voting my conscience. I was voting for Will, for his generation, for my children and grandchildren, and for all those who cherish our American Dream.

I was also voting out of humble gratitude for my father who holds the Purple Heart for injuries sustained in WW II. Along with millions of others in the military, my Dad selflessly defended this nation so that we might enjoy our liberties. I voted out of a heartfelt responsibility that my mother taught me to do what is right. As a politician, I refused to vote for political expediency. Even now, I know that I must vote out of deep conviction and for the public good, not personal gain. Instead of working to enhance my career, I must strive to preserve and protect the country I love.

Long-Term Incumbency: Not What the Founders Intended

The longer I serve, the more I see a nation in trouble because professional career politicians populate the legislative branches of state and national governments. This was never the intent of our Founding Fathers. The interests of career politicians seldom align with the interests of the average citizen. Typically, to sustain a career in politics with job security, the career politician must first bow and submit to party leadership in order to collect funds, favors from individuals, and interests that get him or her re-elected. Sadly for the nation, goal one is job security for too many politicians. The first priority of the career politician is to protect his "seat," his incumbency.

The original notion of engaging political service for a few years and sharing the burden of representation on behalf of one's community has long been widely abandoned. Few elected officials intend to serve for a time and then return to their hometowns and non-government jobs. The desire for full-time, lifetime, government employment with the power, influence, and perks associated with holding office too often replaces the call to civic duty.

Additionally, many professional politicians now desire to change our culture and governance along the Leftist Progressive lines that have long been prevalent in our educational institutions. Since the 1960s, schools have widely taught that government is too complex for amateurs, that we should trust the self-appointed "professionals," many of whom adopted the faddish liberalism that permeated Ivy League schools.

Another driving force is incumbency. Protecting incumbency requires constant fund-raising, complicated political alliances, slick image-makers, and spin doctors. None of this is fundamentally about representing the genuine interests of the folks back home. Inevitably, payback to a coalition of special interests requires selling out the interests of citizens in favor of lobbyists and power brokers.

Disgracefully, politicians at the federal level have rigged a self-serving system of enormous rewards and benefits involving travel (both foreign and domestic), gold-plated health care coverage, generous salaries and allowances for themselves, for their staff, and sometimes even for their family members. They enjoy pensions representing full salaries for life after their service, plus power and prestige that rival royalty. It all adds up to a package of privileged benefits that motivates incumbents to hold on to their careers at any cost. They even have the gall to propose that taxpayers should finance elections by implementing rules that always favor the incumbent.

The acrimony, even hatred, felt by citizens against today's legislative system comes from the entrenched lust of *both* major political parties, Democrats and Republicans, to protect their power at any cost. It is a desired end that justifies their means.

A legislature, refreshed at reasonable intervals with people who have the interests of the voters uppermost in their minds, would have no need to resort to the vitriolic language used to cling to their seats that we witness today in the political arena. Self-service has widely prevailed over national service. That puts our nation in peril.

The siren call to re-elect incumbents because they will use their seniority to "bring home the bacon" is a deception that keeps this dysfunctional system in place. In practice, the professional politician pays little heed to the things that matter most to the hard-working taxpayer. Ask yourself this: Would stopping illegal immigration, balancing budgets, electing good judges, and minimizing bureaucratic hurdles to businesses be difficult tasks for a truly civic-minded citizen legislature rather than career politicians? No, it would not.

Our system of government will only function properly again when the voters understand the simple concept that career politicians, those hungry to appear "above the fold," are a clear and present danger to our Republic, to our State, and to our freedoms.

I am jumping into the deep water of politics with the courage of my convictions and my faith in Nevada's citizens to carry me.

Why I Decided to Run for U.S. Senate against Harry Reid

Harry Reid was born in Searchlight, Nevada, but educated in Las Vegas and Utah. Harry Reid has enjoyed a lifelong political career, steadily moving up in Democrat politics from an attorney to state legislator to Lieutenant Governor to Gaming Commission to U.S. Congress to the U.S. Senate, where he has been entrenched since 1986. After South Dakota voters ousted Tom Daschle, Harry Reid became Minority Leader and then Majority Leader of the United States Senate. Reid is an orator who convinces with words and ideas, but he has a reputation for making deals and holding the Democrat Party's caucus together to pass or block legislation.

By 2010, and after numerous outrageous deals to pass the Obama agenda, people across the country rejected these policies. Under the new regime of Reid, Pelosi, and Obama, Nevada led the nation in unemployment and mortgage foreclosures. Nevada citizens felt a national mandate to send U.S. Senate Majority Leader Harry Reid back home to Searchlight. (I do not mean to besmirch Searchlight, but many know the truth that Harry really lives in a posh Ritz Carlton condominium in Washington, D.C.). This modest volume answers, in my own words, "why" I decided to run against Harry Reid.

In our civics class we learned, or should have learned, the lessons of the Founding documents that pertain to the rules of representative government. As we observe real political life today, few seem to be following the rules. The disconnect between principles and reality has caused a deep schism of cynicism in many Americans. So great is the disgust and frustration with what can only be termed *corruption*, that fifty percent, or less, of those eligible to vote even register: only fifty percent or less of those registered even cast a vote. I interpret the large number of absent ballots as a vote of no confidence in the way our representative government functions today.

I believe that America's Founders meant to vest the greatest range of authority within the respective states. It is within the individual states where the people's representatives live closest to those affected by their actions. I invite you to get involved. Register to vote. Attend a precinct meeting. Be a precinct captain. Get active in your local party organization. Become a candidate for an office of public trust, at some level.

The cure for the rotted core of incumbency is for citizens—we the people—to the take back the reins of government. The 2010 election was a good start. Although Nevada was unable to break the yoke of Harry Reid, we kept him busy. He was unable to spend his millions meddling in other races across the nation. We matched him dollar for dollar. We exposed the voter pressure and the voting anomalies. The people spoke in one loud voice for the Constitution, and Congress heard. On opening day, Republican Congressmen stood to read that wonderful founding document that begins "We the people…"

"I received the *Ronald Reagan Freedom Medallion* in 2004 from the Claremont Institute for my fight to preserve the Nevada Constitution."

Chapter Two

REAGAN REMAINS RELEVANT

The Reagan revolution was one of common sense. It revived the constitutional principles of limited government. I embrace those principles of limited government, lower taxation and more freedom.

RONALD REAGAN CAME to prominence the year my son Vince was born. I was twenty-six years old. I registered as a Republican at twenty-one, the earliest age to vote at that time. My parents and grandparents were Republicans. It was the natural thing for me to do, even though Nevada was mostly Democrat. I voted for Nixon in 1972 on the day my daughter Joye was born. My parents said he was the best choice. I voted for Ford in 1976, and later wondered if I should have voted for Carter because, like me, he was a Southern Baptist. I was not politically tuned-in, but I did take my duty to vote seriously.

When my son failed kindergarten, I was denied the right to home school him, even though I had a Bachelor's degree and had been teaching for years. I fought back, as every mother does when her child is threatened. I appealed to my Legislature to change the home school law. For me, this was a turning point. Since that first appeal, I have been determined to bring about change in the law, for every parent and family that feel threatened by their government.

They Just Could Not Hold Their Noses

I was not following Reagan closely when he spoke at the Conservative Political Action Conference (CPAC) in March 1975. Not until 2008, did I appreciate the prophetic value of his words. The opening of his 1975 speech entitled *Let Them Go Their Way* could have referred to the 2010 election and the first two years of the Obama Administration.

Since our last meeting, we have been through a disastrous election. It is easy for us to be discouraged, as pundits hail that election as a repudiation of our philosophy and even as a mandate of some kind or other. But the significance of the election was not registered by those who voted, but by those who stayed home. If there was anything like a mandate, it will be found among almost two-thirds of the citizens who refused to participate.[5]

In December 2008, I examined the voting results in Nevada. Obama defeated McCain by 120,000 votes. I looked at the election abstracts for Reno and the rural counties. I compared the results to the Bush-Kerry race in 2004. I found that about 24,000 people who voted for Bush in 2004 left their presidential ballot blank in 2008. (I confirmed anecdotal evidence of this "off voting.") People, especially those who had voted for Congressman Ron Paul and yellow dog conservatives, would rather vote for a yellow dog than a liberal, or for a so-called moderate Republican or Democrat. Some of these voters told me they just could not hold their nose and vote for McCain, not even with Sarah Palin on the G.O.P. ticket. They left the presidential category blank. Doing anything other would have meant abandoning their principles and political philosophy.

Running Right, Voting Left

Reagan continues in his March 1975 speech:

Bitter as it is to accept the results of the November election, we should have reason for some optimism. For many years now, we have preached "the gospel," in opposition to the philosophy of so-called liberalism, which was, in truth, a call to collectivism.

Now, it is possible we have been persuasive to a greater degree than we had ever realized. Few, if any, Democratic Party candidates in the last election ran as liberals. Listening to them I had the eerie feeling we were hearing reruns of Goldwater speeches. I even thought I heard a few of my own.[6]

When I read this paragraph, I remembered that Obama invoked

Reagan's name to appear more moderate during an interview with the *Reno Gazette Journal* in 2008. He was in Reagan country. Obama had the *right spin* using Reagan's name along with such words as *clarity, optimism, and entrepreneurship.*[7] After a first term of historically socialist liberalism, Obama once again courted conservatives with Reagan values rhetoric.

It is clear now that the disingenuous compliment to Reagan helped with Obama's election. For the loony Left, any means is justified by their end. On October 14, 2010, Harry Reid used the same tactics in the debate with me, citing conservative Anton Scalia as his favorite judge, and patting his breast pocket where he claimed to have a copy of the Constitution. After voting to seat Justices Elena Kagan and Sonia Sotomayor to the U.S. Supreme Court, his claim was laughable to the educated; as it was clearly an attempt to score points with those naïve enough to believe that Reid embraced their values.

Reagan knew how the Left plays this game, and he warned us. Unfortunately, we forgot his words.

> But let's not be so naive as to think we are witnessing a mass conversion to the principles of conservatism. Once sworn into office, the victors reverted to type. In their view, apparently, the ends justified the means.
>
> The "Young Turks" had campaigned against "evil politicians." They turned against committee chairmen of their own party, displaying a taste and talent as cutthroat power politicians quite in contrast to their campaign rhetoric and idealism. Still, we must not forget that they molded their campaigning to fit what even they recognized was the mood of the majority. And we must see to it that the people are reminded of this as they now pursue their ideological goals—and pursue them they will.[8]

Think back to the media attacks on Hillary Clinton during the 2008 primary debates. Concerning health care, Hillary Clinton's goal was universal healthcare coverage for everyone. The Obama team countered in an attack ad in *The Daily Iowan* on December 21, 2007, charging Hillary Clinton with forcing uninsured people to buy insurance.[9] The Democrat voters turned against the Clintons as Obama molded his campaign rhetoric to fit the mood of the majority, especially younger voters. After the election in 2009, Obama (along with his henchmen, Reid and Pelosi) persuaded, coerced, made shady deals, and ultimately passed *Obamacare*. All the while this was completely counter to the transparent and "popular" campaign attacks he made against Hillary Clinton and her universal health care… only months prior!

Reagan Was a TEA Partier

Reagan gives a clear picture of a movement today that the press calls the TEA Party.

> I know you are aware of the national polls which show that a greater (and increasing) number of Americans—Republicans, Democrats and independents—classify themselves as "conservatives" than ever before. And a poll of rank-and-file union members reveals dissatisfaction with the amount of power their own leaders have assumed, and a resentment of their use of that power for partisan politics.
>
> In another recent survey, of 35,000 college and university students polled, three-fourths blame American business and industry for all of our economic and social ills. The same three-fourths think the answer is more (and virtually complete) regimentation and government control of all phases of business—including the imposition of wage and price controls. Yet, 80 percent in the same poll want less government interference in their own lives![10]

How prophetic! His description of Democrats in 1975 applies to Democrats today. He described their desire for government intervention into business, into banking, into healthcare, and into every aspect of our lives.

Reagan could not have known that, soon after his death, the day would come when the federal government would control banks, run automobile manufacturers, and attempt to rule healthcare and energy. He did foresee a political party that would embrace the redistribution of wealth and an ever-expanding federal government.

Reagan did not foresee, however, an awakening of the sleeping giant of conservatism that crossed party lines, gender lines, ethnic lines and age lines. This giant will not sleep again. This giant wears "Don't Tread on Me" t-shirts and carries homemade protest signs. This giant turns out by the thousands on the hottest summer day or the coldest winter evening to declare its support for constitutional principles and candidates who will be true to those principles. This giant movement inspires loosely-knit-together organizations such as the Tea Party Express, Tea Party Patriots, Nine Twelvers and Glenn Beckers. This is a giant movement made up of fiscal conservatives that have been Taxed Enough Already. The TEA Party movement is Main Street America fighting for freedom in peaceful assembly that would make Martin Luther King, Jr. proud. Reagan is still "one of us." Reagan was a Tea Partier.

What Works…Soft Socialism or Conservative Principles?

Again, Reagan speaks:

> In 1972, the people of this country had a clear-cut choice, based on the issues—to a greater extent than any election in half a century. In overwhelming numbers they ignored party labels, not so much to vote for a man or even a policy as to repudiate a philosophy. In doing so they repudiated that final step into the welfare state—that call for the confiscation and redistribution of their earnings on a scale far greater than what we now have. They repudiated the abandonment of national honor and a weakening of this nation's ability to protect itself.
>
> The mandate of 1972 still exists. The people of America have been confused and disturbed by events since that election, but they hold an unchanged philosophy.
>
> Our task is to make them see that what we represent is identical to their own hopes and dreams of what America can and should be. If there are questions as to whether the principles of conservatism hold up in practice, we have the answers to them. Where conservative principles have been tried, they have worked.[11]

Then as now, so-called elites have pushed liberalism and socialism; then as now, liberalism and socialism have failed the American people.

When George Bush defeated John Kerry in 2004, there was a national mandate *against* the welfare state and *for* homeland security. Four years later, conservatives failed to nominate a candidate who could articulate our principles of freedom and security. Today the people of America are confused and disturbed by massive spending, mismanagement of the economy, the enormous budget deficits, and an ever-increasing government intrusion into our lives.

As Senate Majority Leader Harry Reid (who claims to be the *Obama Whisperer*[12] and voted ninety-six percent of the time with liberal Democrats) implemented Obama's master plan for government takeover, stunned voters clung to the hope and change they were promised. Polling numbers plummeted for Congress and the President. Citizens realized that the government had robbed them, their children, and their grandchildren of a prosperous future. They had eroded our God-given freedoms, which are the underpinnings of conservative thinking. With the 2010 election turnover of sixty-nine seats giving the majority in the House to Republicans (plus 680 seats in State Legislatures and several Governors' Offices turned over to Republicans as well), the revolution has begun.

California Proved It

Once again, Reagan seemed to see into America's future:

> If you will permit me, I can recount my own experience in California. When I went to Sacramento eight years ago, I had the belief that government was no deep, dark mystery, that it could be operated efficiently by using the same common sense practiced in our everyday life, in our homes, in business and private affairs.
>
> The "lab test" of my theory—California—was pretty messed up after eight years of a road show version of the Great Society. Our first and only briefing came from the outgoing director of finance, who said: "We're spending $1 million more a day than we're taking in. I have a golf date. Good luck!" That was the most cheerful news we were to hear for quite some time...
>
> We instituted a policy of "cut, squeeze and trim" and froze

the hiring of employees as replacements for retiring employees or others leaving state service.

That was four years ago. Today, the needy have had an average increase of 43 percent in welfare grants in California, but the taxpayers have saved $2 billion by the caseload not increasing that 40,000 a month. Instead, there are some 400,000 fewer on welfare today than then.

Forty of the state's 58 counties have reduced property taxes for two years in a row (some for three). That $750-million deficit turned into an $850-million surplus, which we returned to the people in a one-time tax rebate.

We also turned over—for the first time in almost a quarter of a century—a balanced budget and a surplus of $500 million. In these eight years just passed, we returned to the people in rebates, tax reductions and bridge toll reductions $5.7 billion. All of this is contrary to the will of those who deplore conservatism and profess to be liberals, yet all of it is pleasing to its citizenry.

Make no mistake; the leadership of the Democratic Party is still out of step with the majority of Americans...[13]

My faith in Reagan's conservative message of common sense soared when the people of California rejected several tax-raising ballot measures in a 2009 election. The voters rejected it soundly by sixty-five percent in a special election.[14] The *tax rebellion* had not ended but instead signaled the beginnings of the new conservative movement nationwide.

If the welfare state to Nevada's west, one that some call the "Socialist State of California," can reject taxes, then I have hope for *real* change, and not just a campaign slogan. I have faith in the grassroots, salt-of-the-earth American voters' willingness to take a stand for freedom.

Reagan continues his defense of freedom:

Inflation has one cause and one cause only: government spending more than government takes in. And the cure to inflation is a balanced budget. We know, of course, that after 40 years of social tinkering and Keynesian experimentation that we cannot do this all at once, but it can be achieved.

Balancing the budget is like protecting your virtue: you have to learn to say "no."

Shorn of all side issues and extraneous matter, the problem underlying all others is the worldwide contest for the hearts and minds of mankind. Do we find the answers to human misery in freedom as it is known, or do we sink into the deadly dullness of the Socialist ant heap?

Those who suggest that the latter is some kind of solution are, I think, open to challenge. Let us have no more theorizing when actual comparison is possible. There is in the world a great nation, larger than ours in territory and populated with 250 million capable people. It is rich in resources and has had more than 50 uninterrupted years to practice socialism without opposition.

We could match them, but it would take a little doing on our part. We'd have to cut our paychecks back by 75 percent; move 60 million workers back to the farm; abandon two-thirds of our steel-making capacity; destroy 40 million television sets; tear up 14 of every 15 miles of highway; junk 19 of every 20 automobiles; tear up two-thirds of our railroad track; knock down 70 percent of our houses; and rip out nine out of every 10 telephones. Then, all we have to do is find a capitalist country to sell us wheat on credit to keep us from starving![15]

We have watched countries go bankrupt from socialism, for it has never succeeded except in the academic minds of elitist university professors. Quality of life is sacrificed, and, as often as not, life itself is eventually threatened and lost.

Tear Down This Wall

As our country teeters on the edge of socialism and Americans are asked to accept less while our leaders exempt themselves from the components of an increasing misery index, I yearn for national leaders who will cry out, "Mr. Obama, Mr. Reid and Mrs. Pelosi, tear down this wall!" Tear down the wall built by the Democrat brand of socialism that is erecting a nearly insurmountable barrier to any hope for future prosperity, for security, and for continuation of the freedoms Americans now take for granted. They are busy building their version of the Iron Curtain that enclosed the socialist paradise of the last half of the 20th Century.

Reagan continues on security:

> Our people are in a time of discontent. Our vital energy supplies are threatened by possibly the most powerful cartel in human history. Our traditional allies in Western Europe are experiencing political and economic instability bordering on chaos.
>
> We seem to be increasingly alone in a world grown more hostile, but we let our defenses shrink to pre-Pearl Harbor levels...
>
> Can we live with ourselves if we, as a nation, betray our friends and ignore our pledged word? And, if we do, who would ever trust us again?
>
> We did not seek world leadership; it was thrust upon us. It has been our destiny almost from the first moment this land was settled. If we fail to keep our rendezvous with destiny or, as John Winthrop said in 1630, "Deal falsely with our God," we shall be made "a story and by word throughout the world."[16]

When Al-Qaeda attacked the United States on September 11, 2001, we did not provoke it. Americans were not to blame and should not feel any compulsion to apologize to foreign nations. The act thrust the United States into a war against cowardice that terrorizes strong nations and intimidates weak nations into harboring their efforts. For his part, Harry Reid called for surrendering the mission of our brave troops in Iraq, not just by cutting military budgets to pre-Pearl Harbor levels, but also by invidiously declaring: "This war is lost."

At the October 14, 2010 debate, I challenged Harry Reid, "Senator you said 'This war is lost' and General Petraeus was 'dishonest.' You owe our military, our veterans, and their families an apology." We are still waiting.

I lived through the Vietnam era. When uniformed soldiers returned home from Vietnam, I saw them spit upon as well as physically and verbally attacked. Meanwhile, politicians, the media, and academia whipped up public sentiment against the war. We lost that war, not in Vietnam, but in Washington, D.C. because of elitist politicians who promote appeasement and who apologize for America's role as the world's super power. Reagan knew these types of politicians. Here is how he felt about those in his own party:

> Americans are hungry to feel once again a sense of mission and greatness.
>
> I don't know about you, but I am impatient with those Republicans who after the last election rushed into print saying, "We must broaden the base of our party"—when what they meant was to fuzz up and blur even more the differences between ourselves and our opponents.[17]

When I read this paragraph, I remembered Reagan's *Eleventh Commandment*. During Ronald Reagan's 1966 campaign for Governor of California, Republicans established the so-called *Eleventh Commandment*: "Thou shalt not speak ill of any fellow Republican." Clearly, Reagan was embarrassed and frustrated by Republicans in Name Only (RINO).

My opponent in the 2008 primary election to Nevada State Senate was an entrenched Republican incumbent who voted for the largest tax increase in Nevada history. He had an epiphany during the campaign, declaring he would not raise taxes if elected. After he won the election, he broke that promise and voted to raise taxes. Typically, liberals (regardless of party) "run right" and "vote left."

To manipulate their silence, old guard RINO Republicans pummel conservatives with the *Eleventh Commandment*. Reagan plainly counseled us to have no patience with Republicans who say we must sacrifice our principles in order to broaden the party base. I can only imagine what Reagan would say about the 200 Left wing Republicans (so-called RINO *Republicans for Reid*–headed by Reid's former "ad man" and a key advisor to Senator Paul Laxalt, and joined by the Republican Nevada State Senate Majority Leader and two Republican mayors[18]) who stated that Nevada needed Reid's "clout" to bring home the pork and earmarks. The incentive was eight billion taxpayer dollars that Reid inserted into a bill to build a high-speed rail line project called the Desert Xpress in Nevada that was an investment of the former ad man. The proposed passenger train to nowhere would run between Las Vegas and Victorville, California.[19] Keep in mind that for thirty years Reid had fought for the competitor, a 269-mile magnetic levitation train from Anaheim to Las Vegas. [20] Now that the "ad man" had raised so much money for Reid's campaigns (indenturing Reid and, by default, his constituents), Reid flip-flopped and promoted a "new" plan (Desert Xpress) whereby the taxpayers paid this money (this "favor") back on Reid's behalf. [21]

Prison Sentences Cross Party Lines

Deal cutting within both parties led to bipartisan prison sentences. For instance, Sandy Berger (Democrat), former Clinton security advisor, pled guilty to a misdemeanor charge of unlawfully removing classified documents from the National Archives in 2005.

Kyle Foggo (Republican), Executive Director of CIA, was found guilty of bribery February 17, 2007.

Lobbyist Jack Abramoff (Republican) was found guilty of conspiracy, tax evasion, and corruption of public officials in three different courts in a wide-ranging investigation. He is serving seventy months in prison, and was fined $24.7 million.

Congressman William J. Jefferson (Democrat) received media attention when, in August 2005, the FBI seized $90,000 in literally cold cash from his home freezer. His Louisiana constituency re-elected him in 2006. In August 2009, Jefferson was found guilty on eleven of sixteen charges, including RICO violations. His sentencing is pending as of this writing.

I could go on, but you follow the news. One after another, legislators come under investigation, explaining why they did not pay their taxes, or failed to honor and keep their marriage vows. Just Google "U.S. political scandal." [22] No wonder voters are disgusted with both political parties!

The Republican Brand

The Republican Party Platform has clearly stated fiscally and socially conservative values embraced by most Americans. These values transcend party lines but are the Republican brand. Republican politicians on the campaign trail often speak those values but do not always vote those values once elected. Even some of our military heroes have been caught speaking of the merits of conservatism to get elected, only to vote eventually with the liberals when they are tested in the furnace of Washington, D.C. politics. This separation causes voter cynicism. Voters refuse to vote, claiming that there is no sufficient difference now between the parties. Reagan addressed the inconsistency problem of the "Republican Brand" with his common sense solution.

> Our people look for a cause to believe in. Is it a third party we need, or is it a new and revitalized second party, raising a banner of no pale pastels, but bold colors which make it unmistakably clear where we stand on all of the issues troubling the people?
>
> Let us show that we stand for fiscal integrity and sound money and above all for an end to deficit spending, with ultimate retirement of the national debt.
>
> Let us also include a permanent limit on the percentage of the people's earnings government can take without their consent.
>
> Let our banner proclaim a genuine tax reform that will begin by simplifying the income tax so that workers can compute their obligation without having to employ legal help…
>
> Let our banner proclaim our belief in a free market as the greatest provider for the people. Let us also call for an end to the nit picking, the harassment, and over-regulation of business and industry, which restricts expansion and our ability to compete in world markets.
>
> Let us explore ways to ward off socialism, not by increasing government's coercive power, but by increasing participation by the people in the ownership of our industrial machine.
>
> Our banner must recognize the responsibility of government to protect the law-abiding, holding those who commit misdeeds personally accountable.
>
> And we must make it plain to international adventurers that our love of peace stops short of "peace at any price."
>
> We will maintain whatever level of strength is necessary to preserve our free way of life.
>
> A political party cannot be all things to all people. It must represent certain fundamental beliefs, which must not

be compromised to political expediency, or simply to swell its numbers.

I do not believe I have proposed anything that is contrary to what has been considered Republican principle. It is at the same time the very basis of conservatism. It is time to reassert that principle and raise it to full view. And if there are those who cannot subscribe to these principles, then let them go their way.[23]

Reagan's words inspire and empower me. When he took office, the Iron Curtain was as great a threat then as Radical Islam is now. Reagan defeated the Evil Empire, the U.S.S.R. He created a thriving economy, adding 20,000,000 new jobs and creating the longest period of growth and prosperity in American history.

Not only are Reagan's words prophetic in being relevant to today's problems, they are essential to facing our nation's biggest challenges ahead. The Reagan revolution was one of common sense. It revived the constitutional principles of limited government.

I embrace those principles of limited government, lower taxation and more freedom. I pledge to promote them, as did our Founding Fathers… with my life, my fortune, and my sacred honor.

Chapter Three

PAY BUCKS FOR POWER–THE POLITICS OF CORRUPTION

Senator Reid, you came to the Senate from Searchlight with very little. Now you are one of the richest men in the Senate. On behalf of Nevada taxpayers, we want to know how you got so wealthy on the government payroll.

ARE ALL POLITICIANS CORRUPT? Is the system corrupt? Neither politicians nor the system *has* to be corrupt. Our Founders were well aware of the histories of Greece and Rome wherein power bred greed and venality among the rulers. The Founders were also aware that the lower classes insisted on more and more welfare, gifts, and services until the Democratic Republic went bankrupt, both morally and financially. The Founders were careful to guard against corruption, but they knew that the ultimate responsibility would rest with individuals and their ability to discipline themselves against the temptations of power and celebrity. John Adams put it this way:

> We have no government armed with power capable of contending with human passions unbridled by morality and religion. Avarice, ambition, revenge, or gallantry would break the strongest cords of our Constitution as a whale goes through a net. Our Constitution was made only for a moral and religious people. It is wholly inadequate to the government of any other.[24]

Just as greed and sloth can tear down a nation, honesty and integrity can preserve our liberties and values. I was first shocked, and then saddened, by what I found when I became a legislator. The fixes are rather simple: reduce the money and power that government has, and elect people with a proven track record of not being part of the system of corruption. Elect people who are unwilling to sell their heritage of freedom and liberty for campaign cash and personal financial gain.

Saying No to the Money

"You have an appointment with the most powerful lobbyist in the Legislature tomorrow morning at ten a.m.," said the female voice on the phone.

It was my first day as a State Assemblywoman, having just won election to my first term in the Nevada State Assembly with shoe leather (walking door-to-door) and no help from the Republican Party, casinos or unions. I thought the legislator and the lobbyist had a lot of nerve demanding a command performance. I remembered my training, "Be slow to anger, slow to speak, and quick to listen." I listened.

When I did not respond immediately she added, "But he's honorable." I was tempted to snub the interview, but curiosity got the best of me.

I reached the top floor of the downtown Reno building, where two tall, well-dressed men escorted me to a room that contained a huge mahogany table surrounded by twenty large leather upholstered chairs. The room was elegantly masculine in rich wood paneling and heavy tapestry draperies. I took the chair at the head of the table and exchanged small talk with the men for a few minutes. When the door swished open, a tall white-haired middle-aged man with a pleasant smile and blue eyes that matched his suit entered the room. The two men jumped to attention. I was surprised at their reaction. I stood, too.

"It is a pleasure to meet you, Sharron," he said smoothly as he took my small hand between his two large hands. "I've heard so much about you and the wonderful campaign that you ran."

"Thank you. It is a pleasure to meet you, as well. I've heard that you're the most powerful man in the Legislature, but an honorable man." I smiled back as he motioned for me to sit.

He chuckled, "Well, that's good enough for me," and pushed a folded check in front of me on the table. I did not reach for it, but left it lying there as we talked about my campaign and my philosophy of government.

"Now, I'm truly convinced," he smiled in approval and slid the check close to me.

"I hope you will not be offended, but I cannot accept this check. You see, my constituents are very skeptical and believe that casino money is the root of corruption in the Legislature. I promised them that I would not take money from casinos or unions as an act of good faith. I mean no disrespect but as a casino lobbyist, I hope you understand," I smiled and pushed the check back to him without looking at it.

"Now I'm more convinced than ever," he said respectfully. "What if I wrote you a check for one thousand dollars to your favorite charity?"

"That is very kind, but giving to my charity would be the same as giving to me."

"Well, what if I wrote a personal check to you for one thousand dollars?"

"Sir, my average donation is ninety-six dollars and eighty cents. Everyone knows who you are, and one thousand dollars is hardly average."

That was the first, and last, time the most powerful lobbyist in Nevada invited me to his office.

The seductive power of money is real. Many of my colleagues and friends down through the years when I was a legislator chastised me for my "foolishness." They scolded me for squandering golden opportunities to ask for the maximum contribution and fund my campaigns the easy way.

During campaigns, the money looks good when lobbyists offer it. Campaigns need a lot of money, and there is nothing harder than "dialing for dollars." The phone calls are humbling. Calling lobbyists and big donors for support requires the bravado of a slick salesman. I had to learn the art of *closing the deal*. What seems to work is making them speak first after you have popped the question, "So, Ben, is it okay if I come by this afternoon about three for the check?" Most donors know that art. Some can outlast you through the deafening silence on the phone. So when a donor comes to *you* with the check before you have to ask, there is a sigh of relief for the easy money, but beware of Greeks (or lobbyists) bearing gifts.

Questions arose from that encounter with the powerful lobbyist that could only be answered by experience. For example, why was a Democrat lobbyist interested in a freshman Republican legislator? Why would he care about my vote on legislation that would pass with or without me? After just one session, I realized it was part of a game like the old *The Price is Right* television show. Some lobbyists want to know what a legislator's price is in order to play *"Pay Bucks for Power."* My response got around after that first interview with a message of "requires no special treatment." Every constituent of mine received equal treatment. I was not for sale. I did not intend to become part of politics as usual. Voters elected me as an outsider, and that is still not a bad place to be. I was not going to be riding the whale of avarice through the net of the Constitution, even if everyone else was doing it. I value personal liberty and my country's freedom too much.

In 2003, I had a conversation with the same powerful lobbyist outside the Assembly Chambers. "Sharron, I think we have a bill that you can vote for. I'd like to come to your office and show it to you. It is a tax increase, but it is not a gross receipts tax. I know you will not vote for a tax increase. And I told the other guys, but they made me promise to talk to you anyway. So, I've talked to you, and we both know it would be a waste of time for me to come to your office," he blurted out breathlessly and then turned on his heel, heading toward the elevator.

"I'm always ready to listen," I called as he walked away. He turned and smiled, but kept walking.

The Payback: A Personal Favor

Alfred came through the door with a kiss for my cheek. I was suspicious. After the niceties of meaningless exchange, he smiled and said, "Sharron. it would be a great personal favor to my client if you would vote for his art tax exemption." The bill would exempt his client's casino art collection from taxation. It was probably the ultimate tax-free investment, which only underlines the need for correcting the income tax structure in this country.

I smiled, "You know, I do not owe your client any personal favors."

He took a small black address book from his breast pocket and flipped through it, finally putting it back into his jacket pocket. To his dismay, my name was not in his book of those who had received campaign donations. There were no strings or expectations attached to me! In fact, I had purposefully returned checks during the campaign that came from casinos and unions because those are the two main groups that voters consider the source of most government corruption—at least in my district. Independence and trust are most important for a representative to build and preserve with their constituency. By refusing that money, I maintained my independence and built a trust that has served me well throughout the years.

"Well, Sharron, the owner would really appreciate it if you would vote for his bill."

"Come look at this, Alfred." I led him to a worktable in my office where a clipboard lay containing a sheaf of papers perhaps an inch thick.

"They do not like our bill," he said as he glanced at the top page of names and addresses that had come in through my e-mails on this bill.

I went through page after page for him. "They hate your bill, and I'll be voting no," I said.

He walked out of my office that day without my vote. Word got around. Lobbyists would poke their head in my office door and call, "So Sharron, what do your constituents think of our bill?"

I would call back, "That's the right question to ask, I'll check." It is the right question to ask a representative of the people, but it is not the question that most lobbyists ask.

Many a legislator has told me that they can take the money and still vote against poor legislation pushed by special interests. That is possible, but there is enormous pressure to find a reason to vote for your contributor's bills. This was the lesson I learned in another session of the Legislature.

The Price for Saying No after You Said Yes

In the middle of our second special session of 2003, legislators complained that lobbyists were diving into their offices and threatening them if they did not vote for the gross receipts tax on business. I went unmolested by those my colleagues called the "carpet sharks." I did not have to play because they had not paid me—no *Pay Bucks for Power* in my office. My stand had been clear from the beginning. I had not taken their campaign contributions, so their threats had no leverage. Others, who had taken the money and then voted against their benefactors, did not fare so well.

"Sharron, Sharron, come quick...*he's* got him in the bushes!" she said. A young woman intern came running into the Assembly Chambers after we recessed. As the Minority Whip, I looked around the room counting the fifteen Republicans I was expected to keep at the ready to vote "no." One was missing. I followed the intern into the night and found *him*, a tall muscular lobbyist, pounding the chest of one of my freshman legislators. He had my freshman backed into a tree, and he was spitting words into his face.

"What do you think your pulling here, you m---f—er! We f---ing own you!" Each word punctuated by a thrust of his open hand into my colleague's chest.

"Hello there," I called as jovially as I could. "They're getting ready to call us back, so we have to get going." I grabbed my shaken but courageous colleague by the arm and escorted him into the building. "Do not go anywhere alone anymore," I whispered quietly to him.

The fifteen of us stood strong through the regular session and two special sessions. We were in the midst of a huge court battle over a Nevada Supreme Court decision to throw out a constitutional two-thirds legislative vote requirement to raise taxes. However, in the middle of that second special session, a deal cut with the oldest member of our caucus in a closed-door meeting cost us mightily when this case went to the Ninth Circuit Court of Appeals and the United States Supreme Court.

We could watch the four lobbyists that we called the Power Rangers—they included two Democrats and two Republicans—emerge from their unmarked office across the street from the Legislature. From my third floor office window, we could not hear their words as they huddled for one last briefing. Then *shazam*, two went to the legislative building, one to the Supreme Court building, and one to the Governor's office. One Assemblyman felt the pressure. In a closed-door meeting the leadership of both parties convinced a senior member of our caucus (from a safe Republican district) that he would be protecting some of the younger members of our caucus (These members had unadvisedly promised the Governor they would vote for a tax increase.) while providing a courageous service to Nevadans when he voted for the tax increase. He came to me after the meeting.

"They told me that I was the only one who could vote for the tax and still get re-elected," he told me. "I've got to take a bullet for the team. Do you think it will hurt our court case?" He looked at me sheepishly, wanting me to say it was okay.

I was angry, but I measured my words. "If you vote for this tax, you weaken our case. If we want the higher courts to hear this case, there has to be damage. If you vote for the bill, they get their required two-thirds majority and go on as if nothing ever happened. It is a bad move. I do not know how they can guarantee you your seat when you're in a conservative Republican district." I watched him go to his seat. Sadly, I knew he would vote for the tax.

His vote cost us the case at the U.S. Supreme Court that ruled "no harm-no foul" and dismissed the case for lack of harm after his switched vote gave the Democrats the required two-thirds majority vote. Later the state Supreme Court Justices, who made the bad decision to strike down our two-thirds vote requirement for tax increases, lost their seats at the ballot box. The new justices reversed the decision and restored the requirement. In 2008, the flip-flopping Assemblyman was defeated in his re-election bid. It took five years, but his opponent only had to tell the voters that the Assemblyman voted for the largest tax increase in Nevada history. The voters remembered.

The Not-so-Subtle Sell-Out

There is a saying that the difference between a statesman and a politician is that a statesman is looking out for the next generation while a politician is looking forward to the next election. Sadly, it is too true. I do not think that anyone running for office intends to sacrifice his or her high ideals on the altar of incumbency, but it happens. It is so seductive that most never realize the compromise.

We walked down the hall of the legislative third floor together. It was my first term as a Nevada State Assemblywoman. She was in her third term. I respected her and welcomed her mentoring.

"I love your bill," she was saying enthusiastically. I could hear a "*but*" coming. We were talking about my "no smoking in the grocery stores" bill recommended to me by a seven-year-old constituent. Stephanie and her mother had come to see me to ask if I could sponsor the bill. Stephanie is asthmatic. Cigarette smoke triggered asthma attacks that put her in the emergency room for four to five hours of treatment.

I sympathized with her mother. My son has asthma. I had spent hours in emergency rooms with him, hoping that we would not have to stay the night, praying that it would not progress into pneumonia. I knew the fear of having to rock my son through the night. Rocking him allowed my son to sleep while sitting up, to breathe, and to be reassured. I would not let him stop breathing. I had listened to Stephanie's story, remembering how my heart ached in response to his labored wheezing.

The casino lobby was a roadblock to my bill. Nevada is unique in the U.S. because slot machines are everywhere. In the airport, as you step off the plane, the "one-armed bandits" jangle and beep a figurative "Welcome to Nevada!" There is a law against smoking in grocery stores *except* where banks of slot machines sit near the checkout counters. It is impossible to come into, or go out of, a store without walking through a cloud of smoke. "Why permit this?" you may ask. The casino lobby testified that addictive personalities gamble, smoke, and drink. The habits go together. If a rule prohibits one, profits on the machines go down due to lack of play.

As we continued down the hall, she articulated the "*but*" I anticipated. "I have to vote against your bill because I took money from the slot route operators PAC." I was stunned.

"You can say you hate the bill. You can say that it is unconstitutional for government to interfere with regulations on private business. You can say that it is not Republican and would send the wrong message about its support of less government regulation. But, do not *ever* tell me you've been bought." I said it so coldly that I shocked even myself. She was stunned, too.

"I have not been bought!" She was emphatic.

"Really?" I said. "Let's review our conversation."

My respect for her declined. We walked on in silence. My friend did not realize that she had been sucked into the corruption. Even after I exposed it, she still voted with her political friends. For her, the next election's campaign funds had become more important than the issues.

It takes courage to resist. It takes insight to recognize the trap. Some do; many more do not. Easy money is the lobbyists' deadly Kool-Aid. It is the same corruption that John Adams recognized and said would destroy our Republic.

The Culture of Corruption

It happens at every level in politics. Political sex scandals can threaten national security and erode the trust of the American people for politicians such as Presidents Harding, Kennedy and Clinton, and, more recently, Senator Ensign and Governor Stanford. It seems that corruption has escalated recently, but perhaps it is that the technology of the Internet and television brings it instantly into our living rooms from a press all too eager to report bad news. The Democrat leaders cheered over Republican ethics charges claiming that the culture of corruption was a Republican norm. The Democrat Illinois Governor's bribery case turned the corruption tables.[25] Democrats used voter anger by hammering home the message of Republican corruption to take back Congress in 2006 and the presidency in 2008.[26] Democrats know that Republican rank-and-file voters will reject their own party's corrupt officials. Democrats hide their dirt under the rug with the help of a willing media. Then, even when it is exposed, Democrats seldom object to corruption. With Senators Dodd and Burris, and Congressmen Frank, Rangel, Murtha and Jefferson, and Governors Spitzer and Patterson, plus too many tax cheats to list, the Democrats' complaints about a Republican culture of corruption sound hypocritical. Corruption anywhere (and yes, on both sides of the aisle) sickens me. Hypocrisy (predominantly Democrat) about corruption only adds insult and stench to the injury. Corruption for personal gain can reap large rewards, usually in the form of pork-laden bills that give advantages to the legislators and their friends. Yes, corruption has become a way of doing business in both parties, but it is not always just lobbyists handing out cash.

Bloggers and *The Los Angeles Times* Reveal Harry Reid's Corruption

A *Los Angeles Times* article dated October 11, 2006, entitled "Harry Reid and the Culture of Corruption" exposed the real-estate deals that netted him $700,000 by selling land he did not own. A casino lawyer who was Reid's old friend and who was connected to political bribery and organized crime, masterminded the transactions.

Remember the most powerful lobbyist in Nevada? He employed Reid's family members and between 2000 and 2006 made campaign contributions of over $45,000 to Reid and $20,000 to the Democrat Senate Committee, as well as campaign contributions to Reid's son's campaigns. The article asserts that lucrative favors followed. In a 2002 land bill, Reid relocated a power corridor to make 10,500 acres of public land available to the lobbyist. In 2005, Reid and Ensign worked together with the EPA to eliminate the environmental impact on that same land. The *Times* reported lobbying partners (including Abramoff), and clients donated $65,000 to Reid.[27] The Nevada newspapers did not carry the story.

In the October 14, 2010 debate I asked, "Senator Reid, you came to the Senate from Searchlight with very little. Now you are one of the richest men in the Senate. On behalf of Nevada taxpayers we want to know how you got so wealthy on the government payroll."

Stunned, Reid stammered, "That was a low blow." He continued to prattle about being a successful attorney putting five children through college, and then this career politician bemoaned that now he lives on a "fixed income." It was an insult to those who actually do live on fixed incomes. The Senator would not answer the question.

The Art of Flip-Flop

The Assemblyman was artful as he argued *against* a bill I had read but had not understood the unintended consequences now brought to our attention. I was convinced as I punched my red *no* button. The final vote tally passed the bill and to my amazement, the eloquent Assemblyman was among those who voted *yes*.

The Assembly recessed, and I caught up with my Republican colleague. "Why did you vote yes after you spoke against that bill?"

He smiled, patted my shoulder patronizingly, and drawled, "Well, Right Angle, if my constituents call and tell me they hated that bill, I'll tell them I agree, and that's why I spoke against the bill. If my constituents call and tell me they loved that bill, I'll tell them I agree, and that's why I voted for the bill."

So, What Can We Do?

There are solutions to the problem of corruption. Are the legislators willing to implement the solutions? The first and best solution is strength of character. A politician doing the right and honorable thing makes politics an admirable profession, rather than one of the least trusted occupations – just above lawyers who are just above lobbyists. Right now, it appears that ninety-nine percent of politicians give the rest of us a bad name.

We do not have to settle for "everyone is doing it" or "it's just the system." The Founders wrote that freedom and liberty could only govern moral people and would not survive wholesale corruption. As more and more politicians regard "pursuit of happiness" as a variation of "party on," our freedom and liberties will be lost. Consequently, more people will feel free to use their political power to enrich themselves rather than pursue the common good. George Washington and the Founders believed this: "Your love of liberty—your respect for the laws—your habits of industry—and your practice of the moral and religious obligations are the strongest claims to national and individual happiness."[28]

Another Revolution?

Some think our only option is another revolution. As unemployment climbs, the markets fall, and home foreclosures continue to cause instability in the economy, more good American citizens are mobilizing and participating in a grassroots movement for reform. Thomas Jefferson said, "The tree of liberty must be refreshed from time to time with the blood of patriots and tyrants. It is natural manure."[29]

I am obviously using Jefferson's words *figuratively* here. To be clear (and counter to how my detractors have tried to paint me...falsely), I am *not*, on any level, advocating violence, nor am I advocating an armed revolution. Instead, I am conveying that there is a very real awakening of the populace who are trying to communicate with the elite, unresponsive, and arrogant centralized ruling class. It is time for this ruling class to clear their ears, listen to their constituents, take these good Americans seriously, and get a grasp on the level of frustration permeating this great country of ours. Are you hearing us, Washington? We are fed up!

Disturbingly, in a display of politics at its worst, some liberals in their penchant to waste no crisis, for furthering their own self-interests, exploited the grief of families and ignored the facts to twist my words regarding the history of the Second Amendment. They attacked me in the immediate aftermath and context of the horrible tragedy in Tucson, Arizona, involving Representative Gabrielle Giffords and others. This repugnant and opportunistic display of hateful partisanship was embarrassing for our nation and most importantly, unconscionable in its level of disregard and disrespect for the victims and their families.[30]

The TEA Party protests are an outpouring of the fear that our country is being lost to the corruption of political greed and lust. The best solution is not to overthrow the government but to dismantle repressive laws that have fostered corruption and then enforce the laws designed to prevent it. Government regulation and the income tax are the chief means of corruption. We have seen one Democrat after another dodge taxes. We have watched businesses and unions look for tax breaks, (or even create them via expensive and powerful lobbyists) privileges, regulations, and subsidies, all in order to make millions. Like Diogenes, we wonder if there is one honest person left. As Samuel Adams said:

> If you love wealth, more than liberty, the tranquility of servitude better than the animating contest of freedom, depart from us in peace... May your chains rest lightly upon you and may posterity forget that you were our countrymen.[31]

Our Internal Revenue Code is a mess for a reason. Special interests pay for special favors. Whether the tax breaks are set in fine print or spelled out in bold type, there are plenty of places for our politicians to hide kickbacks. Meanwhile, all the exemptions, deductions, exceptions, and special provisions reduce the tax base, which means higher tax rates and smaller incentives for individuals and companies to produce income. Thomas Jefferson saw the potential of corruption from government taxation:

> They are not to do anything they please to provide for the general welfare, but only to lay taxes for that purpose... It would reduce the whole instrument to a single phrase, that of instituting a Congress with power to do whatever would be for the good of the United States; and as the sole judges of the good or evil, it would be also a power to do whatever evil they please...Certainly no such universal power was meant to be given them. It was intended to lace them up straightly within the enumerated powers and those without which, as means, these powers could not be carried into effect.[32]
>
> To take from one, because it is thought that his own industry and that of his fathers has acquired too much, in order to spare to others, who, or whose fathers have not exercised equal industry and skill, is to violate arbitrarily the first principle of association, 'the guarantee to every one of a free exercise of his industry, and the fruits acquired by it.[33]
>
> Place economy among the first and most important virtues, and public debt as the greatest of dangers to be feared. To preserve our independence, we must not let our rulers load us with perpetual debt.[34]

James Madison agreed:

> If Congress can employ money indefinitely to the general welfare...The powers of Congress would subvert the very foundation, the very nature of the limited government established by the people of America.[35]

No tax system is perfect, but ours is so awful that fundamental reform is the only fix. The manipulation of the tax system is the foremost source of corruption in our government. It is just too easy and tempting for lobbyists and politicians to enrich themselves with a few hidden and complicated items in the tax codes and in government regulations. Fundamental reform is not just a necessity; it is also an opportunity to stop taxing income and start taxing consumption. By switching from taxing wage and capital income to taxing consumption, we can significantly improve economic efficiency and growth.[36]

A consumption tax of some kind will directly cause those that spend more to pay more taxes. The income tax was never part of the Constitution nor is it a realistic way to fund the government. To help pay for the American Civil War, the United States government imposed the first personal income tax. The rate was three percent of all incomes over $800—those making about two-and-a-half times the average wage. To make up for tariff reductions, the Democrats in the 1894 Congress passed the first peacetime income tax at a rate of two percent on income over $4000. In 1895, the United States Supreme Court ruled in *Pollock v. Farmers' Loan & Trust Co.* that a tax based on receipts from the use of property was unconstitutional. This had the effect of prohibiting a federal tax on income from property. In 1913, the states ratified the Sixteenth Amendment, which states: "The Congress shall have power to lay and collect taxes on incomes, from whatever source derived, without apportionment among the several States, and without regard to any census or enumeration."[37]

Just as the property tax allows citizens to keep their homes as long as they pay the "rent" of property taxes, the income tax allows citizens to keep an ever-decreasing portion of their incomes. Even though Harry Reid and his compatriots like Rangel, Sebelius, and Geithner treat the income tax as a voluntary tax, the rest of the nation must pay up or go to jail. Frank Chodorov wrote in *The Income Tax: The Root of All Evil* that repeal of the income tax is necessary to restore freedom. Citizens are only free if they can keep and enjoy their earnings. Government taxation sowed the seeds of the fight for independence. John Adams wrote in 1818, "The Revolution was in the hearts of men…before the war commenced." An income tax was unthinkable to the Founders.[38]

Neil Borst contends that the Internal Revenue Service has its foot on the throat of our economy, contributing to unemployment and investment of United States capital overseas.[39] Lawrence Kotlikoff in *Averting America's Bankruptcy with a New Deal* in March of 2007 contends that government fiscal extravagance and the retirement of baby boomers will in effect bankrupt the United States. Economists Jagadeesh Gokhale and Kent Smetter noted a $63.3 trillion gap between the present value of projected spending and the present value of projected revenues. This translates into massive and crippling debt for our children and grandchildren.[40] The liberal solution for this debt is more taxation and holding fast to the income tax. It is mathematically impossible for income taxes to pay our way out of this debt.

There is however, a movement advocating the abolishment of the income tax. Kotlikoff explains it would be possible to replace federal income and payroll-based taxes with a national retail consumption tax, a rebate of federal sales tax paid on spending up to the poverty level, and dollar-for-dollar federal revenue replacement. This would set the stage for the repeal of the Sixteenth Amendment. It would replace federal personal and corporate income taxes, payroll (FICA), gift, estate, capital gains, alternative minimum, and self-employment taxes with one federal retail sales tax without the accompanying IRS bureaucracy. Existing state sales tax authorities would act as the primary administers of this type of tax. A consumption tax, instead of an earnings tax, would tax us only on what we choose to spend on new goods or services.

In a 2005 article on the Fair Tax for *The Wall Street Journal*, Kotlikoff suggests that a consumption tax could replace all other taxes fairly and give a choice to every potential taxpayer to pay taxes or not. The affect would reduce by approximately two-thirds the burden on taxpayers while providing a broader tax base and improved fiscal efficiency.[41]

Some have suggested the Value Added Tax (VAT), the flat tax, or a federal retail sales tax as the answer to tax simplification and reform. A federal consumption tax plus a rebate is the most straightforward reform. The monthly rebate to poor households would mean, in net terms, they would pay no sales taxes.

Limited growth of government is ultimately the only way we can eliminate the fiscal gap and retain a strong and healthy economy. Doing so will require the radical reformation of Social Security, Medicare, and our nation's healthcare system. The government has bankrupted these systems by making promises they cannot keep (robbing the general funds of taxes that should have gone to Medicaid, Medicare, and Social Security) and creating a Ponzi scheme in the trillions.

We may have to turn to an inflation-protected, individual, personalized, investment annuity retirement system as an option and alternative solution to the brokenness in the current Social Security system if future workers are going to have a retirement income and health care. Such a system would enable workers to bequeath their savings while offering them protection from the loads, commissions, and fees of Wall Street and insurance companies who will otherwise take advantage of a huge investment pool.

Abolishing the Income Tax System Solves
Some of the Political Corruption

Over seventeen thousand pages of Federal tax law and code does not raise enough revenue to cover the government's expenditures. The tax code is complex, expensive, inefficient, and inequitable. The number of lawyers, accountants, and auditors that work full time, plus the taxpayers' compliance costs, add up to billions of dollars in wasted resources. The distorted incentives of tax deductions and advantages sought by special interest lobbyists encourage the corruption of politicians.

Ken Dalanian in his article "Obama, Clinton Helped Contributors Secure Special Tax Breaks" discusses the advantage that special interests take from the tax structure. As an Illinois Senator, Barack Obama received $54,350 for his presidential campaign from members of a law firm that requested he introduce a tax break for a Japanese drug company operating in Illinois. It became law in December 2006, with an estimated cost to taxpayers of $800,000. In 2000, Hillary Rodham Clinton accepted $162,800 ($110,000 to committees supporting Clinton and $52,800 directly to her campaigns) from Rienzi & Sons, a food importer in Queens, N.Y. In 2002, as New York Senator, she introduced a tax refund provision of tens of thousands of taxpayer dollars in duties on imported tomato products, which became law in December 2004.[42]

Obama took millions from bundlers, unions, and lobbyists' friends and co-workers, while the other politicians raked in millions from corporations, unions, and lobbyists directly. It is hard to see how this is an improvement or how it makes Obama more righteous. He quickly accepted tax cheats, lobbyists, and profiteers into his administration, installing them in positions of power by creating dozens of czars or czarinas not vetted by the Senate (just another example of this self-proclaimed "*constitutional scholar*" disregarding and operating outside of the Constitution). The mainstream media was all too willing to turn a blind eye to the most outrageous indiscretions of these czars no matter how outlandish their beliefs and behaviors, how greedily they enriched themselves, or what little experience or skills they brought to the tasks at hand. These unconstitutional "advisers" need to be defunded. The President can have friends, but the American taxpayer should not pay for those friends.

Obama brought Chicago-style patronage and thug politics to the national level and showered his cohorts with billions of dollars. Auto unions, teachers' unions, service unions and A.C.O.R.N. have received billions. The largesse has just begun.

The Internal Revenue Code and government regulations make easy pickings for corrupt politicians, lobbyists, and those willing to play the *Name That Tax Provision* game. A simple tax system would end most of the game. The other problem of getting special concessions and bills for personal enrichment out of Congress is more a matter of character. Trial lawyers, a large predominantly Democrat special interest group, have paved the way for outrageous corruption. David Freddoso, Washington Examiner commentary staff writer, exposed the *Pay Bucks for Power* within the Trial Lawyer's lobby. Trial lawyers have contributed $762 million to Democrat lawmakers since 1990. In exchange, a single provision for a $1.6 billion tax break for trial lawyers was tacked onto a bill.[43]

We have reached a point where we must decide: will we have a government run by special interests, lobbyists, corrupt politicians, trial lawyers, unions, and their stooges, *or*, will we have a government run by and for the people? People must stand up and return to the Founders' belief in small limited government, with fair and just taxation. We must vote for representatives that will keep the people's trust, not "bring home the bacon" in ever-growing pork projects and ever-growing promises of government largesse and programs.

The Founding Fathers knew history. They had read of the fall of Greek Democracies and the Roman Republic as largely due to following the same policies that the Democrats are now promoting. Unelected bureaucrats and czars dispense billions to their special interests and cronies.

This must stop!

Our children and grandchildren deserve the same liberties and the right to pursue and enjoy the same prosperity our parents and we have enjoyed. We hope they will have even greater liberty and prosperity. This will only happen when the pursuit of happiness again means the pursuit of virtue, not the pursuit of avarice and power.

In almost every speech I deliver, I ask voters to examine my record. The electorate is cynical because they have been lied to and because they have seen the games that are played by politicians. It is not just a politician's voting record demanding scrutiny. Like the movie character Jerry McGuire, we must demand that they "show us the money."

When I first ran for public office, I knew that the love of money was the root of evil in politics. I was determined to be different. I have returned large contributions and refused to ask for money from lobbyists notorious for demanding a favor during the legislative session.

Perhaps my greatest compliment during the 2010 Nevada Senatorial race came from a young mother. "I've been telling my nine-year-old son that he can grow up to be the President. But, I wasn't sure I believed it because so many politicians are independently wealthy and campaigns cost so much money. You showed us both that it was possible to be an ordinary person with an ordinary income and run for high office." She was referring to the $14.3 million dollars I raised during the third quarter of the race–ninety-four percent came from donations of $100 or less. We were many people with a little money directed at the same goal.

Some of my colleagues have laughed at me saying, "You should take the money. I do. You can always say no to the favor. Just be smart." The trust of those people I represent is far more valuable to me than a few campaign dollars. I know it is right to "just say no." I have, on many occasions. I know I can resist the pressures of lobbyists and big donors. I have, on many occasions. When a constituent asks, "How do I know that you have not been bought?" I can truthfully say, "Simple…because I don't take the money."

David Victor Bruce Sharron

"My brothers and I posed for a *back to school picture* in front of the motel—our family business and home."

Chapter Four

SMALL BUSINESS–THE LIFE BLOOD OF AMERICA

Frankly, the only way the troika of Reid, Obama, and Pelosi will stop their assault on the American Dream, the economy, our wallets, and our freedoms is by defeat at the ballot box.

THE AMERICAN DREAM is the promise of a plentiful life based on opportunity, ability, potential, and accomplishment. It is not purely a hope of material wealth, although many have become rich. It is a vision that all men and women have value and can reach their own greatest potential by working hard while gaining the respect of others. The American Dream has attracted immigrants from around the world who were escaping the despotism and the subjugation of class or cast obstacles in older societies.[44]

This dream drew past generations, who lived within their means, to build that dream on the motto, "Use it up, Wear it out, Make it do or Do without." The Greatest Generation came knowing that the fruits of their labor would not be confiscated and given to "each according to his need." My father and mother took a risk on the promise of that dream, as did their parents before them.

After his honorable discharge from the Korean War, my father drew out his share of the equity in the family potato farm and invested it in the Atlas Motel in South Reno. He worked the graveyard shift at a *Union 76* filling station because the motel income did not stretch far enough to make the mortgage payment, pay for the motel maintenance, and feed the family. He had four children under five years old who grew up embracing a dream that hard work would produce success.

Dad and Mom bought the motel when I was three, and by the time I was nine, I was making beds with my dad. My parents were always there. When we came home from school, Mom would be getting dinner started, making cookies, or doing the bookkeeping. Dad was moving sprinklers, shoveling snow, or painting trim. It was rare that they were ever gone unless they had to take a second job. If they did leave us, even when we were teenagers and too old to need a babysitter, Mrs. Hannah (a lady in her late sixties) was there to take care of the motel. My parents feared that one of us might be "snatched away" if we were exposed to some of the more disreputable public.

There was always room for our relatives and friends to visit, and they came often. When they came to gamble, they did not pay for the rooms. My father handed out promotional coupons delivered to him by the downtown Reno casinos for our customers. These "Lucky Bucks" were good for a free roll of nickels—the siren call from the one-armed bandits. Sometimes Dad would bring back the nickels for us after a night out with the friends who came to visit.

Customers drank a lot of soda pop, leaving the bottles in the rooms for us. Every three or four months Dad would take us to the grocery store with a load of those bottles to cash in on the three cents for every empty bottle return deposit. It was wonderful! We would each have four or five dollars to spend on, well, whatever, but we usually just saved the cash. Mom and Dad had convinced us that we all wanted to go to college, and we would need that money for our educations.

I can only remember one time that my father spanked me. It was a group spanking. We were in our "playpen"—a three-sided chicken wire fence that attached to a five-foot stucco fence. The twenty by thirty foot enclosure had a padlock on the gate, a shaded lean-to, and a swing set. Highway 395 ran in front of the motel so Dad built the pen to keep his four preschool children off the highway and to keep us from "being seen" by would-be predators while he and my mother cleaned the rooms. As we grew up, we continued to play in the pen.

In the summer, Dad would throw a garden hose over the stucco fence so that we could have water to make mud pies and run through when we got too hot. One hot summer afternoon the mud pies became mud grenades for the biggest war the boys ever waged against the girl and the baby. In the middle of the war, my father appeared red with rage, turning the air blue with curses. He lined us up by age (I was nine, Vic seven, Bruce six, David four) and spanked us.

After the corporal punishment we found out it was not the mud grenade war that had made him furious, but the mud that flew over the stucco fence onto his clean white towels and pillowcases he had hung on the clothesline. He would have to do the entire wash again.

"I'm spanking the first kid who touches this sign!" Dad declared, as he hung a sign on the clothesline, and we knew he was not making an idle threat. The green sign with white letters simply said, "$4.00 A Couple." It was one in a series of four-foot square signs he had made over the last few months. Every other day he would repaint a sign with a new price. He called it the "price war," and we knew it was a fight for the family's survival.

After lunch, we drove toward town, finding the other motel signs that said, "$4.00 A Couple." When we returned, Dad made his own sign. He would hang it about 4:00 p.m. when the first customers would start looking for a room for the night.

"It is hardly worth cleaning them," my mother had said when she heard the price was $4.00. How could they pay the mortgage and provide for their family? The question haunted them day after day, but we children were unconcerned as we played our game of tag.

"I got her! I got her!" Vic yelled to the other two boys as they chased me around the corner of the stucco building. *Twang!*

I had forgotten about the sign. Looking back to see how close my brothers were, I hit it squarely while running as fast as I could. I flew backwards in the air landing on the ground with a terrific thud that knocked the wind out of me. I could not even cry. My whole body ached as I tried to catch my breath. I touched the huge green knot that had already begun to swell on my forehead.

"Oh no! Oh no!" My three brothers screamed in mass confusion, as my Dad appeared from inside the office-house where we lived.

To my great surprise, and the relief of my three siblings, mass spankings did not begin. Instead, Dad got a rag with turpentine and nearly rubbed the skin off my face and arms. It stung, and I stunk. Looking back, I wonder if Dad decided this was a greater punishment.

I remember our first black and white TV. My mother was convinced that it would rob us of family time. My brothers and I shared a room until I was twelve. Mom sang to us every night and read us the classics (*Tom Sawyer, Huckleberry Finn*) even after we were old enough to read them ourselves. We liked the shared experience and discussion. Dad taught us to play pinochle, hearts, and dominoes. We dug a fort out of the hard rock bed of the Virginia and Truckee railroad right-of-way Dad bought for our back yard. We had a knot swing over the pond in the neighbor's horse pasture. We had onion fights in the field next door where they eventually built the Reno-Sparks Convention Center. We all learned to drive a standard transmission International Scout in the Convention Center's big parking lot.

For four kids, growing up at the motel was all good. It was not always good for my parents. The competition was fierce. The margin of profit was narrow. The government taxation and regulation stepped up incrementally until my mother lost her confidence and turned the bookkeeping and the liability for mistakes over to a CPA.

Income Tax Code: Its Assaults on Small Business

Taxpayers today, like my mother, have found that the length, depth, height, and breadth of the tax law is so onerous that the average person must hire someone else to do their income tax preparation. Not surprisingly, the dictionary definition of onerous uses the income tax return in an example sentence and the word *taxing* as a synonym for *onerous*. "Onerous adj. 1: not easily borne; wearing; 'the burdensome task of preparing the income tax return'; 'my duties were not onerous; I only had to greet the guests'; 'a taxing schedule' syn: burdensome, onerous, taxing."[45]

Consider the example of senior citizens who typically have modest retirement savings. Right now, the government forces seniors to use complicated forms and wade through even more complicated instructions for those forms. Simplifying the process should be a priority.

Harry Reid says that paying income tax is voluntary.[46] Apparently, Harry Reid has not heard that nothing is certain except death and taxes. It is possible that Senator Tom Daschle, Obama's first HHS nominee, HHS Secretary Kathy Sebelius, Treasury Secretary Tim Geithner, Performance Officer Nancy Kelleher, Labor Secretary Hilda Solis, and U.S. Trade Representative Ron Kirk believed Reid when he said from the perspective of his Washington, D.C. Ritz Carlton condo ivory tower that income taxes are voluntary? Technically, it is only voluntary to present the information and send in the form but the form must be sent in and the tax paid. That is not voluntary according to about 300 people each year indicted for federal income tax evasion.[47]

The Sixteenth Amendment to the Constitution gave the Federal Government the power to tax income. Some say the ratification of the Amendment was not proper. Some of the copies that went to the states had errors in them rendering the Amendment supposedly invalid because the states ratified different versions of the document. Some people consider this argument frivolous. Case law overwhelmingly requires income tax be paid.[48]

The Federal Government in an honest moment in 2002 agreed that the codes needed to be simplified. The then Treasury Secretary evaluated the tax code as an "abomination…not worthy of our free society." He admitted that the tax code was so complicated that it was nearly impossible for the IRS to understand. The Secretary estimated that taxpayers spent $70 to $125 billion a year and millions of hours trying to comply with the tax code. If the IRS cannot understand the tax code that they enforce, how are average taxpayers supposed to understand it? The conclusion is that they don't. They hire accountants to handle the unending paperwork and attorneys to find loopholes. The money and work-power dedicated to the task of code compliance translates to lost productivity for businesses. All of these additional costs could be eliminated with a simpler, fairer, flatter tax code, creating savings that would be passed along to consumers in the form of less expensive products.[49]

There are some alternatives to the Federal Income Tax that are worthy of consideration. The Fair Tax is one. The simple and fair Flat Tax is another. Once again, there are solutions, from simplifying the codes and regulations to repealing the Sixteenth Amendment. To embrace these solutions would mean freedom for individuals and businesses. Implementing new alternate tax codes would break the juggernaut that is stalling the economy now, just as it would have when my parents were doing business.

As we got older, we got more involved in the business. We cleaned the rooms when Dad could not afford to pay a maid because the cost was more than just wages. Taxes, health and retirement benefits, worker's compensation, and withholding require an additional forty percent more than the wage the worker takes home. We had to pay the mortgage, even in the slow winter months when we were not able to rent all the rooms. We still had to pay it when a fire burned down power lines and we could not rent rooms without electricity and water pumped from our well by our electric pump. The bills still had to be paid when a huge storm dumped nearly six feet of snow and no customers could travel to rent a room. No one sent disaster relief when Little Wheeler Lake burst its dam and flooded all the rooms. And, I might add, my parents neither wanted nor expected a government bailout.

We learned to budget for government regulation and taxation that cut into a slim margin of profit. We learned to save for the rainy days that always came. We believed Mark Twain when he said, "No man's life, liberty, or property is safe when the Legislature is in session."[50] We learned that if there was not enough profit then it was time to get an outside job. Mom had her degree in accounting from Kansas State. Dad had two years of Agriculture at Cal Poly, San Luis Obispo, when he enlisted in the Navy in 1942 for World War II, and then later he got his broker's license and sold real estate.

The American dream, with hard work, paid off in financial security for my Dad's retirement. After selling the motel my father sold real estate and made investments. My parents taught us the foundations of the American Dream: going to college, getting a good job, owning a house, and having our own families. I earned tuition money for my bachelor's degree from college by waiting tables at Bob's Big Boy. I married, raised a family, worked in a field I loved, and pursued public office. My brother, Vic, started his own international off-peak electrical refrigeration business and invented a formula that freezes water at 43° to 48° F. Vic also plays bass guitar in his wife's variety dance band. Bruce was a crane operator and worked on the Alaska pipeline. David worked in the coal industry as a mining engineer then as mine manager and finally retired to Maui. Ted and I still manage rental properties. My parents taught my brothers and me that our potential was limited only by our imagination. Our lives are an example of the American Dream lived out in America generation after generation.

The American Dream is a non-discriminatory dream intended to be attainable by all Americans. Every American child, with few exceptions, has heard that they can be anything they want to be, even the President of the United States. The entrepreneurial spirit perpetuates the American Dream. Most Americans want to own their own business, be their own boss, and control their own destiny. Most Americans want to be free to pursue the

American Dream unfettered by bureaucratic red tape, regulation, and burdensome tax and fee structures.

Extortion and Patronage, Chicago-Style: Government Gangsters Take Over

The American Dream is not held so dear by those who call themselves Progressives and have hijacked the term *liberal*. Since January of 2009, the government of this nation has declared war on businesses, big and small. Those who have made their million dollars by sweat equity are vilified like Shylock and Scrooge, and becoming the victims of government-provoked "class envy." A million dollars really is not much. Almost every American is going to make a million dollars. Do the math, $20,000 a year for fifty years is a million dollars.

The General Motors takeover by the Federal Government was nothing short of "Chicago extortion" of businesses for patronage to political allies. Prosperous dealers all over the country were forced to give up dealerships, some of which have been in their family for over eighty years. It appeared to be nothing short of partisan revenge against 2008 Republican campaign donors, and this was a move to cut off the money supply to Republicans by the Democrat party. Some said it was a Robin Hood taking of rich dealerships and giving them to "friends" of the Obama administration. Others said it was elitist ignorance of the free market system.

My granddad, whose ancestry traces back to the patriots of the Revolutionary War, worked at a Studebaker dealership. Few people remember the Studebaker that died a natural death like the buggy whip. Companies like Studebaker, Nash-Kelvinator, Packard, Hudson, Stutz, Pierce-Arrow, and Desoto were not too big to fail and are now a piece of history preserved in museums and paraded at Hot August Nights, a classic car event in Reno, Nevada.[51] We have seen automobile companies come and go since Henry Ford made it an American industry, but never before has the auto industry been bludgeoned by government gangsters and union thugs. The Reid-Obama-Pelosi regime used taxpayer money to team up with the United Auto Workers to bailout companies deemed as "too big to fail." They delivered by FedEx a form letter Notice of Closure to 5,969 thriving franchises, some had been in business for generations. The Participation Agreement or Wind-Down Agreement sent on June 2, 2009, gave General Motors (GM) franchises until June 12, 2009, to sign and return the documents to GM. Government had inserted itself into private enterprise with taxpayer dollars, giving GM no option to fulfill agreements with dealers, and the dealers were given no opportunity to appeal.[52]

A New Jersey attorney said the "level of coercion is dramatic."[53] The dealers were forced to sign this disclaimer, "In executing this Agreement, Dealer acknowledges that its decisions and actions are entirely voluntary and free from duress."[54] Those dealers who signed the agreement could continue to do business until January 2010, but could not sell old inventory back to GM or buy new inventory. Franchisees who did not sign the agreement were terminated immediately and became part of GM's "bad assets."[55] One Florida attorney described the conditions of the "wind-down" as "an ultimatum along the line of 'take it or leave it."[56] The call to action against this mob-style thuggery has been challenged in bankruptcy court by thirty-seven state Attorneys General.[57]

It is shocking and frightening that our government would demand its citizens relinquish their businesses and their civil and legal rights.

Lest we think this is an isolated incident of government takeover, consider the banking industry where banks that were solvent were forced to take the bailout to protect those that were foundering. A "stress test" was applied which those same banks failed because paying back the bailout money would once again expose the banks that the government gang was protecting. If a bank refused the bailout, the bank's charter and CEO might come "under review." This loan sharking would make Al Capone proud.

Moreover, of course, tax evasion does not lead to Alcatraz anymore; it leads to becoming the Secretary of Treasury.

Fraud and Abuse: Washington, D.C. Style

Is the Cap and Trade scandal (based on a lie of Marxist socialism and attached to a popular cause like environmentalism) a created "crisis," conveniently calling for the government to take over the industry as the solution? The fantasy of man-caused global warming is being used to deal a mortal blow to the oil and coal industries. The policy will embolden and enrich our enemies who supply nearly seventy percent of the oil to our country. It will force the American citizen to pay for power sources that will, at best, double our utility bills and raise the cost of every product made of plastic, transported, or requiring electricity as part of its manufacturing. Let's expose it for what it is: Cap and Trade is a hidden tax. It is scientifically impossible that carbon dioxide at 280-800 parts per million, .000028 percent (that we and all other animals breathe out and plants "breathe in," and to which all industry contributes a small fraction compared to what is produced by natural processes) can have any effect on global warming.

In 2008, anecdotal evidence for a cooling planet exploded. China had its coldest winter in one-hundred years. Baghdad saw its first snow in all recorded history. North America had the most snow cover in fifty years; with some places like Wisconsin, the highest snow cover since record keeping began. There were record levels of Antarctic sea ice, and record cold in Minnesota, Texas, Florida, Mexico, Australia, Iran, Greece, South Africa, Greenland, Argentina, and Chile. The list goes on and on.

This is no more than anecdotal evidence, to be sure, but hard scientific fact supports the evidence. All four major global temperature-tracking outlets (Hadley, NASA's GISS, UAH, and RSS) have released updated data. All show that global temperatures had dropped precipitously. (Daily Tech, February 26, 2008)

Real global warming allowed Leif Erikson to sail to Vinland (America) a thousand years ago and plant grapes in Nova Scotia. Just think of all the car exhaust and coal fired electrical plants in 1000A.D.! I wonder if Mr. Sun might have something to do with temperature fluctuations. Manmade carbon dioxide is infinitesimal in relation to carbon dioxide created in nature. Nevertheless, we supposedly have a crisis that requires government to grab more of our money and freedoms. If certain politicians and bureaucrats had it their way, they would be regulating everything from utilities to cow flatulence, light bulbs, toilets, and automobiles–every breath you exhale. The selected few may get wealthy selling indulgences called *carbon credits*.[58]

But wait! There is more. With the push for universal healthcare, American seniors could be herded into those "Soylent Green" (referring to the 1973 film *Soylent Green*[59]) factories of healthcare rationing. Government healthcare is another artificial solution to a crisis that does not exist. Most Americans are satisfied with the quality of healthcare, just not the cost. Removing government meddling is the solution to lower costs in healthcare.

Removing the government regulations that limit access to insurance across state lines and removing government mandates for unnecessary coverage are just two free-market solutions.

Another blow to the economy are millions of illegal aliens (about half of the "uninsured") who were promised amnesty by the Obama Administration. The depressed market place will be flooded and overwhelmed by people demanding free services paid by taxpaying, law-abiding citizens. Illegal aliens cost us a low-ball estimate of $200 billion in welfare, health, education, and incarceration. Strangely, California's deficit of $22 billion is almost the exact amount that illegal aliens cost Californians, but any attempt to rein in the benefits have been tossed out with charges of racism by Democrat politicians and California judges. Immigration is great! We are all immigrants, but illegal aliens are not prepared to join the American democracy because they are hiding in the alternate economy.

Shining City on the Hill Solutions

I hear the fear in the not-so-silent-majority as I attend TEA Parties across the United States. With our national security compromised, our dollar losing value, unemployment soaring and our businesses reduced to bankruptcy by our very own government, will America remain the *Shining City on the Hill*? In 1992, Reagan told us, "America's best days are yet to come. Our proudest moments are yet to be. Our most glorious achievements are just ahead."[60] Over-regulation, taxation, and the good old boy "reward your friends and punish your enemies" system creates a stifling environment. The American Dream and the American entrepreneur are still alive, but will they continue in this government takeover atmosphere?[61] The answer is yes...if we vote to take America back and if we are the majority. The solutions are in the free market and capitalism. The policies of less government regulation and lower taxation will cause our economy to bloom once more. Free market policies encourage people, like my parents who owned a small motel, my paternal grandparents who farmed potatoes, and my maternal grandfather who sold Studebakers, to take a risk.

Our Founding Fathers envisioned a nation whose strength and vitality would emerge from the ingenuity of its people and their commitment to individual liberty. They understood that a nation's prosperity is dependent on the freedom of its citizens to pursue their hopes, dreams, and creative ambitions. The miracle of the marketplace set in motion the forces of economic growth that made our nation uniquely productive. This pattern of economic development has inspired people throughout the world to look to America for a better life.[62]

Martin Luther and John Calvin translated Bible verses—such as, 2 Thessalonians 3:10, "If anyone will not work, neither shall he eat;" Proverbs 10:4-5, "He who deals with a slack hand becomes poor, but the hand of the diligent makes one rich;" and Proverbs 14:23, "In all labor there is profit"—into what many today call the Protestant Work Ethic.

Progressives have chipped away at the Protestant Work Ethic with numerous incremental laws and public policies that promote an entitlement mentality which rewards idleness and sloth; taking money away from those who have earned it and giving it to those who have not, including many who are not even citizens of the country. This philosophy known as "redistribution of wealth" empowers the government to decide who has worked too hard and earned too much. American taxpayer wealth (not elite Leftists', of course) is given to those the government deems more worthy. The game now is to become one of the "more worthy" and not work or pay taxes. The parade of Obama appointees was forced to reveal their respective lapses in tax payment, the likes of which would land you and me in jail. Jay Leno and others have joked, "It is no wonder the Democrats do not mind raising taxes, they do not pay them." The undermining of America's culture with anti-God, anti-work, anti-American politics, has deliberately produced class envy and division.

It is time for government, as well as private business and all Americans, to re-embrace the values of integrity, honor, thrift, diligence, self-reliance, self-discipline, responsibility, accountability, deferred gratification, and hard work. We must elect representatives that will return government to the people and free the people from the bureaucratic elite. As Reagan said, "The government is for the people; the people are not for the government."

We hear so much about the greed of business. Well, frankly, I would like to hear a little more about the courage, generosity, and creativity of business. I would like to hear it pointed out that entrepreneurs do not have guaranteed annual incomes. Before they can turn a profit, they must anticipate and deliver what consumers want. The truth is, before entrepreneurs can take, they must give.[63] In addition, we need to give business a break—a break from regulation and a tax break. Small business creates most new jobs in America, and most small businesses pay their taxes at the personal rates, not the corporate rates. The personal tax cuts will create jobs. Those who oppose it only handcuff employers and further hurt the unemployed.[64]

In short, illegal aliens, welfare recipients, and poor men and women do not hire us for jobs. United States Senators and Congressmen do not create jobs (at least not enough jobs to stimulate and stabilize an economy), but they do create the regulatory and tax environment that either encourages or stifles job creation. It is the role and responsibility of legislators to create a business-friendly environment. Entrepreneurs create jobs. Rich men and women, or those trying to become rich, create jobs. Hardworking people, like my Dad, create jobs.

Winston Churchill said that some see private enterprise as a predatory target to be shot, others as a cow to be milked, but few see it as the sturdy horse pulling the wagon. Workers, savers, investors, and the entrepreneurs of America have been milked and shot at long enough![65]

Small business is the lifeblood of America. Obama, Reid, and Pelosi would do well to heed the warning, "Do not eat the blood for the blood is the life."[66]

Frankly, the only way the troika of Obama, Reid, and Pelosi will stop their assault on the American Dream, the economy, our wallets, and our freedoms is by defeat at the ballot box. The election victories that throw them out will send shockwaves through the Beltway, and the cockroaches will run from the light. Only true conservative principles can pave this road to recovery of the economy and restart the engine of small business that powers our economy.

"The Gold Standard offers stability to an economy. Outside Tonopah, Dad and I pose with a freshly poured gold button worth $100,000 in 1992."

Chapter Five

WHO IS REALLY RUINING THE ECONOMY?

When the latest beggar for more public money cries, "It is for the children," it reminds me that my Dad worked for his four children.

"IT'S THE ECONOMY, STUPID!" James Carville, Bill Clinton's political strategist in the 1992 presidential election, placed this sign over his desk in the Little Rock campaign headquarters. The current version of that statement according to mainstream Americans who have lost their jobs and homes is, "It's the Government ruining the economy, stupid!"

Wherever I talk about the economy today, I hear people respond with desperation in their voices about their jobs, retirement accounts, investments, and their grandchildren's debt. The old sayings, "What goes around comes around" or "Whatever you sow, you shall you reap" find their fulfillment today in the fervid spending of our political class. The weeds of the stimulus bills, bailouts, pork payoffs, and double-digit unemployment (all with price tags of trillions of dollars) are piling mountains of debt on our children and grandchildren by expanding the size and scope of government to unprecedented levels. To the Hallelujah Chorus of Pelosi, Reid, and the national media, Obama has piled up more spending and debt than all other presidents combined! We need to rip these weeds up by their socialist roots!

We are at a national crossroads. Throughout the United States, the most sustained threat to life, liberty, and property is coming from our own government. No private individual has ever come close to inflicting the damage caused by the tyranny of political power. Across time, throughout the world, hundreds of millions of people have lost freedom, property, and their lives to the aggressive and tyrannical behaviors of their own governments. It pains me to see, and to say, that this is actually where our great country is heading.

The Founding Fathers put severe limits on politicians and government. The Constitution focuses on what the government *cannot do,* and the Founders harnessed government through the separation of powers. Many of today's politicians lack basic understanding of our liberty, our Constitution, and capitalism. Capitalism is the cornerstone of our freedom and prosperity.

No other liberty can survive without economic liberty. Economist Milton Friedman said economic freedom was "the most basic of human rights and an essential foundation for other human rights."[67] (The misuse of this statement by Barney Frank is the basis for the abuses of Fannie Mae and Freddie Mac.) People free to use their property, earn from it, and profit from its sale and they contribute more to the overall economy of a nation, as long as this freedom is not hindered by government force, fraud, or theft. National economies supported by robust personal property rights structures and markets have a growth rate double to national governments with anemic coercive approaches to property rights. [68]

Property taxes by nature are constitutionally dubious. Payment is required, or property is forfeited, making the property owner a tenant to the government landlord. Yet liberal socialist minions recoil at the mere mention of restraint through legislation like Proposition 13, championed by Howard Jarvis and passed in California. Chile has just entered first world economic status by embracing capitalism's free-market economics that enable freedom to thrive. China and India are becoming more and more democratic as they embrace capitalism and raise their peoples' standard-of-living.

Unless we make a sharp right turn, the United States will collapse from First to Second World status, just as Argentina declined under the national-socialist Juan Peron, and Cuba did under Fidel Castro. Full-blown socialism, once found under the National Socialism of Germany and the Soviet Socialists of Russia, as well as the softer socialism of the mixed economies in Europe and South America, create more government control over the economy. By definition, government control leads to fewer freedoms, period.

The Loss of Economic Liberty and the
Destruction of a Great Nation

From 1836 (the last time we paid off our national debt) to 1913, we had limited government and no national bank. Since the 1913 passage of the Federal Reserve Act and the Income Tax Amendment, the government has been adding unaccountable special boards and commissions, thick federal departments, unelected lifetime bureaucrats, and now a myriad of "czars" accountable only to the President. Americans are ruled ever increasingly by fiat. Power is corrosive.

The Department of Energy (DOE) is just one example of how modern U.S. Government works, or rather, does not work. The DOE was created in 1977 to deal with the oil crisis. (The word *crisis* should always pique a conservative's interest since Saul Alinsky in his *Rules For Radicals* gave us the Left's guideline on how not to waste a crisis, which is code for promoting big centralized government expansion and takeover.[69]) Thirty-two years and several hundred billion dollars later, the United States has made no real strides toward solving the energy crisis. Hundreds of billions of dollars have gone to special interests like big agriculture's ethanol and various conservation plans with government busybodies telling us what to eat, what to drive, and which light bulb and toilet to use. This is what Alinsky meant by a crisis being an opportunity. It allows politicians to take hundreds of billions of dollars from the people to give to their supporters and their favored special interests, while expanding government control over our economy. The common sense approach of meeting an energy crisis by producing more energy (more oil, nuclear, coal, natural gas) is not even considered.

Government has nothing except what it takes from others. A crisis is an opportunity for those in government power to take more away from us. Government is not a profit center. It is a cost center. Bloated government, with its attendant regulations, mandates and subsidies, has violated the genius of the Constitution that called for a limited federal government. We developed into the most prosperous nation in world history based on the bedrock of freedom: individual liberty, free enterprise, and sound money. Government does not grow the economy. We, the people, do!

Keynesian economics, named after the British economist John Maynard Keynes, embraces the theory that the government can pump money into the economy to "encourage demand" and "create jobs" during an economic downturn. Keynesian economics, as practiced by Franklin Delano Roosevelt and perpetuated by Jimmy Carter, Bill Clinton, and Barack Obama, have pushed us away from prosperity. The United States, once the largest *creditor* nation, is becoming the largest *debtor* nation. Keynesian economics advances the fallacious ideas that government can spend more and create massive deficits to create prosperity. Both ideas are absurd on their face. Government is famous for wildly wasteful spending. When Keynesian economics on steroids rules the economic landscape, government is the only part of the economy that grows. Ballooning deficits are bankrupting Social Security, Medicare, and Medicaid. Our government is moving toward devastating inflation and financial collapse. Once the largest *producer* nation, the United States has become a *consumer* nation. This is not a process of natural social evolution. As government consumes more and more, regulates more and more, and taxes more and more, it becomes too costly for businesses to operate. Businesses, especially small businesses, cease operations altogether, or relocate abroad. For most families, one spouse works to support the family, and the other works to pay the taxes. Two family members earning income is not social evolution; it is a necessity that comes with the expanding intrusion of government.

Once we were rich with products "Made in the USA." Now we are deep in entitlement debt as we spend other nations' money, while massive federal and state government taxations require us to give more and more of our own money to government.

The Worst Economic Crisis since the Great Depression?

My father and mother lived through the effects of the Great Depression. Dad still tells stories about bartering because there was no money. My grandfather would walk to town with a bucket of fresh eggs to trade for flour and sugar. My mother told us about the rationing of sugar, gasoline, and nylon stockings during World War II. She said she would draw a line up the back of her legs with her eyebrow pencil to simulate the seam in a nylon stocking so that people would think she was wearing them. The Greatest Generation lived through the Great Depression and has not seen the likes of it since—not yet, anyway.

Why do some politicians invoke Roosevelt and the Great Depression? The purpose is clear. Fear is one of the most powerful emotions. References to the Great Depression strike immediate fear in the hearts of Americans and thus divert our attention from the *real* crises of the *current* economy

Democrats today are trying to justify the expansion of government, spending us into massive debt, and infringing even more on our liberties. The focus is less on growing the economy and more on the redistribution of wealth to their political allies. Today, most economists recognize that the *New Deal* prolonged and deepened the Depression.

Washington insiders ignore John Kennedy's and Ronald Reagan's successes based on reducing the marginal tax rates in order to grow the economy. Instead, politicians follow the massive government expansion of Roosevelt and Carter. Inside the Beltway politicos engage in deficit spending on an unprecedented scale along with the nationalization of industries in the spirit of Mussolini, Chavez, and Castro.

In the 1930's, the U.S. experienced the worst economic collapse in the nation's recorded history. Washington's deficit spending and increased government intervention stifled long-term economic growth potential and delayed full economic recovery. Keynesian economics can work for a brief period. However, when this tactic becomes standard operating procedure, the cumulative effects on a national economy are inevitably devastating.

Friedrich von Hayek and Milton Friedman discredited Keynesian practices in the 1970's and Reagan dumped Keynesian economics. By emphasizing supply-side policies and allowing businesses and individuals to keep more of their own money, which Reagan called "common sense," the economy boomed for twenty-five years. One by one, beginning with the first Bush administration, the policies of Reaganomics were traded for increasing taxes, expanding government, and more deficit spending. The result was the first stimulus bill of 2008.

Left-leaning politicians aim to remedy the alleged failure of capitalism by hearkening back to Roosevelt's *New Deal*. This time they are increasing the same debt, the same government intervention, and the same bureaucratic regulation that caused the housing and stock bubbles to build and burst in the first place. Politicians are repeating history! And most of the bad parts of history, at that. The government took advantage of prosperous times to grow itself, regulated where it saw profits, and refused to intervene when its policies pushed the economy into disaster. Now it is using that disaster as an excuse to grow government while stealing our money to pay off allies and special interests. It is the greatest con game in the world: "Heads, I win; tails, you lose."

Joe Biden warned Americans that we would not like what was going to happen if Obama was elected President. What an understatement! Stimulus money in the trillions is tearing through the economy yielding massive debt. Most of the money will take years to spend. Much of it went to Democrat special interests, unions, government growth, and pork projects. Counter to promises made by the Obama Administration, less than ten percent is going to "shovel-ready projects," creating actual productive jobs for working people.

The Economic Recovery Plan that has Always Worked

Friedrich von Hayek refused to join communism in a time when all of Central Europe was celebrating it. He managed the Austrian Institute of Business Cycle Research. He was an economist, statistician, and an administrator. In 1931, Hayek became Tooke Professor of Economic Science and Statistics at the University of London. In 1944, he published a small volume, *The Road to Serfdom*. Hayek showed how the Nazi economic system held the same general economic principles of the American Left— the self-styled Progressives, the planners, the socialists, and the Roosevelt *New Dealers*. Hayek was a champion of capitalism and the free economy, but above all, he was a defender of liberty.

The "Virginia School" of economics, The Locke Institute at George Mason University in Virginia, is something of an heir to the Austrian Institute School and is dedicated to combating the Keynesian school of deficit spending that rules Washington. Accordingly, and consistent with most conservatives, "The Virginia School" champions the four pillars of "Reaganomics:"

1) Reduce the growth of government and spending
2) Reduce marginal tax rates on income from labor and capital
3) Reduce government regulation of the economy
4) Control the money supply to reduce inflation.

France, Germany, India, Brazil, Canada, and even Communist China have experienced economic growth by embracing the fiscal restraints heralded by Hayek.

Reducing unemployment and restoring economic health will only come with a return to free market capitalism, lower taxes, repealing tariffs, and trade barriers, reducing the minimum wage, limiting union power, encouraging private business job creation by less regulation, lowering the corporate tax rate, and passing tort reform. Furthermore, we cannot restore market discipline by bailing out failing banks.

Government bailouts remove the natural limits to risk-taking by removing, or severely limiting, the element of consequence. The resulting unchecked and artificially raised level of risk-taking lines the bankers' and investors' pockets with billions of *our* dollars while failing to expose the very government regulations (and, ironically, lack of proper oversight and accountability) that caused the credit bubble in the first place!

Offering socialized healthcare for everyone in order to solve the invented healthcare crisis will only create another bankrupt government program. This new socialistic program will cost trillions of dollars and destroy the best health care system in the world.

The Cap and Trade scheme designed to enrich and expand government while rewarding the liberals' favored allies will raise our taxes and utility bills and cripple industry. Liberals want to accomplish all of this via a "manufactured man-caused global warming crisis."

Socialization of the industrial base through government ownership of banks and automakers will destroy the banking and auto industries. By adhering to their mentor Alinsky's commandment not to waste a crisis, the liberal parties in power are bringing us another Great Depression.

There are steps we can take to put this Humpty Dumpty economy back together again. However, we cannot expect the people who pushed the big egg off the wall to help. Their solution is to march Dumpty's family and friends to the wall and push them off, too. The bigger the mess is, the more opportunity to gain power and money. No government ever spent itself into prosperity, and national prosperity has never come from government programs. The cost of government spending will be paid by our children and grandchildren, forced eventually to live in an impoverished and less free nation.

Where to Start? Audit the Fed

To understand what is going on with our economy, here is a brief primer on how our banking system and government financial institutions are structured. This understanding exposes how the nation's ruling class enriches itself at our expense.

In early 1781, Congress, under the Articles of Confederation and at the urging of Alexander Hamilton, created a private national bank. Thomas Jefferson and James Madison were strongly opposed to its creation. Objections of "alarming foreign influence and fictitious credit," favoritism to foreigners, and the fear of competition with state banks issuing their own bank notes, quickly surfaced. Pennsylvania refused to let the national bank operate in that state and almost killed the idea.

In 1791, the federal government started the First Bank of the United States, ultimately shut down by President Madison. The second central bank met a similar fate under President Jackson. Political opposition to central banking and corruption were the main reasons for shutting the government banks down. From 1837 to 1921, there was no central bank; instead, an independent treasury system existed.

The third national bank, The Federal Reserve System (referred to informally as the Fed) was created in 1913 by the Federal Reserve Act and is currently the United States' central banking system. The Federal Reserve Act passed with more Democrat than Republican votes. Rural and western states' politicians were suspicious of the "Eastern establishment" and wealthy bankers like J.P. Morgan and John D. Rockefeller, Jr. The Fed was the federal government's "fix" for the crisis of 1907 and a series of financial panics or bank-runs that followed.

The Fed serves as a banker's bank and as the federal government's bank. The U.S. Treasury keeps an account with the Federal Reserve for federal tax deposits, government payments, government securities (such as Savings Bonds and Treasury bills), as well as for selling and redeeming notes and bonds.

The American public believed that the Federal Reserve System would bring about financial stability. In 1929, that belief was shattered when the stock market crashed, and there were runs on banks. Banks held (and still hold) only a fraction of their deposited money in reserve, using the majority of their deposits for investing. During the 1929 bank runs, too many of the bank's customers withdrew their savings. The Federal Reserve, designed to prevent or minimize bank runs, was to act as the lender of last resort by covering outstanding deposits. Some economists, including Milton

Friedman and Ben Bernanke, believe that the Federal Reserve System was partly to blame for the Great Depression because it refused to lend money to small banks during the 1929 bank runs.

Like all government bureaucracies, the Fed's roles and responsibilities have expanded as its duties evolved. The Fed influences monetary and credit conditions, which in turn affect employment, prices, and long-term interest rates. The Fed, charged with stabilizing and containing the risks in financial markets, also regulates banking institutions as a protection for the nation's financial system and for the credit rights of consumers. Finally, the Fed has a major interest in operating the payment system and providing financial services to banks, the U.S. government, and foreign institutions. The Fed has been (and still is) regarded as a quasi-public bank because it has aspects of both a government-run system and a private enterprise.

As an independent institution, the Fed acts without prior approval from Congress or the President, but there are Congressional oversights and statutes. The President appoints the Fed's Board of Governors. The Federal Reserve is self-funded (not funded by Congress), with the majority of its funding coming from the interest on the portfolio of Treasury securities, as well as capital gains/losses that may arise from the buying/selling of the securities and their derivatives as part of Open Market Operations. The Federal Open Market Committee (FOMC) of the Fed is the overseer of national monetary policy. There are twelve privately-owned Federal Reserve Banks located across the country (Boston, New York City, Philadelphia, Cleveland, Richmond, Atlanta, Chicago, St. Louis, Minneapolis, Kansas City, Dallas, San Francisco) that act as agents for the U.S. Treasury and for numerous private U.S. member banks. At the top of the Fed bureaucracy are various advisory councils.

The Fed distributes coin and paper currency, but the U.S. Treasury, through the Bureau of the Mint and Bureau of Engraving and Printing, produces the nation's cash and sells it to the Federal Reserve Banks at manufacturing cost (currently about four cents, per bill, for paper currency). The dollar was based on a specific weight in gold until 1933, when the government nullified American holdings in monetary gold, but allowed foreign banks to redeem U.S. currency at thirty-five dollars an ounce. In July 1944, forty-four nations designed a system of fixed exchange rates by establishing the U.S. dollar, based on the gold standard, as a reserve currency, and requiring each country to adopt a monetary policy that maintained its exchange rate with gold. The International Monetary Fund (IMF) and the International Bank for Reconstruction and Development (IBRD) regulated the system.

In 1971, Richard Nixon declared that the United States dollar was no longer convertible to gold, thereby making the United States dollar, not gold, the reserve currency for nations that had signed the agreement. Inflation soared until Paul Volcker, Chairman of the Federal Reserve Board, tightened the money supply by using money-supply aggregates as guidelines for controlling inflation.

Inflation results from the increase of the money supply, which in turn devalues the purchasing power of money. Rising prices are the result of inflation. The economist Ludwig von Mises asserted that governments always try to get people to focus on prices as a cause of inflation rather than increasing the money supply as the root cause of inflation. By focusing on prices, government shifts the solution from demanding that the Fed quit increasing the money supply to a solution based on wage and price controls. The Fed has managed to insulate itself largely from such criticism. The Fed no longer reports the "M3" (total money supply), claiming that it costs more to gather the information than the value the information provides.

The effects of inflation are:

1) Workers will be hurt if their incomes do not increase at the same rate as prices.
2) Seniors on fixed income will be hurt if their savings do not increase at the same rate as prices.
3) Savers and those with financial assets lose value (dollars) and will experience decreased purchasing power.
4) Businesses and people find it hard to plan for costs of future projects or to pay for existing costs, such as employees.
5) Interest rate-sensitive industries, like mortgage and real estate, suffer as monetary inflation drives rates up.

Average people lose some of their savings and pay higher prices due to inflation. The government profits at the direct expense of everyone else, as a net debtor paying debts in cheaper money and gaining income from higher interests it charges banks and institutions. Inflation becomes the hidden tax, and wages become one of the last things that are increased. Continued inflation forces businesses to reduce costs by cutting jobs, benefits, or other expenses just to maintain a margin of profit that keeps their businesses alive. An increase in unemployment, business failures, business relocations offshore, employee benefits reductions, and automation that replaces workers with machines can result from inflation.

Inflation has its risks. When the increased money supply makes paper money worth less than anything it can buy, inflation snowballs to hyperinflation. In 1923, Germany, workers in the French Ruhr Valley were encouraged to strike by the German government that printed money to pay their salaries. When the people realized their money no longer had the same buying power, they rushed to buy anything that had more value than the paper money. The more they spent, the higher prices rose, until marks were only good to burn to keep warm in the winter. Adolf Hitler found hyperinflation to be a crisis he could not waste, drawing increased support as he rallied his countrymen around the common enemy of hyperinflation.

Knowing about the Fed and exposing its role in the collapsing economy is the first step to recovery. An audit of the Federal Reserve will scrutinize the banking practice of fractional-reserve lending. Bankers lend deposits with only a portion of those loans covered by money reserves, which expands the apparent money supply and drives inflation.

In any other world, artificially taking and using other people's property without their knowledge or consent is embezzlement. The U.S. courts "fixed" that inconvenient flaw by following the British ruling in *Foley v. Hill and Others* in 1848. The court ruled in that case that money left with a banker is, "to all intents and purposes, the money of the banker, to do with as he pleases."[70] The money belongs to the bank not the depositor. Because the money belongs to the bank, the bank escapes legal accountability for precarious investments or loans that create two claims to the same money—depositor and borrower—that cannot be paid at the same time.[71] An audit of the Federal Reserve would expose a central banking system that appears bent on a horrendous expansion of credit, money supply, and an inflationary policy that will make us a second Weimar Republic or Zimbabwe.

Even China is lecturing us on the dangers of inflation. Premier Wen Jiaboa called on Washington "to honor its words, stay a credible nation, and ensure the safety of Chinese assets."[72] China has diversified its $2 trillion foreign exchange reserves, although it remains the single largest holder of US government debt, which accounts for about half of its stockpile.

Washington needs to continue selling treasury notes to fund the $787 billion stimulus package. Secretary of State Hillary Clinton urged Beijing to maintain its stock of U.S. Treasury Notes as she visited China because there has been so much discussion about continuing to buy treasuries.[73] As the monopoly supplier of bank notes and regulator of our economy, the Fed has legal privileges that exempt it from the free market. This is similar to Fannie Mae and Freddie Mac being exempt from oversight thanks to Senator Dodd and Congressman Frank, as they and their cronies pocketed millions in contributions from the agencies they were supposed to regulate. Both the politicians and the agencies assure us they are doing us a public service. What we know about the Federal Reserve raises questions for an auditor to ask:

1) What does the government get in return for the privileges it grants to the Fed?

2) What connection does the Fed's ability to create inflation and print money have with the government's involvement in economic, political, and military wars?

3) Would the economy improve if money and banking were privatized?

4) Should government be able to create inflation to pay off its expanding debt as China fears?

5) Does a centralized bank cause economic recession?

The Long-Term Solution: Bring Back Free Market Capitalism

Capitalism did not fail and cause the Great Depression, or the latest economic recession. These financial disasters happened because leaders failed to implement the principles of capitalism. Instead, they opted for a failed premise of government control and regulation. As Reagan knew and as our Founding Fathers feared, once again the government is not the solution but the problem.[74]

Government is not God, or even godlike. The purpose of governments is not to make everyone equal by redistributing wealth, or to provide all our needs from the cradle to the grave. The role of government is not to protect everyone from everything, including their own poor choices. It is not the role of government to determine our future by quantifying our individual benefit to society. This big government ideology is national idolatry. The Founders, and each successive generation that followed, have driven a stake through the heart of this false god. Sadly, in each generation there are those who resurrect this old devil in the new garments of hope and change.

The monetary and big government intervention policies of Hoover and Roosevelt pushed the economic recession over the cliff of economic depression and kept recovery down in the 1930's. The Reid-Obama-Pelosi Administration dusted off those policies and put them into hyper-drive. Today my father's generation of the Depression and World War II is dying. The baby boomers are taking their place without the institutional history or self-reliant occupations to deal with rationing, inflation, and poverty. There is trouble ahead.

When government rescues businesses that should be allowed to fail, when profits are confiscated from successful businesses and citizens, when the motivation to maximize profits safely is lost, there are consequences. They include a growing desire to avoid taxes through shelters, loopholes, or moving abroad. Plus, the whole society hunkers down to avoid risk. The result is less investment and fewer jobs created.

On the other hand, if government dismantles the regulation barriers to the free market and reduces taxes, it will provide real stimulus that allows people to spend or save more of their earnings. The dismantling of big government will incentivize and energize businesses to work hard to earn more money that will, in turn, fuel a prosperous economy and add revenues to government coffers. It is just common sense; free market solutions work.

A Dream inspired America's freedom. That Dream has inspired people throughout the world to come to America ever since our Founders declared independence from the tyrannical taxation of a greedy government that called itself a benevolent monarchy. The freedom to pursue hopes and ambitions, unfettered by government intervention, is the miracle of the marketplace that unleashes ingenuity, productivity, and economic growth.

The natural breed of entrepreneur has no guaranteed annual income. They must anticipate and deliver what the customer wants. My Dad used to remind us, "The customer is always right. If they are not happy, we do not eat." Most small business owners, like my Dad, are courageous, generous, and creative. They create new jobs and pay taxes at personal, not corporate, rates. They support the infrastructure that finances the essential constitutional mandates of a government that mainly deals with defense and commerce. Unfortunately, our government now looks at business as a way to get "a piece of the action" in taxes, to justify employing government bureaucrats, and as sources for campaign financing and even personal profit.

The private sector did not ask for public options. They never agreed to fund government education, government healthcare, government energy production, government auto manufacturing, government banking, or the litany of alphabet soup acronym socialist programs that never die no matter how incompetent, unwanted, or wildly expensive. The politicians and bureaucrats refuse to create zero-base budgeting. Instead, they allow every program an automatic increase each year. Anything less is called a "cut." Businesses earn their increases the old-fashioned way, by producing better products and services. The government gives automatic "cost of living" raises and faces any deficit by taxing future generations through deficit spending and inflation. Businesses balance their budgets by cost reduction, productivity increases, and money management. In other words, businesses survive and prosper by providing products people want and need at prices that are fair and reasonable.

When the latest beggar for more public money cries, "It is for the children," it reminds me that my Dad worked for his four children. He saved for our futures, and he saved for his own future so that he would not be a financial burden to us in his old age. He did it for his children, his grandchildren, and his great grandchildren.

The implementation of a free-market approach is still the remedy for the United States economy, just as it was after the Carter recession. We should remember what Reagan said: "The ten most dangerous words in the English language are 'Hi, I'm from the government, and I'm here to help.'"[75] The only way that government can help is to get out of the way and leave the economy alone. When government is limited, people are free. As government grows, our liberties shrink.

In August 2009, I joined a cross-country caravan that covered thirty-four states and stopped on the steps of the nation's capitol in Washington, D.C. The TEA Party Express embraced its own acronym "*Taxed Enough Already.*" As the people across America gathered by the hundreds and thousands to greet the buses when we rolled into small towns with interesting names like Winnemucca, Elko, Ely, and Alamo, or with familiar names like Reno and Las Vegas, the liberty chants were all the same. The Star Spangled Banner and the "Don't Tread on Me" flags waved everywhere. It is the same spirit of freedom of those willing to dump British tea into Boston Harbor whose patriots declared, "Give me liberty, or give me death." The American people get it. They understand the common sense of Ronald Reagan. He once said this:

> This is not the time for political fun and games. This is the time for a new beginning. I ask you now to put aside any feelings of frustration or helplessness about our political institutions and join me in this dramatic, but responsible plan to reduce the enormous burden of Federal taxation on you and your family.
>
> During recent months many of you have asked what can you do to help make America strong again. I urge you again to contact your Senators and Congressmen…Tell them you believe this is an unequaled opportunity to help return America to prosperity and make government again the servant of the people.
>
> …Congress will stand at the fork of two roads. One road is all too familiar to us. It leads ultimately to higher taxes. It merely brings us full circle back to the source of our economic problems, where the government decides that it knows better than you what should be done with your earnings and, in fact, how you should conduct your life. The other road promises to renew the American spirit. It is a road of hope and opportunity. It places the direction of your life back in your hands where it belongs.
>
> I've not taken your time this evening merely to ask you to trust me. Instead, I ask you to trust yourselves. That's what America is all about. Our struggle for nationhood, our unrelenting fight for freedom, our very existence—these have all rested on the assurance that you must be free to shape your life as you are best able to, that no one can stop you from reaching higher or take from you the creativity that has made America the envy of mankind.

One road is timid and fearful; the other bold and hopeful... It has been the power of millions of people like you who have determined that we will make America great again. You have made the difference up to now. You will make the difference again. Let us not stop now.

Thank you. God bless you. And good night.[76]

"Four generations of Angles, like the majority of American families, can't afford *Obamacare* and other big government programs."

Chapter Six

UNIVERSAL HEALTHCARE FOR EVERYONE BUT HARRY, BARRY AND NANCY

Americans understand that government-run healthcare begs for higher taxes. However, Washington's political elites are trying to jam down our throats (against the majority of public opinion and desire) an oppressive healthcare system from which they are exempting themselves! A healthcare system good enough for the average American should be good enough for the elite Beltway crowd.

"YOU KNOW, DARE," Dad said to me (my baby brother, David, could not say Sharron when he first learned to talk. He called me "Dare," and the nickname stuck with my father), "growing old is hell." My dad spoke flatly, as he looked into the mirror.

It is hard for me to see my strong Dad so dependent, especially dependent on me. He says I am his favorite daughter...because I am his only daughter. I am Daddy's little girl, but in his later years I have become one of his caregivers as well. He never complains, but I know it is humiliating and frustrating for him to have me feed him or take him to the bathroom. Sometimes after I tuck him into bed and the lights are out, I pull up a chair to play my guitar and sing the old country-western songs, folk songs, and hymns that he loves. The role reversal is odd but comforting to us both.

While the neurologist calls his symptoms *Parkinsonisms* (related to a stroke he had a few years ago) Dad does not have all the classic symptoms for Parkinson's disease, and he has other problems that are not Parkinson's. Injured during World War II, he suffers from epilepsy related to that injury. Recently he wrote about that injury.

On November 19, 1943, I was at my station at night on

a 20mm anti-aircraft gun on the Hollywood Deck of the USS Dale (DD-353). There was a belt harness around my gizzard holding me up in the gun. They said if we saw a plane attacking to shoot it. So I thought I saw it and started firing. The elevator guy and the ammo guy were supposed to warn me when the 5-inch gun above us was swinging over us. But they left me. I do not know where they got to. The number two 5-inch gun over me started blasting. I was strapped into my seat. Suddenly, there was an explosion, and I thought we had taken a bomb from a "Betty" (Japanese) bomber. The residue out of the muzzle of the big gun went into my eyes. I do not know how I got out of the gun. The next thing I knew, I was in sickbay. They bandaged my eyes and gave me a shot of morphine. I did not see the Makin Island campaign (part of the Gilberts just north of the equator). The other guys described the action on the beach to me. I was awarded the Purple Heart because of my injuries.[77]

I am proud of Dad's military service. Dad saved for his retirement, but not enough to cover all of his doctor bills and prescriptions. Dad has Medicare and supplemental drug prescription coverage, yet he falls into the "gap" or "donut hole" of Medicare coverage about March each year, and he does not get out of that hole until October. This $2,500 gap is the responsibility of the patient. He also has coverage with the Veteran's Administration. With all this coverage, Dad still has about $800 per month out-of-pocket prescription drug expense not covered by any insurance. His nearly free government insurance company (Medicare and the VA) has decided that he should have generic drugs for his problems. His doctors say "absolutely not." Dad needs the specific brand drug for his conditions.

In 2006, my brothers, Vic and David, and I relocated Dad from a pending admission to a nursing home in Kansas. He was unable to speak to us except to answer with an emphatic "no" when I asked him if he wanted to go into a nursing home. Vic has a handicap-accessible home because his wife's parents needed those accommodations when they went to live with Vic. It was the natural place for Dad to go. Through intensive physical therapy, speech therapy, and the care of good doctors, my father regained most of his faculties—except his balance. It would be foolish for us to take a chance on reversing that progress by switching to the generic drugs that the government says he should have. We trust the doctor, who knows my dad by name and by sight. This doctor answers immediately when there is an emergency. Dad's doctor has used every tool at his disposal to give my father quality of life—to enjoy spending time with his three children, five grandchildren and twelve great grandchildren—as well as quantity of life.

My father travels at least three times each year. He spends four months in Southern California with Vic, four months in Hawaii with David, and four months in Nevada with me. People are envious when they hear that schedule! He has a quality of life that includes everything from political rallies with me, dancing to Vic's wife's country-western band, and riding in the outrigger canoe with David and his team of ocean paddlers. At 88, life is more challenging, but he is still at home with us. Even though end-of-life issues are hard and Dad's healthcare is expensive, this stage in my father's life is a blessing for all of us.

We trust Dad's doctor. We do not trust government pill counters.

Government-Controlled Healthcare Is Life-Threatening

When the Reid-Obama-Pelosi troika introduced warmed-over Clinton Care, I shuddered. The scope of a government-controlled healthcare agenda consolidates the proposals for a socialist takeover that have been proposed and refused during previous administrations. This manufactured crisis is about the role of government in the economy. Healthcare is the Trojan horse for government takeover of the insurance industry, which is part of a much larger government takeover series including the housing industry, banking, automakers, and AIG. Government-run healthcare forced on the American people, with a government-run "public option" insurance plan, would place Washington bureaucrats in control of healthcare services, which would limit choices for all Americans. The predictable consequence is rationing, making healthcare unobtainable to the very young, the very old, and the very sick.

Many of the statistics that claim Americans receive substandard care have flaws that give good reason for doubt that there is a real crisis. For example, a 2003 study by the Rand Corporation stated Americans receive only fifty-five percent of the recommended care, but two-thirds of the those contacted in the telephone interviews refused to participate and, of those who did participate, Rand had incomplete medical records to accurately document the care. Based on the records, Rand found that only fifteen percent of the patients interviewed received flu vaccine but in actuality eighty-five percent of the patients said they received the vaccine. The World Health Organization ranks the U.S. thirty-seventh in the world in quality but they based this score on two primary factors. 1) Americans do not have universal coverage and 2) the financial burden for care is on the individual.

Single-payer government-run healthcare is standard practice in the United Kingdom (U.K.) and Canada with many disconcerting results. Withholding drugs that prolong life for cancer patients is common because "there is a limited pot of money" and the drugs are of "marginal benefit at quite often an extreme cost." The U.K.'s National Institute of Health and Clinical Excellence (NICE) board restricted the use of macular degeneration drugs to one in five sufferers. Those who were allowed to use it could do so only in one eye with the explanation, "When treatments are very expensive, we have to use them where they give the most benefit to patients."[78] Aricept is one of the drugs my father takes. In the U.K., it is restricted because it was not "cost effective." They also restrict surgical procedures such as pap smears for young women under age twenty-five. Many young women denied pap smears, a cervical cancer early detection test, develop cervical cancer. There is no appeal to a higher agency. Government-run health care inevitably leads to rationing in order to cut costs.

The consequences of this rationed care based on cost efficiencies were published in the 2008 Concord Study. The British cancer survival rates are the worst in Europe (also a purveyor of government-run healthcare) and are significantly lower than in the United States. For example, the five-year survival rate for breast cancer is eighty-four percent in the United States verses seventy-three percent in Europe; the survival rate for prostate cancer is ninety-two percent in the U.S compared to fifty-seven percent in Europe. The first people to get rationed care are the elderly. Obama himself recently said that an elderly woman should not get a needed pacemaker for her heart. "Just take pain meds," he said.[79]

This political snake oil will hijack over ten percent of the American economy. Americans understand that government-run healthcare begs for higher taxes. Cost-control measures take away medical options. The elderly and newborn will be the first Americans to experience rationing. It is a bitter pill to swallow when one realizes that the best healthcare system in the world will become a system of medical rationing as determined by a government bureaucrat. Americans do not trust government to decide their healthcare options. Government-controlled healthcare is like watching an anesthetist crank up the gas to euthanize the greatest healthcare system in the world, while the surgeon cuts out the heart of what makes our healthcare system the best in the world.

Loss of options and rationing of healthcare would be nightmarish enough, but some have proposed the government force us into "healthy lifestyles," by deciding what we can eat and drink and how much. It is not just about taxing Dr. Pepper but also foods that contain salt and fats, plus the requirement that one maintain his/her ideal weight through diet and exercise. Americans will be fined or lose their healthcare if they do not comply. A government nutritionist will be looking over your shoulder to assess every bite you eat, sip you take, and breath you breathe. To help pay the trillions necessary for government healthcare, it may be necessary to make deep cuts to Medicare and Medicaid and/or tax health benefits.

The Architects of Government-Run Healthcare

As healthcare policy unfolds, the real authors of that policy surface as czar Advisors. The Czar Appointment process completely circumvents the constitutional requirement for Presidential appointees to face Senate vetting and confirmation. In 2009, one of these czars, a physician and the brother of the White House Chief of Staff, ironically blamed the Hippocratic Oath for the abuse of individual, personal, and first class patient care given by doctors. This Czar would redefine doctors' ethics based on the needs of society and cost efficiency. He refers to a "complete lives system" which calls for a doctor to make a "value to society" assessment based on projected productivity and anticipated length of life of the patient. The Czar places a priority on care for those fifteen to forty years of age.[80]

These principles are chilling. The first of the 2009 healthcare bills seemed to reflect the move toward cradle-to-grave care that will ultimately decide whose life is valuable to society and whose life is not so valuable.

Free Healthcare: Not a Guaranteed Constitutional Right

"We hold these truths to be self-evident, that all men are created equal, that they are endowed by their Creator with certain unalienable Rights, among these are Life, Liberty and the pursuit of Happiness." [81] These rights from natural law were called by America's Founders rights of birth—life, liberty, and the pursuit of happiness. These are political rights, or "negative rights." The government has no right to take them away.

The Constitution guarantees citizens' rights that protect them from an oppressive tyrannical government. Article 1 Section 8 restricts the federal government to enumerated powers. The government can only do those things expressly permitted in the Constitution and nothing more. Restricted government allows liberties free from government interference. These liberties are not entitlements to government giveaways that take from some people to give to other people. Simply put, providing government healthcare is not one of the clearly and expressly enumerated powers afforded the federal government by the Constitution.

Providing government healthcare is an area where the states can experiment, and where some have. Massachusetts and Maine paid the price for this experiment. The Massachusetts insurance-for-all plan with no cost constraints is driving the state to the brink of financial bankruptcy. Not only did many drop their current insurance to sign up for free government insurance, but the state government also refused to allow new enrollments and increased taxes. Rationing quickly began. As one would reasonably expect, forced tax increases paid for Massachusetts failed experiment. Having anything besides this same expectation (but on a far grander scale) for our federal government to be able to pay for *Obamacare* is naïve and irresponsible, at best.

Maine also enacted universal coverage in 2005. Premiums have risen by seventy-four percent and many residents have dropped coverage. This renders universal healthcare in the state nearly worthless as it struggles with an uninsured rate of ten percent, a level barely lower than the pre-reform level.

The federal government's deficit spending is unrestrained by the Constitution. States, unlike the federal government, have laws that force balanced budgets, so they make cuts and begin rationing relatively quickly. If the citizens do not like the results of socialism, they can move to another state. My home state, Nevada, has received countless refugees fleeing from California's rush to socialism. If the federal government succeeds in taking over the healthcare system (over ten percent of our economy) and implements this national socialist system, there will be no fleeing to another state to avoid it; there will be no escaping it. That, by definition, is a severe infringement on freedom and liberty. That, again by definition, is tyranny.

Healthcare has been "rationed" by the reduction of payments to doctors and other medical professionals. These reductions may seem equitable but they quickly lead to doctors refusing to see patients insured by Medicare and Medicaid. When government is the only insurance, doctors simply leave the profession to pursue professions that are more lucrative. Good compensation is one reason we have the best and brightest doctors in the world. If medicine becomes just another low-paying, paperwork-heavy government job, the U.S. will have a shortage of doctors just like Britain and Canada do.

Free citizens should have the right to choose where, when, and to whom we go to for the medical care and the help we need. "No one in a free society should have a 'right' to anything that requires others to toil against their will on behalf of those unwilling to provide for themselves."[82] Reducing access to medical care creates another form of rationing, prolonged waiting. In both Canada and Britain treatment for cancer, hip, or knee replacements can take years. Tests for cancer, MRI and CAT scans often require patients to wait for months. David Gratzer chronicles horror stories of people dying while they waited for care in his book *Code Blue: Reviving Canada's Health Care System.*

The Consequences to Seniors

I always think the best of people until they reveal their Machiavellian dark side. The holocaust of National Socialism (abbreviated Nazi) and the gulag of International Socialism (called Communism) are both examples of abandoning the "right to life" and "unalienable rights" that we in America all too often take for granted. To the socialist and the communist, all is done in the name of the common good. Individual rights are sacrificed for the assumed group benefits. ("From each according to his abilities, to each according to his needs," Karl Marx, *Communist Manifesto*.)

History shows that taking from the able and giving to the needy requires a government big enough to control every aspect of your life, and one powerful enough to kill those the government feels are unworthy, (Withholding or rationing care from those who need it is another form killing.). In the past, the "unworthy" were the elderly, the disabled, the unborn, the non-German, the Jew, the rich, the capitalist, and the dissident communist. "The government big enough to give you everything you want, is also big enough to take away everything you have."[83]

It appears the first on the "unworthy" chopping block are the elderly and the unborn. Ezekiel Emanuel (President Obama's Healthcare Czar) wrote in *The Lancet Medical Journal* that if healthcare has to be rationed, he prefers the "complete lives system," which "discriminates against older people."[84] Over ten years ago in an article for the Hastings Center Report regarding guaranteed healthcare, Emanuel wrote about rationing care, "individuals who are irreversibly prevented from being or becoming participating citizens...an obvious example is not guaranteeing health services to patients with dementia."[85] Lest we think such practices are still in the stages of wishful thinking for America's universal healthcare Socialists, several states like Oregon[86] are already using "comparative effectiveness research" that dictate to doctors the treatments they prescribe and the cost of the treatments.

Is this really an "unfortunate interpretation," or is this the cold hard truth that "affordable" really means that some lives are not worth caring for, as determined by a government bureaucrat?

The first House of Representatives Health Care Bill HR 3200 contained the intent to limit healthcare to the elderly. As written, as the insured gets older, a federal bureaucrat would make cost-benefit analyses and would have the "power" to deny coverage simply based on age and the increased costs associated with it. Soon, there will be a duty to die, just like in the 1973 film *Soylent Green*.

Consider the topics of the following pages in the controversial H.R. 3200, the first Government Healthcare Bill of 2009.

1) Outcome-based measures (pp.336-339);
2) Advance Care Planning Consultations (p. 425);
3) Instruction and consultation regarding living wills, durable powers of attorney (p. 425);
4) Approved list of end-of-life resources (p. 426), including "the use

of antibiotics; and the use of artificially administered nutrition and hydration"(p.430),

5) Orders for end-of-life (p.427) and "orders regarding life sustaining treatment" may include an ORDER for end of life plans (p.429).[87]

Perhaps the most telling part of this proposed bill was that some members of Congress exempted themselves from the bill's provisions and later voted to repeal the bill.

The Consequences to the Unborn

There are other agendas within the universal healthcare plan, *Obamacare*. Government will pay for and encourage abortions. If abortion is not explicitly prohibited in legislation, abortion is included as a "minimum benefit standard." History demonstrates that unless abortion is explicitly excluded, administrative agencies and the courts will mandate it. This will require provisions like the amendment to the Medicaid statute in 1979 by Henry Hyde. If explicit prohibition of abortion is not included in every piece of healthcare legislation, every health plan, and every hospital receiving federal funds or accepting Medicaid, Medicare, or the new health plan will have to pay for and provide abortions. Pro-life taxpayers with grave moral objections will be forced to subsidize abortions with their tax dollars under universal healthcare.

The Consequences to Small Business

Very few politicians creating new laws in Washington, D.C., have the experience of meeting a payroll each month. Small business creates two-thirds of all new jobs. Government healthcare takes direct aim at small business owners. The "play or pay" mandate for businesses means they will pay healthcare premiums based on the dollar amounts of their payrolls. Penalties as percentages of payrolls and fines for non-participation in the government plan amount to taxation. The penalties apply to those who do not provide health insurance and to those who do not participate in the government-run system. The average margin of profit for most business is eight percent. Public option healthcare would eat away that profit margin (and more), effectively putting most businesses out of business, eliminating millions of jobs.

Mussolini, Hitler, and Stalin targeted small businesses with taxation and regulation after taking over heavy industry and financial institutions like the banks, insurance companies, and automobiles manufacturers. All three turned over the industries to the unions that supported them. Subsequently, those governments took over the unions. Sound familiar? The lifeblood of our nation deserves better.

The Consequences to Our Economy

There has been a fundamental shift of our economy from the free-market to the government takeover of banks, insurance companies, auto companies, energy, and healthcare. Government intrusion into a free economy was unimaginable and specifically prohibited by the Founding Fathers and Framers of the U.S. Constitution.

Most government programs spend three of every four dollars on overhead. For example, my friend David Elliott used to work for a federal agency. He was required to fill out pages of forms in quadruplicate to order a six-dollar box of donuts for the therapy group he conducted. Frustrated by the wasted time it took to fill out the forms, he asked the finance department how much it would cost to process all the paperwork. The estimated cost totaled $140 (not counting David's hourly wage).

Government's intervention through Fannie Mae and Freddie Mac (government-sponsored public mortgage lending institutions) into the mortgage market promoted lending to those who could not normally afford housing loans, especially minorities. Banks made irresponsible loans under the threat of losing their charters or facing discrimination lawsuits from their own government. The heads of Freddie Mac and Fannie Mae (appointed by government officials) received millions in bonuses for making unsecured, risky loans. Senator Barack Obama and Senator Chris Dodd (Democrat, Connecticut) were the biggest receivers of campaign contributions from Fannie and Freddie.

Over ten years ago, some politicians, many economists, and hundreds of interested parties brought to Congress' attention the fact that there was a looming crisis in the housing market. Government-backed competition in the banking and lending private sector distorted the market. The federal government through Freddie and Fannie agreed to guarantee all the risky loans, bundled large pools as securities and sold them by the hundreds of billions. This lending craziness, compounded with low interest rates set by the government, led to waves of loans to unqualified individuals with no proof of income or citizenship needed, and no credit check. Irresponsible lending practices approved and encouraged by the federal government drove out competition from banks offering loans not guaranteed by Fannie and Freddie.

With the economy spinning out of control from the Fannie and Freddie "public-private" experiment, the Reid-Obama-Pelosi government justified federal intervention into every area of American life. Government intervention destroyed a sector of the economy (housing) and the government turned to bailouts and subsidies.

Across the board, government intervention only proved the truth of the definition of insanity, "doing the same old thing and expecting different results." So how can we expect a different result with the government intervention called *Obamacare?* The only thing different would be that the catastrophe will be much bigger.[88]

This removal of free market competition (which controls not only costs and quality to consumers, but also guarantees the ability to earn an income commensurate with the training and skill of service providers) will lead to diminished services and fewer healthcare providers as well as increased costs. This is what F.A. Hayek meant by "the dead hand of government."[89] Government intervention inevitably kills whatever it touches. "Help" the poor family; the family is destroyed. Daniel Moynihan makes this case in *The Negro Family: the Case for National Action.*

The very policies touted by Congress as a way to save small family farms are instead helping to accelerate their demise, according to economists, analysts and farmers. "Help the family farm; it disappears." *Ideological Usurpation of Government to Destroy Family Farms* by Carol W. LaGrasse documents the problem. Owners of large farms receive the largest share of government subsidies. They often use the money to acquire more land, pushing aside small and medium-size farms, as well as young farmers starting out.[90]

We can conclude from the examples that a government-subsidized-and-mandated system will take away the incentives for bright young would-be doctors. Those who earn medical degrees do so knowing that they will have to pay off student loans for their eight to ten years of college education debt, then take on the skyrocketing medical malpractice liabilities of the profession and manage a small business. Historically, all of this has been worth it because these young doctors love what they do, and they believe they could afford the debt and provide a good living for themselves and their families once they set up their practices. However, all that will change dramatically for the worse with *Obamacare.*

With government limiting a doctor's ability to earn enough to overcome the initial cost, will they choose a less financially demanding field? I talked recently with a medical doctor who put eight stitches into my father's forehead after an accident. The doctor was a compassionate professional. As we talked about his debt and the opportunities within his profession, he told me, "If I had known what I know now, I would have become a nurse. They have union protection and none of the liabilities, plus they can do almost everything that I'm doing now and for better pay." He is far from alone in his sentiments.

In the Military

There is, however, a place for government healthcare. Within Article 1 Section 8 of the Constitution, the last half is devoted to the establishment and maintenance of the military. It is necessary and proper to provide healthcare for these brave men and women as well as their families, whether they are active duty, reservist, or retired. Military personnel have the same healthcare issues as all Americans, but they are the only able citizens who should have *guaranteed* government-covered healthcare. As a nation, we are especially responsible for Department of Defense and Veterans Administration healthcare, and outreach to wounded warriors and their families.

My son-in-law decided to join the Marines just before his twenty-fifth birthday. He made a personal sacrifice to volunteer to defend our country. My daughter and two grandchildren lived in poverty while he deployed around the world. For four years, they lived on food stamps, Women Infants and Children (WIC) milk subsidies, and other government programs. As a combat engineer, my son-in-law was required, among other duties, to disarm land mines. This hazardous duty placed his young family in a position of potentially losing their father and husband. He was a good Marine, receiving awards and rank increases, but it was not enough. Because of poverty wages, he left the Marine Corps after his first tour of duty.

The experience of more than seven years of war has highlighted the fact that our military personnel and weapons have been vastly over-stressed. The Progressive Left has undermined one of the most basic reasons for the federal government to exist by its relentless attack on those who support the military mission as being "warmongers." The members of the U.S. Senate have allowed Harry Reid to go undisciplined for his unconscionable (and demoralizing to our brave military) declaration regarding our military's brave efforts in Iraq that "This war is lost." After North Korea fired thirteen missiles over the Fourth of July 2009 weekend, Harry Reid supported a $1.2-1.6 billion cut in missile defense appropriations for 2010. These are cuts to the very program intended to defend the U.S. homeland against rogue nation missiles!

The Reid-Obama administration deliberately downsized our military forces below the levels needed to meet international conflicts. They delayed force increases by adopting overly optimistic hopes for early resolution of the war. They deferred action to replace aging weapons systems and war-worn equipment. They shifted money from funding operations to quality-of-life and "people programs". As if that was not enough damage to our national defense, the government imposed one hundred percent of wartime national sacrifice on one percent of the population, our military families.

Our focus should be on rebuilding an overstretched volunteer military force for future readiness, as well as homeland and personnel protection. While most politicians acknowledge the sacrifice of our brave military, it is only lip service if they do not provide for the needs of active, reserve force and retired personnel and their families. At the forefront of these needs is guaranteed *quality* healthcare.

In the context of that unique example of a legitimate, government healthcare system, the size of the active duty force should match the mission. Military pay should be comparable to the private sector. We should authorize currently serving families the use of pre-tax health and dependent care programs. We need to fix the TRICARE payment rate formula to promote provider participation. We should restore VA survivor annuities for widows who remarry after age fifty-five. We can do better!

I Am for Healthcare Reform!

As I have stated earlier, I feel the United States has the best healthcare system in the world. Do I feel it can be improved upon and needs reform? Absolutely. Do I think the several-thousand-page abomination (or "Obamanation") called *Obamacare* is the answer? Absolutely not.

First, any legislation voted upon by our U.S. Congress (especially that which will result in a government takeover of more than ten percent of our overall economy) should be read in its entirety by at least ONE Congressman or Senator before the vote takes place! It is beyond absurd and irresponsible to me that our Congress voted on this monstrosity before anyone even read it.

The healthcare reform I advocate could be accomplished in the same way that Clinton implemented Reagan's welfare reform and would be far simpler and more efficient by including the following elements:

1) Increase competition among health insurance companies by opening interstate competition across state lines (like the automobile insurance industry). There is nothing like free market competition to bring the best value and price to consumers.

2) Make allowances for pre-existing conditions. By allowing the expansion of insurance pools to group memberships (such as Chamber of Commerce members, service clubs, etc.), the costs are spread over a larger number of premium payers which also spreads the cost of care—even the most expensive care. We are the wealthiest, most advanced, and most compassionate nation in the world. Our own citizens, willing to pay for health insurance, should not be kicked to the curb and treated as second-class citizens simply because they have a malady.

3) Introduce real tort reform. The unnecessary and unethical cost to, and burden on, our healthcare system by the number of frivolous malpractice suits is astronomical. The only ones who have benefited from these egregious suits are the lawyers involved. With the power of the legal lobby in Washington, it is no wonder real tort reform is yet to be introduced…and passed.

4) Increase the penalties and consequences for the criminal acts of insurance, Medicare and Medicaid fraud. This has been the "gift

that keeps on giving" for too many, for too long, and at great cost to our taxpaying public.

5) Have remedies in place for those who truly cannot afford healthcare coverage (see "compassionate nation" in number two above). However, we should not be providing free healthcare to those who are in our country illegally. We should not be providing free healthcare to those who just decide they do not want to pay for it. We do far too much of this today, and it is bankrupting our country.

6) Allow for personal Health Savings Accounts. Each individual should save and be responsible for their own and their families' healthcare choices. This savings account would eventually replace employer provided benefits, which are deducted from the employee's total salary package but are not completely at the discretion of the employee; they must be used for medical costs.

There seems to be a panicked desperation to pass healthcare reform but not to pass the cure. Healthcare costs will remain one of the most poignant issues facing our nation into the indefinite future. The cures do not involve a public option. The hand of government needs to release its death grip on the best healthcare system in the world. Iowa Senator Charles Grassley said, "Government is not a competitor, it's a predator."[91] If real reform is about cost and not control, then we need to consider more appropriate and better solutions worthy of our nation and society…worthy of *we the people.*

Excessive government mandates and domineering regulations on healthcare practitioners and health insurance companies are the chief causes of skyrocketing healthcare costs. Also, increased regulations and mandates in certain states makes it cost-prohibitive for some insurance companies to offer coverage.

In a state with particularly onerous mandates (and there are many such states), fewer insurance companies are willing to do business there, leading to diminished competition within that state. And because, as stated above, we do not have true interstate competition among insurance companies, consumers in these states are held hostage by these intrastate mandates, having fewer options for their healthcare needs than their peers just across state lines. Having limited options and diminished competition leads to increased costs for the consumer. Further, Americans should be able to choose which insurance coverage they need and should have the option *not* to pay for specific coverages they do not need. Reducing the number of mandates reduces costs. Nevada is tenth in the nation with fifty-two government mandated coverages. A 2009 autism mandate added one hundred dollars per year to every premium.[92] The Nevada law intended to help children with autism get the services they need but only twenty-five percent of those suffering from autism were covered. As a parent, I had a child with different educational and medical needs. As a former educator, I have taught children with autism. I am painfully aware of the struggles these families face. Effective legislation would recognize autism as a real medical condition and encourage companies to provide affordable insurance coverage choices for autism without penalizing unaffected citizens with higher insurance costs.

As a Nevada state legislator, I proposed a bill that allowed the creation of larger insurance pools through business or fraternal federations such as the Chamber of Commerce, labor unions or even Kiwanis or Rotary clubs. Larger risk pools allow for lower costs because insurers compete for the business of all patients including those with pre-existing conditions. The insurer can charge enough to cover the cost instead of passing it on to others. Those rare condition "orphan diseases" that are currently considered "uninsurable" because they require a lifetime of special care would be appropriate to cover in a Government subsidized program such as Medicare. In 2006, states were encouraged to create "high risk" pools where those with pre-existing conditions would receive care at the same cost as healthy Americans. This safety net cost would be spread across the pool

Government made a promise to millions of Americans when the Medicare laws passed. The promise remains but must not be expanded to the entire population. The system is unsustainable even at current levels. Real reform of Medicare is necessary. Cutting the waste, fraud, and abuse in Medicare would save funds that could be used to pay market rate for services. According to the FBI, Medicare fraud accounts for three to ten percent of all healthcare spending. According to the Medicare Payment Advisory Commission (Med-PAC), Medicare reimbursements to hospitals are only 94.1 cents of every dollar actually spent treating Medicare patients.

Medicare was well-intentioned, but as it stand today, it is antiquated, at best. It is based on a 1965 fee-for-service model without regard for disease management programs, wellness and prevention, or care coordination. Reducing the Medicare regulations and paperwork burdens that inflate costs would cut expenses to providers and in turn to patients. Providing the quality of healthcare Americans have come to expect requires an investment in advanced medical technology, salaries for well-trained technicians, nurses and doctors, and well-equipped facilities. The answer is not Medicare for all. Experts estimate that Medicare will be bankrupt by 2017. Expanding this entitlement will only increase the deficit. Commercially insured Americans currently subsidize the Medicare shortfall. Medicare already rations care to seniors by limiting hospital stays and by not covering one-hundred percent of health costs. Medicare needs reform. Encouraging choices such as Healthcare Savings Accounts will ease the pressure on the current system.

Tax-advantaged Healthcare Savings Accounts would bring individual cost efficiencies into the equation by encouraging everyone to shop for the best healthcare deal. Dollar-for-dollar tax credits for health savings accounts, insurance premiums, and medical expenditures would incentivize individual responsibility for healthcare. By paying for insurance with pre-tax dollars, individuals could save about thirty percent. Decreasing government regulations to allow people to change their coverages commensurate with specific changes in their health status and medical expenses will help offset and reduce global increases in premiums for everyone based on general criteria like aging, as is the norm today.

Our entire healthcare system, and therefore our entire citizenry, would be well served if we personalize much of what currently falls under Medicaid and Medicare. For example, those who truly cannot afford health insurance on their own could apply for, and receive, healthcare stamps from the federal government. With these stamps, our poor and "helpless" could purchase private insurance of the same grade and quality as those who can afford it on their own.

Our Internal Revenue Code incentivizes employer-provided healthcare, which is roughly sixty percent in America. Insurers do not have to market to consumers, only satisfy employers. By allowing health insurance choice across state lines, the competition at the consumer level will drive insurance costs down. There are more than thirteen hundred insurance companies competing for American healthcare dollars, but government regulation has limited our access to those services. Patient choice is a simple free-market solution.

Trial lawyers, after unions, are the largest contributors to the Democrat Party. This is a deep conflict of interest. As lawyers by trade, many federal legislators, like Mr. Reid are unable to distance themselves from the very disease that drives medical costs through the roof. Frivolous lawsuits are a major cause of rising healthcare costs and a chief obstacle that drives good doctors out of business. Defensive medicine is the fretful mixture of fear of lawsuits and a desire to provide the best patient care. Doctors authorize tests and procedures in part to reduce potential liability (real or perceived) and legal expenses from lawsuit risk. Malpractice insurance premiums, claims paid, and legal fees are key to the soaring costs of healthcare.

Tort reform (reducing pain and suffering damages for malpractice, and diminishing lawsuit risks so doctors are not compelled to practice defensive medicine) will lower medical costs on the front end. When providers have lower costs for liability insurance with the cost of frivolous lawsuits by ambulance-chasing trial lawyers significantly reduced, the savings will pass through to patients. The 2003 Medical Malpractice Initiative passed in Texas proved that capping liability awards at $250,000 for non-economic damages (such as pain and suffering) reduced the number of malpractice lawsuits. Medical liability insurance rates dropped an average of twenty percent. Nearly one-fourth of the doctors realized a fifty percent decrease in the cost of their premiums.[93]

Finally, immigration reform, refusing all but emergency healthcare to uninsured illegal aliens, will reduce hospital costs, and those savings will pass through to the overall healthcare system. The thrust is for common sense solutions that work. The uninsured place a significant burden on public services and inflate insurance costs. The need for choice-based tax-exempt health savings accounts and flexible spending accounts persuade millions of uninsured to get coverage. Market-based changes to the existing healthcare insurance system will empower doctors and patients and foster competition and choice. Government competition in the private sector undermines and dominates all other participants.

Americans understand that government-run healthcare begs for higher taxes. However, Washington's political elites are trying to jam down our throats (against the majority of public opinion and desire) an oppressive healthcare system from which they are exempting themselves! A healthcare system good enough for the average American should be good enough for the elite Beltway crowd of Harry, Barry and Nancy.

Until the time when all Americans:

1) Are free to make their own health decisions privately as they and their respective doctors see fit (not as a one-plan-fits-all widget and not as a Department of Motor Vehicles-styled bureaucracy that decides if a person is valuable enough to receive treatment)

2) Have cost-effective healthcare (not a bureaucratic nightmare with poor care, long waits, rationing, and ever-rising taxes to pay for its far-reaching waste and inefficiencies)

3) Reject healthcare based on the failed systems such as Canada, Britain, and Europe...

Be afraid...be very afraid!

"True western conservatives, Ted and I drive a truck, but we also have a car that gets nearly thirty miles per gallon of gas."

Chapter Seven

SCIENCE FICTION IS NOT SCIENCE

Energy production does not have to be at the expense of the environment. Conservation and clean air, along with a robust and prosperous energy-driven economy, are compatible.

SINCE THE START of 2009, the government under Reid, Obama, and Pelosi has moved to take control of our individual life choices by massively increasing taxes, gasoline prices, utilities bills, and all other purchases heavily dependent on energy. The control begins with the cars we drive, how we heat and cool our homes, what light bulbs we use, and the appliances in our kitchens. If left unchecked, all of this will bring soaring utility bills, spiking gasoline costs (and, in turn, higher cost for food and all consumer items because of gasoline related production and transportation increases) and higher income taxes.

The Left's "Cap and Trade" legislation is the same type of governmental limitation (or cap) used in agriculture and industry to reduce output and raise prices. Now the target is "pollutants."

Our government is regulating American citizens toward ever decreasing amounts of substances deemed as pollutants. Those who reduce their emissions by a greater amount than the limit of consumption that the government allocates to them receive credits. Those manufacturers that do not reduce their emissions, or production, must buy these credits from those with accumulated credits. Of course, administering the Cap and Trade scheme requires a massive new government bureaucracy passing the cost increase of this scheme to the consumer in increased fees[94] and increased costs for goods and services.

As my friend, staunchly conservative Nevada Senator Don Gustavson who joined me in the 2003 fight against the largest tax increase in Nevada history, said, "A fee is the same as a tax."

Government control and limitation (Cap and Trade) in agriculture manifests as government payments or subsidies that result in paying farmers not to produce with the hope of reducing production and, thereby, increasing demand which raises prices. My cousin, a Kansas wheat farmer and cattle rancher, sold his cows and put all his wheat land into "set aside." Fertile farmland that once provided family income for three generations has now returned to prairie grass. Why? Because, the government pays him more for fallow environmentally-friendly ground than my cousin can make on the open market selling wheat. My cousin avoids the headaches of watching prices fluctuate and the risk of hailstorms wiping out his crops.

The Cap and Trade policies for energy are just another attempt to curtail energy production by artificially manipulating the market with government regulation. This will breed government corruption by creating a system that fosters favors that enrich a few while raising prices and taxes on all energy. All of this is justified by the fantasy of global warming.

The frenzied delusion over man-caused global warming or climate change has promoted an alleged carbon dioxide emissions crisis. Proponents of this manufactured crisis demand that the government raise taxes on energy producers and increase the cost of energy for all Americans. Cap and Trade, or "scam and tax," is a thinly disguised way to ration energy by increasing energy prices through taxation.

By raising taxes on the price of electricity and gas, Americans will consume less. Prices will go up on every manufactured good, from food to vehicles, because of the increased government cost (tax) on energy used to produce or transport products. The dominoes fall when consumers cut back on spending, reducing production, resulting in fewer new jobs and higher unemployment.

Clearly, the attack on fossil fuels, especially coal, brings added burdens to middle class America, to workers in the energy industries, to truck drivers, to everyone but the chosen few who administer "carbon credits." Coal-fired electricity generation provides over fifty percent of the energy for many states including Indiana, Missouri, New Mexico, Pennsylvania, West Virginia, and Wyoming. Lower and middle class wage earners will spend a higher percentage of their incomes on gas to drive to work, increased grocery costs due to escalated energy cost for shipping, and swollen utility bills. Cap and Trade is a wealth redistribution plan that takes from besieged working folks and gives to wealthy investors who know how to leverage legislated entitlements.[95]

Shock waves went through America as we realized that our government meant to tax us for energy use. Cap and Trade destroys any hope of energy independence. The federal government is determined to force our reliance on alternative energy sources—which are not prepared to meet the demand—by taxing anyone who uses energy produced by fossil fuels.

The "energy reform" masquerade amounts to a citizen tax based on three areas of increased cost. First, costs for mandated increases in the use of "clean" energy such as wind and solar and the cost of new "green" standards for appliances and new construction pass through to consumers. Secondly, taxpayers will pick up the costs of building a national "smart grid" to transmit "green" energy from wind farms on the coast and solar arrays in the southwest. Thirdly, the Cap and Trade legislation with its set of punishments to energy users completes the energy bundle.[96]

The incredible redirection of our energy production away from fossil fuels to experimental, or even imaginary, sources of energy (all in the name of the contrived crisis of man-caused *global warming* and/or *climate change)* is an outrageous power grab by the liberal Left. On closer inspection, the entire plan is comprised of half-truths, outright lies, and poor science. The goal of Cap and Trade is a massive increase in government bureaucracy and taxes. The complete man-caused global warming theory is suspect, even within the ranks of those who purport to be its true believers. A University of Colorado disaster trend expert called the U.N. Secretary's report at the Global Humanitarian Forum "a poster child for how to lie with statistics," doing a "disservice" to those serious about climate change.[97]

With the debunking of the man-caused global warming "crisis," the initial reason for the necessity of the draconian Cap and Trade package on energy production is on shaky ground. The next plank of alternative energy sources is equally as specious.

Conservation: Love and Respect for the Environment

My three brothers all chose to work in the energy field: Vic in off-peak refrigeration, David in coal, and Bruce on the pipeline in Prudhoe Bay. In my family, I was the exception in my choice of vocations. While my three brothers all went into engineering, I chose liberal arts. As the only girl, I did not share my brothers' interests. Engineering seemed instinctive with them. They would use shovels to dig in the hardpan Virginia & Truckee

Railroad bed that ran behind our motel. They built a "fort" four feet deep and ten feet by ten feet square and covered it with boards then camouflaged it with dirt. It had a trap door so we could sit on the dark cool earth during the hot summer.

We had second-hand bicycles when I was ten. I liked to ride, but the boys became mechanics. When Vic was 14, he bought a Vespa bike. He took it apart down to the axles, and then put it back together, just to see how it worked. He rode it until he could afford a car, then he took the car apart.

Once, my mother came home to find our perfectly good toaster in pieces on the kitchen table. Vic promised it would be operational by morning. It was, but she laid down the law about not tinkering with her kitchen appliances.

Vic became a mechanical engineer, earned an MBA, and started his own business. Inventions fascinated him. He holds a patent on freezing water at 43 to 48 degrees Fahrenheit. Vic started out working for an engineering firm in solar energy. Then he became a partner in an off-peak electric refrigeration business that he bought and turned into an international source for low cost electrical air conditioning for large buildings.

Bruce and David planned to be miners. Bruce liked working outside and could not see the benefits of school, so he started working on heavy equipment for construction projects. Bruce joined the Operating Engineers Union and went to Alaska to work on the pipeline as a crane operator.

David became a miner. He earned a degree in Mining Engineering from the University of Nevada's Mackay School of Mines and went to work in the coal industry. When he retired, he was the manager of a Wyoming low sulfur coalmine.

When we were growing up, industry and the environment were just beginning to collide. As the environmental movement gained religious fervor, preservation rather than conservation became the goal. Humankind was demonized as the cause of all climatic and environmental problems. Around 1968, the condition of the land became sacrosanct, although in reality the earth is constantly changing. The camper's code of take out what you bring in, exercise fire safety, and leave the land as you found it was not good enough. Now, wilderness meant that it was off-limits to any human activity, recreational or industrial.

Growing up in Nevada, our family was close to nature and spent hours, days, and months exploring the wilds and caring for the land. We were the original "no-trace" campers with a great love for the outdoors and natural beauty. Farming, ranching, hunting, and mining all coexisted then in relative harmony. We Westerners generally have a love for the land. We take stewardship of the land seriously.

Strife began when big city eco-liberals demanded compliance with unrealistic and unnecessary regulations. Westerners resent their arrogance and ignorance, as well as their wanton disregard for sound science. God made us stewards of the land to use and conserve it, not keep it as it was in 1968 in some sort of vacuum-sealed preservation with a look-but-do not-touch mentality.

My husband, Ted, got his degree in wildlife management, and began his career with the Department of the Interior Bureau of Land Management in watershed inventory. He scouted and recorded many miles of the Nevada Desert. He spent thirty-seven years in natural resources. He is an avid hunter and fisherman, something of a modern day Daniel Boone.

As a conservationist, I know there is a wise and appropriate use of natural resources that is both productive and protective. From a Washington, D.C., office, it is hard to understand land use beyond the concrete and asphalt of the Beltway. In their intellectual arrogance, the big city, eco-liberals seem to believe they know better how to use the western lands than the people who live on the land. Sometimes eco-liberals even profit financially from their pseudo knowledge.

The Nevada "land swaps," which include water rights, have been the source of suspected Reid-for-profit ventures. Politicians pick government land to swap for private lands, making sure that they and their friends profit. The land seems to have only two uses: wilderness that is off-limits to human beings, and wilderness ripe for cities sucking water from underground aquifers across the state to pour into Las Vegas casino fountains. Both ventures garner campaign contributions as swapping land from one category to another brings millions into some politicians' bank accounts.

Green Verses Greenbacks

Energy literally runs the U.S. economy. Cheap and abundant energy has not only made everyone's life richer, but it has also provided the riches for our country, enabling our industries and individuals to clean up and reduce pollution. Yet, the Green movement will not peacefully co-exist with the energy needs of the nation. Left wing ecology lobbies want to strangle the lifeblood of our nation, rich in abundant fossil fuels, with government over-regulation, Cap and Trade taxes, and restricted development.

Government has escalated the costs of energy for everyone, and contributed to the loss of U.S. manufacturing. While energy costs used to make up about seven percent of operating budgets of businesses and industries, that number has skyrocketed to thirty percent. Increased energy costs cut into profit margins, raise prices of fuels, and drive U.S. companies abroad, or broke. Talk to a trucker if you have any doubt how this works.

Fossil fuels (coal, oil, gas, liquefied natural gas) have been America's main energy sources for the 19th and 20th centuries. They will be our primary sources for the 21st century. They powered the world's Industrial Age. Forty-nine percent of the nation's power comes from coal, twenty percent from natural gas, and twenty percent from nuclear. Hydroelectric accounts for seven percent and all other sources make up less than five percent.[98]

The invention of the "carbon footprint" as an ecological crisis jeopardizes almost ninety percent of our energy resources. Somehow, the five percent tail of wind power, geothermal and bio-fuels are supposed to wag the dog of fossil and nuclear fuels and decrease dependence on foreign oil. Wind power, geothermal and bio-fuels are surely worth further exploration, but they will not replace fossil fuels in our, or our children's, lifetime. In addition, these shallow alternative sources of power come with considerable negatives and costs.

Solar Energy: A Fantasy in Sunlight

Nellis Air Force Base near Las Vegas, Nevada boasts the largest solar panel field in North America with 140 acres built on a capped landfill. Yet, it is only a secondary energy supply for the base, which relies mainly on traditional supplies for the majority of its energy. The solar photovoltaic array consists of 72,000 panels and supplies thirty million kilowatt-hours, which is twenty-five percent of the total electricity use for roughly 12,000 residents.[99] Few acknowledge the energy source (and enormous "carbon footprint") used to develop the copper, aluminum, and glass components of the solar panels. The amount of land and the previous use of the land play into the Environmental Impact Statement (EIS) that will ultimately dictate which communities will be able to supplement their energy resources with solar.

Solar power represents a minuscule amount of energy produced in the United States. It is best suited for sunny climates where it serves as a small supplement to a main energy source. Nellis would need to expand to 560,000 acres to power a city of twelve million! Paving Rhode Island with wall-to-wall solar panels would not supply the needs of New York City.

Wind Power: Not In My Back Yard!

In 1998, a Norwegian study of wind power in Denmark concluded that it has "serious environmental effects, insufficient production, and high production costs." The study raises grave questions about the wisdom of the United States seeking to increase dependence on wind power. With most of the world retreating from government subsidies for wind power projects, our consideration of wind as a major energy source demands scrutiny.

Denmark (population 5.3 million) has over 6,000 giant turbines that produced electricity equal to nineteen percent of what the country used in 2002. Yet they did not shut down one conventional power plant. Because of the intermittency and variability of the wind, conventional power plants must be kept running at full capacity to meet the actual demand for electricity. Most cannot turn on and off as the wind dies and rises and the quick ramping up and down of those that can be would actually increase their output of pollution and carbon dioxide (the primary "greenhouse" gas). Therefore, when the wind is blowing just right for the turbines, the power they generate is usually a surplus and sold to other countries at an extremely discounted price, or the turbines are simply turned off.

In high winds, ironically, the turbines must be stopped because they are easily damaged. Build-up of dead bugs halves the maximum power generated by a wind turbine, reducing the average power generated by twenty five percent and more. Build-up of salt on offshore turbine blades similarly reduces the power generated by twenty to thirty percent. International leaders in wind production have retreated from the industry.

Denmark, the industry leader, abandoned plans for three offshore wind farms and slated withdrawal of subsidies for existing sites. Spain, Germany, Switzerland, The Netherlands, Japan, Ireland, and Australia have also limited subsidies and purchases from the power source.[100] We might overcome technical problems with science, but wind power lacks public favor when people are asked to support it for their own communities. The negative impact on migrating bird populations has surfaced in California wind farms, and NIMBY (not in my back yard) weighs-in heavily with wind power opposition. Many people think that wind turbines are ugly, they ruin scenery, they kill large numbers of birds and harm ecosystems, they make noise, and they lower property values. People think wind power is a good idea…somewhere else.

The small Nevada ghost town of Virginia City thrives on visitors. Residents packed a county commissioner meeting complaining about the visual impact of a proposed wind farm. These residents did not agree that the $200 million to $400 million wind farm would "enhance" the scenery of their historic town with sixty-nine 330-foot tall windmills and a five-mile transmission line.[101]

Geothermal: An Addition to the Energy Grid

Geothermal energy is renewable heat energy produced from the earth. Its power stations are small and do not have much impact on the environment. Beyond the cost of building the power station, the energy is almost free, much like harnessing hydroelectric power by damming rivers. The main source of geothermal for power generation is steam or hot water flashed to steam, which in turn drives turbines to generate electricity.

A big problem with geothermal energy production is finding suitable locations for a power plant with a type of surface rock that allows for easy drilling. Sometimes the best geothermal sites are located in remote areas with wilderness, scenic, or recreation value. In those settings, transmission lines will impact the environment negatively.

A geothermal site may temporarily "run out of steam," lasting from months to several years, during which time no electricity is generated. Geothermal is difficult to transport, so it must be used to generate small amounts of electricity for localized areas.

Geothermal byproducts include hazardous minerals. It is extremely difficult to dispose of hydrogen sulfide safely. Other troublesome byproducts can include arsenic, mercury, and ammonia. Gases dissipated by released steam often include carbon dioxide (CO_2), methane, hydrogen sulfide, ammonia, nitrogen, and hydrogen. Groundwater contamination is preventable by collection and re-injection, which also maintains underground reservoir pressures to prevent subsidence of the ground. Then there is the likelihood of recurring low-level earthquakes. Although no stronger than magnitude four, they damage homes and foundations.

Finally, cost is a consideration. Geothermal power plant construction is more expensive than large coal-fired natural gas or wind facilities. Because operation and maintenance are affordable and there are no fuel costs, geothermal is becoming more competitive.[102]

Nevada is second only to California in rich geothermal sources, with fifteen plants that supply electricity to local areas like Reno, Fallon, and Elko. Where hot springs exist, hydroelectric plants can be built and contribute a modest percentage to our energy grid with a minimal "carbon footprint," unless, of course, the Greens start over-regulating or advocating the destruction of geothermal projects like they have done with dams for their impact on the environment.

Biofuels: Not Ready for Prime Time

Biofuels, such as ethanol, once viewed as alternative energy sources that reduce harmful emissions, now seem to many to be increasingly suspect. One U.N. reporter called biofuels a "crime against humanity."[103] The creation of biofuels takes away from acreage for food production and requires more land than solar panels. The United States consumes about one-fifth of the corn grown to make ethanol, thereby increasing food prices and decreasing food for export. Manufacturing these fuels drops a large carbon footprint, and actually exhausts more fuel in the production process than it creates. In turn, more natural gas and oil must be imported, increasing U.S. deficits. That does not take into account over $3 billion in government subsidies awarded to producers of biofuels.[104] Nor does it factor in the impact of periodic government subsidy cuts that cause the loss of jobs created by those entitlements as energy fads come and go. Experts in ecology and agriculture are concerned that any significant transfer of land from food production to biofuels will increase starvation in the

Third World. Like the steam powered car, biofuels are an interesting and innovative idea, but not practicable. It is just not realistic to expect biofuels to reduce or replace our dependency on fossil fuels.

Nuclear

From a carbon emissions standpoint, one of the "greenest" renewable energy sources is nuclear. It has zero carbon emissions. Several sci-fi movies have created a public perception of imminent disaster looming from nuclear plants. This perception comes in spite of the fact that the U.S. Navy has cruised the oceans with nuclear reactors for decades. Green opposition's use of fear, aided by Harry Reid, has severely stifled the nuclear industry in the United States. Liberalism is not about intellectual facts. It is about emotion.

France gets eighty-five percent of its electric power from nuclear energy (we get about twenty percent). The 1979 partial core meltdown at the Three Mile Island power plant near Harrisburg, Pennsylvania, although the most serious nuclear accident in United States history, caused no deaths or verified injuries. The 1986 Soviet Union Chernobyl accident is blamed directly for several deaths and remains an ecological problem. Construction standards in the Soviet Union were far behind our own. Output overruled safety in the U.S.S.R. More recently, the earthquake and tsunami in Japan have caused a nuclear reactor crisis. This crisis should not prompt another politically driven regulatory crisis in the U.S.—but rather should prompt hearings to examine and separate facts from fears so that we can improve upon our own technology and safety.

Three Mile Island and Chernobyl sparked anti-nuclear protests and created a virtual ban through regulation on new nuclear power plants in the U.S. By siding with the Sierra Club and Greenpeace, Harry Reid, a major fear-monger, demanded closure of the Yucca Mountain Repository. One-fifth of our nation's electricity is produced by 104 nuclear reactors at sixty-six power plants around the United States. Vermont is the highest user at 72.5 percent. Even man-caused global warming enthusiasts such as Union of Concerned Scientists, Natural Resources Defense Council, and Environmental Defense agree that nuclear power is part of the long-term energy solution. Yet the Sierra Club and Greenpeace argue against nuclear power citing radioactive waste, expensive construction and weapons-grade spent fuel security issues.[105]

Storage of spent nuclear fuel is a problem that our government promised to solve over twenty-five years ago, and has spent billions addressing. The designated site for storage of 60,000 tons of used nuclear fuel from power plants and 20,500 tons from the military is Yucca Mountain which is on the edge of the Nuclear Test Site in the middle of the Nevada desert. Any alternative location requires a legislative change to the Nuclear Waste Policy Act (NWPA). Nuclear power-producing companies have paid 0.1 cents per kilowatt-hour[106] (passed through to electricity customers) building $30 billion in a fund for storage at Yucca Mountain. That is more than $750 million in annual payments into a fund that paid out $10 billion and has a $22 billion surplus that earns annual interest in excess of $198 million.

The spent fuel was supposed to begin moving into the Yucca Mountain facility in 1998. Instead, the power plants' spent fuel is sitting in temporary dry cask storage adjacent to reactors across the country. The Department of Energy currently manages nuclear spent fuels at 121 sites in thirty-nine states. Taxpayers have paid a $560 million bill via the Department of Energy to reimburse the storage costs. The nuclear power companies also began suing the government for breach of contract. They have won 72 cases. Litigation costs taxpayers $500 million annually and may not be paid from the Nuclear Waste Fund (NWF). Estimates for the total potential liability range as high as $50 billion.[107]

Waste is clearly a disadvantage of nuclear energy. The Yucca Mountain site was designed and constructed to help alleviate this real, and national, problem. Unfortunately, like most government projects, politics has again entangled the solution. After the Yucca Mountain site was secured in Nevada, Harry Reid began a fear-mongering campaign against the repository, calling it a "dump." In 2006, he claimed victory and touted the Yucca Mountain Nuclear Waste Storage Facility as "dead."[108]

Obama promised Reid the elimination of the 2011 funding for a review to open Yucca Mountain.[109] While Harry Reid fights over the best way to rid the state of the repository, it will be up to the citizens of Nevada to demand the common sense solution for removing spent fuel rods from nuclear facilities, especially from locations on our seacoasts that are susceptible to earthquakes and tsunamis. A disaster such as the one that occurred in Japan would be devastating to the whole nation (and potentially the world), not just our coastlines.

With the advancement of technology over the past thirty years, spent nuclear fuel reprocessing has become a reality. Nuclear energy fuel can be reprocessed to recover fissile materials in order to provide fresh fuel for existing and future nuclear power plants. Several European countries, Russia, and Japan all have a policy for reprocessing used nuclear fuel, although government policies in many other countries have not yet addressed the various aspects of reprocessing. The major motivation for reprocessing is to recover unused energy from the original uranium and reduce the amount of high-level radioactive waste. As much as ninety-five percent of the fissile uranium energy remains in the spent fuel. The level of radioactivity of reprocessed waste is much lower and deteriorates more rapidly than the spent fuel.[110] In 2009, it was estimated that the fuel available from recycling of current nuclear spent fuels could power United States reactors for nearly thirty years.[111]

For example, mixed-oxide fuel (MOX) is the result of an advanced form of reprocessing.[112] Creating MOX is relatively old technology, but until fairly recently it has hardly been used around the world, even in the U.S. Although MOX was developed in 1963, it was not used commercially until the 1980's. Today about forty reactors in Belgium Switzerland, Germany, and France are licensed to use MOX. The Mixed Oxide Fuel Fabrication Facility (MFFF) at the Savannah River Site in South Carolina is expected to begin converting U.S. plutonium to MOX in 2016.[113]

MOX is not the only reprocessing solution. Another is PUREX, an acronym for Plutonium and Uranium Recovery by Extraction. It is been around since 1972. Using PUREX, nuclear reprocessing can recover weapon-grade materials from spent nuclear reactor fuel.

With reprocessing Yucca Mountain becomes a "renewable" resource for Nevada as well as a safer haven for spent fuels from the existing nuclear energy producers. While Senator Reid works to deny this resource for Nevada (and the nation), the potential has captured the attention of eleven communities in Idaho, Illinois, Kentucky, New Mexico, Ohio, South Carolina, Tennessee, and Washington State.[114]

Nevada could be a big winner. Nuclear energy could reduce our dependence on fossil fuels while producing electricity with zero carbon emissions based on proven science. In addition, research and development facilities housed on, or near, the reprocessing plant have the potential to draw scientists from all over the world, bring grants into the Nevada University system, and attract professors and students into the math and science fields. This renewable resource would, consequently, create jobs in Nevada.

Does the Future Include Fossil Fuels?

Energy independence should be our national goal. It would improve our economy and our security. We spend about $700 billion yearly on foreign oil. Some of that money underwrites terrorism in the Middle East and Latin America.

America can overcome the energy challenges by using domestic fossil fuels as a bridge to energy independence. The United States has fossil fuel reserves, in one form or another, that can last hundreds of years. Just because the Greens have convinced the Democrats to forbid American people access to these reserves does not mean the resources are not there. The United States needs to drill and mine, here and now, to pay less for energy, and to decrease our dependence on the historically unstable Middle East.

Renewable power sources furnish only six percent of the nation's energy requirements. Offering tax credits and subsidies will increase the renewable energy supply to ten percent by 2030. Oil and gas will continue to deliver more than fifty percent of the nation's energy source regardless of climate policies restricting carbon dioxide emissions. Many native petroleum resources are yet to be developed. Nevada has the most abundant North American on-shore artesian oil well, in addition to thicker and richer gas shales than those in the Texas Fort Worth Basin.[115]

As Americans work to develop zero-emissions alternative technologies, we must continue to draw more oil and fossil fuels from American soil to meet our shorter-term energy needs. Our elected representatives should encourage accelerated development and drilling from offshore fields, as well as from those in Montana, Alaska, and North Dakota, and undeveloped sources in Nevada. Refining capacity using the latest in scrubber technology should be expanded and the regulatory blockages removed that have been put in place by environmental extremism and litigation.

The Real Energy Solutions

Solar, wind, biofuels, and geothermal are the hot new designer energy sources. Unfortunately, they remain two to three times more costly to produce in high volumes than fossil fuels. In every test in the past fifty years, none has proven economically "competitive." The T. Boone Pickens windmill plan was based entirely on tax credits. Currently, alternative energy solutions are only feasible on the backs of American taxpayer subsidies. Subsidies will bring higher taxes, as well as higher energy and utility bills. Subsidies cause an artificial business boom dependent on government money. A little discussed, unintended consequence is the closure of those businesses and the loss of jobs that result when those subsidies are pulled and given to the next hot technology. Time is a deterrent to immediate solutions within the alternative fuels industry.

The common sense solution remains a combination approach that does not throw the energy baby out with the environmental bath water. Alternative fuels may be a supplemental power source in the distant future, but clean coal is America's most abundant and affordable energy resource today. We have coal reserves for hundreds of years at the current rate of use. We must encourage new technologies, such as coal gasification, and the development of carbon capture and storage to reduce emissions, that must be encouraged.

Because of Harry Reid's agenda of blocking construction of new coal-fired power plants, Nevada is part of the Democrat stalemate! Slavish dedication to environmental extremists has resulted in shortages, higher prices, job loss, dependence on nations hostile to us, and a looming crisis of gas lines and brownouts. Such shortsighted, environmental extremist games put a chokehold on production, increase prices, and encourage the possibility of commodity manipulation. It is not acceptable in Nevada or in the nation as a whole.

The development of flexible fuel vehicles, as well as vehicles with higher gas mileage, that operate with more efficient engine operation is a key ingredient to reducing energy demands. Recently, Ted and I bought our four-door mid-sized Buick for two reasons: (1) it was American made, and (2) it gets thirty to thirty-five miles per gallon. The American consumer wants to conserve energy and save money. We do not need a government agency with thousands of bureaucrats spending billions of dollars to tell us to save money, conserve energy, and take care of where we live. Ted and I accept our God-given role as stewards of the land.

A common sense plan would keep prices low by increasing fossil fuel supplies and developing alternatives that are competitive at the lower price. This would not allow the typical politician to raise taxes, create massive new bureaucracies, take over the energy industries, or make decisions from Washington, D.C. that result in the loss of individual freedoms. In typical liberal fashion, the British Petroleum oil spill in the Gulf of Mexico was used to close down all production in the Gulf, furthering the liberal agenda to stop domestic production rather than punishing the intolerable actions of one bad player. The Environmental Protection Agency (EPA) did nothing to police or prevent the oil spill. The EPA's only solution was more regulation and shutdowns. Instead of moratoriums and more regulation, the government should set and enforce fair, efficient, and effective safety and environmental standards. Yet Obama's and the EPA's policies, such as a moratorium on drilling in the Gulf of Mexico for U.S. companies (while inviting Brazil to drill in those same waters), only encourages more antics by oil and energy speculators like. J.P. Morgan who are some of the real culprits regarding the higher price of fossil fuels.

Energy production does not have to be at the expense of the environment. Conservation and clean air, along with a robust and prosperous energy-driven economy, are compatible. Energy companies want a reputation of being environmentally conscious. At best, these same companies want the trust of the American people; at worst, they certainly want to avoid huge fines when something goes wrong.

American industries are the most responsible and pollution-free industries in the world. Our industries have the ingenuity that will create possibilities if our government gets out of their way and encourages freedom. Progress follows when free people dream, invent, and prosper. Progress does not happen when Big Brother government strips away individual choice and incentive with a hidden socialist agenda.

Americans need a government they can trust when it comes to national energy policies.

Chapter Eight

OVER THE FENCE OF THE CONSTITUTION

When we sacrifice principles for friendships, America ends up with "good old boy" politics.

THE POET ROBERT FROST wrote, "Good fences make good neighbors."[116] They also keep us safe.

My father built the "pen" for my brothers and me when we were toddlers in order to keep us safe from anyone who might come onto our property and to keep us from going onto busy Highway 395 in front of our motel. We were strictly forbidden to climb over that fence because we could be injured if we tried and fell. He expected us to go through the gate.

In much the same way, our Founding Fathers built a fence around this nation, called the Rule of Law, and articulated it in our Constitution and Bill of Rights. These documents define the character of our nation. American citizens are kept safe within its borders and rules. The Constitution clearly defines the privileges of freedom. It clearly describes how others may achieve those freedoms by becoming naturalized citizens. However, since the beginning of our nation, not everyone has been satisfied with the gate of the Constitution. Some have preferred to circumvent it and climb over the fence.

In my office hangs my State of Nevada Certificate of Election containing my oath of office. It reads:

I, Sharron E. Angle, do **solemnly swear that I will support, protect and defend the constitution and government of the United States, and the constitution and government of the State of Nevada,** against all enemies, whether domestic or foreign, and that I will bear true faith, allegiance and loyalty to the same, any ordinance, resolution or law of any state notwithstanding, and that I will well and faithfully perform all the duties off the office of Member, Nevada State Assembly in and for District 26 on which I am about to enter so help me God.[117]

That oath demanded that I uphold the Constitutions of the United States and the State of Nevada. Little did I realize how that oath would be challenged during my eight years as a Nevada Assemblywoman. The lessons I have learned while honoring that oath have motivated me to be vigilant on behalf of the rule of constitutional law. I have fought those attempting to go over the fence of both Constitutions via judicial activism, oath breaking, election fraud, and by trespassing.

Our United States Constitution has served us well these last two hundred plus years. Recent trends of bending and breaking the Constitution to conform to the whims of the moment, if not stopped, will destroy our nation.

Judicial Activism Goes Over the Fence

"There's nothing we can do." I heard the despair in the Republican Minority Leader's voice as I entered the room.

I asked, "What has happened? Did we hear from the court?"

It was Thursday, and we had been anxiously awaiting the outcome of an unprecedented lawsuit filed in the Nevada Supreme Court by the Attorney General. The lawsuit, filed against the Nevada State Legislature, came on Sunday at the request of the Governor. The lawsuit alleged that the Legislature had misconstrued the State Constitution by abiding with the requirement that the Body could only pass tax increases with a two-thirds super majority. The restriction had been added to Nevada's Constitution by a people's referendum in 1994.

One State Senator justified her support for this action by using the usual Democrat spins that included irrational statements, personal attacks, and name-calling (without naming names, of course). She articulated the time-honored Democrat ploy of "I want to do this and you won't let me, so you're mean and hate children, too." The coups de grace were incendiary invectives of "held hostage" and "obstructionists."[118] These spin tactics suspend reasoned debate, cost-benefit analyses, demand for accountability or any arguments that justify a program that wastes money or makes matters worse; in short, they are diversions, using hollow arguments that cannot stand on their own merits.

In 2003, I was part of that Nevada State Legislature as an Assemblywoman. Fourteen Assembly members and I held firm against an onerous tax increase, vigorously supported by special-interest groups. Nevadans, by ballot, had passed a two-thirds voting requirement to raise taxes to protect themselves from a legislature all too eager to take and spend other people's money for whatever cause or program the Legislature fancied. As in many states, there are a powerful few in Nevada, who seem to control the politics of the state through money and influence. Our band of fifteen, dubbed the "Mean Fifteen" by the press, called these four men "the Power Rangers." Unable to convince or browbeat enough legislators to go along with the largest tax increase in Nevada's history, the Power Rangers went shopping to find judges they knew to be sympathetic to their cause.

Clearly, our small band of freedom fighters knew why we had seen one of the Power Rangers heading to the Supreme Court building while another went to the Governor's office, and two more came into the Legislative building. The ability to watch their activities is an advantage of having the three branches of government all housed in the same complex in close proximity within the same complex.

The answer to my question about the Court's decision was in the grimaces of three of my fellow Assemblymen. Fifteen of us had refused to raise taxes, not only through the regular session, but also through a special session and into the second special session. The "Fearless Fifteen," as we dubbed ourselves, were holding firm and blocking the increase that the Governor and the special interests were determined to achieve. We remembered Ben Franklin's famous caution when asked what government the Constitutional Convention had given the people: "A Republic, *if* you can keep it."[119]

The United States is a Democratic Republic, with an emphasis on Republic. The trouble with a direct democracy, which destroyed Athens and ruined Rome, is that if the majority votes directly, it always votes itself more and more free stuff from the government. Eventually, that destroys the economy and the nation. This would be bad enough, but the history of direct democracy in Athens and Rome has a history of jailing, killing, or ostracizing whoever got in the way of the popular agenda.

Representative democracy ("republic") preserves the bigger picture of the best interests of the nation as a whole, rather than feathering the legislator's nest, enriching the legislator's special interest buddies, or grabbing pork for political payback or favors. A republic has checks and balances between the different branches of government, elections "to throw the bums out," and the right for anyone to petition their legislature, and courts "where no one is above the law."

A republic assumes that the government will be limited by the voting public, thereby protecting and preserving the rights of individuals and minorities against a potentially tyrannical majority. A republic also affords protections from a tyrannical government striving to grow in power, size, and reach. In recent years our own government has been on a power-grabbing binge to feed itself and grow at a pace that, if continued, will destroy—and bankrupt—this great nation from within. Our federal government has grown into such a top-heavy bureaucracy that it takes an average of seventy-five percent of the revenue allocated to any of its programs, right off the top, for self-serving "overhead costs." By comparison, any charity is considered potentially fraudulent if it uses more than ten percent of donations for overhead.

The overwhelming conservative victories in the 2010 elections were a shining example of the protection of our great Republic at work, whereby the people—through the power of the voting booth—began reining in this feeding frenzy and power grab by our government. The people, through the systemic protection of our Republic, sent a resounding message to our leaders all throughout the land: "Get it together...or get out!"

Ben Franklin envisioned a system of government that would keep external powers from conquering, and internal greed and power-mongering from destroying, the new republic. I understand the pragmatism (and the pessimism) in Ben Franklin's motivations for a system of checks and balances. I was never more acutely aware of the need for this pragmatism than that day when I walked into the room among my fellow legislators.

The Assembly Republican Minority Leader deftly typed the end to an e-mail, clicked "send," and turned off his computer with his left hand. He had lost his right arm long ago in a farm accident but had so well adjusted from the loss that almost no one paid attention to his disability. His knowledge of the Nevada political and legislative intricacies was legendary. He could use those intricacies as easily as he had just operated his computer.

I trusted his instincts and in my position as the Minority Whip, I wanted to know what direction we were going to take.

"The Supreme Court has ruled that the two-thirds requirement is procedural and that funding education is essential in the Nevada Constitution so..." Our leader paused a moment to take a deep breath.

I finished the sentence for him. "They're saying that we cannot hold back the tax? They have struck down the Nevada Constitution's two-thirds vote requirement to pass a tax? That means the Democrats can pass a tax with a simple majority vote and we cannot do anything?"

Everyone in the room nodded. Judicial fiat had not only overruled the will of the people, but had done so in a manner that was sheer sophistry. In essence the court ruling said that since the education establishment (as in the teachers' union—a mainstay of the Democrat Party) wanted the money, then they would get it. What the law said and what the people wanted (and was in the best interests of the State) just did not matter to the Court.

Nothing was more important to the Founding Fathers and to the Framers of the Constitution than the separation of powers—an independent judiciary, legislature, and executive branch. Modern Liberalism has made a mockery of this concept by "judge shopping" for opinions that thwart the rights of the people and legislatures. These Progressive Socialists, through judicial fiat, try to annul laws unpleasant to them that have been passed lawfully by the people, such as California's propositions limiting welfare benefits to illegal aliens or defining marriage as between a man and a woman.

Similarly, judge shopping can create completely new laws and rights on issues like homosexual marriage, abortion, loss of property rights to fanciful endangered species (whose endangerment and species identification are often manufactured by the court). The worst nightmare of our Founding Fathers was a judiciary appointed for life and dedicated to rewriting the Constitution by overturning the will of the people as well as legislatures, thus representing the threats of tyranny and factions.

In a Las Vegas newspaper article published a few days after the Supreme Court decision regarding our Nevada tax increase, a reporter revealed the truth about a deal the Supreme Court Justices had made with Nevada legislative power brokers in exchange for their decision. He took heat for not revealing his specific source, citing him only as a "former judge," who had said, "The fix was in" in *Guinn v. Legislature*.[120]

The super majority requirement, part of the Constitution of Nevada, was more recent law than the educational funding requirement and clearly should have prevailed. It curbed the power to tax. The power to tax is the power to confiscate. Governments have an insatiable appetite for spending to accommodate the demands of special interests and pork-barrel projects. The beneficiaries of those projects provide the funding and influence for the legislators' re-elections, so…the legislators raise taxes to pay for their special interest spending sprees.

Re-election to positions of power has become the driving force behind the decisions of most representatives, at the expense of the true needs or desires of the electorate. To protect the interests of the taxpayers, the restraint against cavalier tax-and-spend is enshrined in the Nevada State Constitution. Nothing chafes a legislature more than restrictions on the ability to take taxpayer money and spend it. It comes as no surprise that ever since the two-thirds tax restraint initiative passed in 1994, legislators and lobbyists have been searching madly for a loophole to circumvent it.

The Fearless Fifteen, we who had stopped the tax increase with our steadfast minority votes, sat talking for two hours in disbelief.

The attorneys our caucus contacted advised us that there was no avenue of relief since the Supreme Court of Nevada had the final say in such matters. It was not in my nature to give up. I had to exhaust every possible option from every source. I could hear my mother's voice saying, "Don't quit doing what is right."

The next day, I started calling attorneys and legal institutions. After many calls and numerous voice mails, to my pleasant surprise, I finally spoke with a real person. After stating my case, the response came: "There's nothing you can do."

With mounting frustration I asked, "Is there no one who cares about the Constitution anywhere in the United States?"

The answer came back as, "Well, you might try Dr. John Eastman at the Claremont Institute. He's a professor at Chapman University."

I glanced at the clock as I dialed. It was Friday, 4:30 p.m. *What are the chances?* I said to myself as a secretary answered and then surprisingly connected me straight through to Dr. Eastman.

After a few minutes of introductory conversation he said, "I've been watching your case with great interest, but I don't think there is anything you can do."

"You're my last hope," I said with a tremble in my voice. "Would you please look at it one more time?"

"Okay...I'll call you back in half an hour, but don't get your hopes up too high."

It was the longest thirty minutes in my legislative history, but the phone finally rang. "It is a long shot, but they've definitely violated the U.S. Constitution," Dr. Eastman said. He went on to say he would be putting the case together with his team of graduate students. In fact, they worked night and day with little sleep until he met me in Federal Court in Reno several days later. I was overjoyed and celebrated the Providence of expert assistance from one of the foremost constitutional attorneys in the country.

Two days later, on Sunday evening, I sent rapid-fire e-mails to Dr. Eastman in Irvine, California describing the battle over the largest tax increase in the history of Nevada as it was being "rammed and jammed" through the Legislature without regard to content or consequence. The proposed tax increase legislation passed over the Fearless Fifteen's strenuous objections by a simple majority in the Assembly, not with the two-thirds approval the Nevada Constitution required.

On the advice of Dr. Eastman, our Nevada Attorney filed a request for a Temporary Restraining Order (TRO). On Monday, the TRO was granted by the court, and as the Senate prepared to pass the "illegal" bill approved by the Assembly, the TRO was formally served demanding that the Legislature cease and desist until the case went to court on Wednesday.

The Senate Majority Leader called for a vote over objections made three times by a Senator, who repeatedly made the point that it was an illegal bill. The Legislature's legal counsel advised the Majority Leader three times not to act on the bill. Finally, he relented, being forced to adjourn without a vote on the bill.

Eastman had stopped the steamroller, and the Fearless Fifteen were jubilant. Dr. John Eastman will always be one of my heroes because of that day and the days that followed.

When Dr. Eastman and I arrived at Federal District Court, picketers with big signs were there ahead of us. The signs displayed the names of the

Fearless Fifteen surrounded by the red circle and slash line across them. It was the first time I had been the subject of an organized protest. The court claimed it had no jurisdiction over the matter, refused to rule, and instead lifted the TRO against the Legislature.

Angle v. Guinn (named for my suit against the Governor who had sued the Legislature) went all the way to the U.S. Supreme Court. The efforts yielded mixed results. The Court decided that our claims were moot because the tax bill had subsequently passed with the required two-thirds vote after much strong-arming had persuaded one legislator to switch sides on the issue.[121] After all the dust settled, however, our efforts had claimed three victories:

1) First, the Legislature refused to pass a tax by a simple majority, preferring instead to convince one legislator to change his vote to gain the required "super majority." In the end our efforts caused them to abide by the Nevada Constitution, which they should have chosen to do in the first place.

2) Second, the Nevada Supreme Court Justices who ruled against the Nevada Constitution's two-third requirement in favor of political power brokers were replaced with different Justices after the next election. The voters were outraged by the behavior of those Justices who sided politically with the Governor and his ill-intentioned cronies and, by so doing, had trashed the protective role of a legal and binding Constitution.

3) Third, the new Court reversed the previous unconstitutional opinion and restored the two-third requirement to the Nevada Constitution.[122]

Here is one lesson learned from this story. Liberal Progressive Socialists subvert the role of the courts to enrich themselves from the process and compel opponents to pay the hundreds of thousands of dollars, even millions, in legal fees to overturn the outrageous rulings of their handpicked judges. Enforcing the Constitution (as opposed to making it up as we go along, as some elitists would prefer) requires engaging attorneys, often for long periods of time. Had Dr. Eastman and his students charged for their time, we would have had no way to pay the actual dollars it would have cost to pursue the case. Powerful and well-funded liberal lobbies know very well how to exploit these cost-prohibitive barriers in pursuit of their subversive agendas. That is one more reason to thank God for the likes of Dr. Eastman.

The ACLU, environmental groups, and trial lawyers have successfully pressured Congress to pass laws, which, in turn, force government agencies to pay outrageous legal expenses to defend against those pursuing their own liberal agendas and using issues thinly veiled as alleged "constitutional" violations in the process. A school district defending school prayer, a city defending the Ten Commandments or a cross on public property, free speech rights of assembly for Christian groups, or the Boy Scouts holding meetings on public property…all must hire their own attorneys and sometimes are forced to pay their opponents' attorneys' fees in the process. These are outrageous abuses to our legal system and our taxpayers' money.

These special interest groups get millions out of the public coffers through legal intimidation of their opponents. Judge shopping effectively checkmates opposition to even the most outrageous proposals. Rarely is there a penalty to the judge for making outrageous decisions, especially if the judge is appointed. In short, it is a racket.

The story of how we fought, and prevailed, to preserve the two-thirds majority provision in the Nevada Constitution makes clear the difference between a constitutional Republic and a Democracy; it also makes clear that our Founding Fathers understood and valued this difference. In a Republic, the law rules; in a Democracy, a simple majority of the people or a loud intimidating minority in power can make up the laws and rules as they go along, and as they see fit any one time. No one's home, person, or property is safe. Laws and judges are supposed to restrain the greed and power of individuals, of organized crime, and of the government. Laws and judges are to keep everyone secure and equal before the law. Free people are to be virtuous and self-restrained, not grasping after the money and possessions of others.

Living through this court experience gave me an unforgettable lesson in how fragile our liberties are, and how important it is to have people of courage and principle in our legislatures. While I was deeply honored to receive the Ronald Reagan Freedom Award Medallion for Courageous Client from the Claremont Institute on Constitution Day September 17, 2004, it was not for the award (or any accolade) that I persevered. I fought because I realized it is imperative to guard against the efforts of those who would sell our Constitution for a pittance. I persevered because, while it is difficult to keep a republic, it is worth every effort.

When people ask me to name the highlight of my legislative career, I say it was this 2003 fight for the integrity of our Nevada Constitution. I had kept my oath of office in support of the people even when a majority of the Legislature had ignored their oath, fleeced the people, and enriched powerful special interest groups by jumping over the fence of the Constitution.

It was neither the first nor last time the Legislature passed an unconstitutional law. This was not the only time that I have gone to court to challenge one. I have experienced the twisting of law and legislative intent by activist judges. I have won some of these cases, and I have lost some. I personally have paid out-of-pocket costs to fight some of these battles.

The battle to protect and defend our Constitutions, both U.S. and State, continues. The battle never ends. Liberty is costly in time and treasure, but we must continue to fight if we are to provide an inheritance of liberty and a free Republic to the next generation.

Judge Takes First Amendment Right to Petition

The Property Tax Reform Initiative for Nevada, Nevada's Proposition 13, to limit unpredictable and ever-increasing property taxes, qualified as Question 5 for the November 4, 2008 ballot with the following statement by the Nevada Secretary of State,

> After careful consideration of the allegations contained within a complaint submitted August 1, 2008 on behalf of the Nevada State Education Association and examination of the petitions in question, this office finds no evidence the verification conducted by the county clerks/registrars failed to comply with the law. Accordingly, based upon the verification of signatures by the county clerks/registrars, The Property Tax Reform Initiative for Nevada is deemed sufficient."[123]

The Secretary's declaration should have ended the matter but, on September 8, 2008, The Nevada State Education Association (NSEA), also known as the teachers' union, sued *We the People Nevada* in an attempt to exclude the matter from the ballot. I was the Chairman of this non-profit political action committee in support of this ballot initiative to limit property tax increases. One activist judge's eleventh hour decision declared the Secretary of State's certification and the 64,166 valid signatures (more than enough to qualify for the ballot in all seventeen counties) invalid. Through judge shopping, the teachers' union was awarded an injunction to remove our petition from the November ballot.

A judge disenfranchised Nevada voters! The fix was in. The judge upheld the NSEA's allegation that the petition circulator's notary affidavit, the statement at the bottom of each signature sheet, contained "flaws." These few flaws were simply sophistry, a fantasy. The Secretary of State had accepted the petitions and certified they complied with the laws of Nevada; by law, the Secretary of State's certification should have sufficed.

The National Education Association (NEA) took this opportunity to further their national agenda, bringing their unlimited financial resources to bear against all initiatives limiting taxation across the country. NEA members spend millions from the "Ballot Measure/Legislative Crises Fund" in politics throughout the nation. In 2007-2008, the Florida arm of the union spent $200,000 opposing property tax cuts.[124]

Because of their agenda, activist judges often decide a case before it goes to court. In our initiative petition case, the judge did not reveal that his wife had been a twenty-seven-year school employee and a member of the teachers' union. The judge stated as fact not established in the case or in case law outside the case that the petition would reduce government funding. The judge allowed evidence to be submitted by the NSEA without concurrent testimony by a witness. Since only the teachers' union attorney presented "evidence," *We the People Nevada* could not cross examine to determine testimony validity. The Judge would not allow testimony to be given by *We the People Nevada's* expert witnesses.

The NSEA vs. We the People Nevada was an example of judge shopping at its worst. The appointed judge ignored the law, ruled for special interests; consequently the Constitution was subverted. It is a further outrage that this judge paid no penalty and experienced no consequence for his unlawful behavior on the bench.

The case was not about the merits of our Nevada Prop 13 language. This case was not about collecting enough valid signatures to qualify for the ballot. It was not about fraud (at least on our part). *We the People Nevada* followed the law to the satisfaction of the Secretary of State. The NSEA, with the agreement of this Judge, wrote the law <u>after the fact</u> and created it out of thin air. This "new law" was based upon the judge's opinion of what *should* be the required on the notary affidavit at the bottom of the petition and not based on what was, in fact, actually required by law at the time the Notary Affidavit was used and submitted. Further, per the U.S. Constitution, a judge's role is to enforce existing laws created in the legislative branch. A judge cannot, and should not, create laws from the bench! It was pure unconstitutional fantasy.

Even the judge said, if violated, this "new law's" penalties or consequences would not be enforced; yet he enforced it selectively against us, and the consequence was his throwing the Property Tax Restraint Initiative off the ballot. Laws cannot be applied selectively or only when convenient for a judge to further his personal agenda. What this judge did for his own self-interests was a travesty of justice that resulted in his prohibition of the people's First Amendment right to petition.

Not only did the NSEA encourage the judge to "legislate from the bench" by creating a new law, they admit it was worthless in preventing perjury or correcting the flaws they had manufactured. All of the signatures necessary to qualify this petition for the ballot, validated and certified by the Secretary of State, were invalidated by this sleight of hand and subversion of the legal system. Such threat of lawsuits, the expenses of petitioning, and the unpredictability of success cause many citizen groups not to pursue their right to petition and free speech.[125]

Legal gamesmanship and collusion subvert our most basic liberties allowing us the rights to vote, petition the government, and the right of free speech. This example of judge shopping illustrated what our Founding Fathers called tyranny and factions. The problem is certainly not isolated to Nevada. Across our great land, the judiciary all-too-often nullifies citizen petitions.

Judicial activism is one vehicle that catapults special interests and their self-serving agendas over the fence of the Constitution.

Breaking the Oath of Office

In 2005, the property taxes within Nevada reached an all-time high. Many homes were assessed with up to 200 percent increases in taxation over one year. As my friend *"Good Old"* Bill Fiedrich testified,

1) I came to Reno 50 years ago. I have lived in Verdi for 26 years.
2) I bought a one-acre lot in 1974 for $10,000. The lot across the street just sold for $350,000 – cash.
3) I built my home in 1979 for $115,000 so my total cost for housing was about $125,000. The mortgage is now paid off.
4) The house down the street just sold for $1.2 million. The property taxes on that house are $9,000 per year.
5) My wife and I live on Social Security, which amounts to about $20,000 per year. We do not qualify for food stamps and we do not get welfare. I own two cars – one is old enough to vote and the other is old enough to drink.
6) If my house is assessed at $1.2 million which there is every reason to believe it will be; and my taxes are $9,000 per year. That is $750 per month. I cannot afford that!
7) Now, before someone jumps up and says, "You're lucky Bill. You have a free and clear home worth over a million bucks! You're rich!"
8) I cannot eat my house. If I'm forced to sell, where am I going to move to? Cleveland?
9) With all due respect to those folks in Cleveland, I do not want to live there.[126]

The Nevada Legislature was afraid that citizens would pass an initiative similar to California's Proposition 13 and cut off easy access to more and more taxpayer money. In 1980, legislative intervention scuttled the initiative, enabling Nevada to assess taxes based on the arbitrary appraisal value of comparable sales in a neighborhood. This was a typical government program: Create an agency with hundreds of people to make appraisals on a make-it-up-as-you-go basis without oversight, appeal, or any real basis in market value. Spend lots of (taxpayer) money, and hire friends and relatives to make these capricious appraisals.

Not surprisingly, by 2002, longtime residents were being forced out of their homes because they could not afford to pay the property taxes. Senator Don Gustavson and I led the fight for an affordable, stable, and predictable cap on all property taxes through our Nevada Property Tax

Restraint Initiative patterned after California's Prop 13. Polling showed that this initiative would pass by seventy percent, if we could get it qualified for the ballot.

Assembly Bill 489 was the legislative preempt to our citizen's initiative. This bill promised a "cap" by splitting the property tax rolls into a three percent top rate increase for residential properties, and an eight percent top rate for commercial properties. The Nevada Constitution states that property taxes must be uniform and equal and forbids a different property tax based on use. Everyone is to be equal before the law. Semantics, coupled with the reality that no business would challenge the law because eight percent was better than the runaway taxation they were experiencing without the cap, enabled this law to pass. The headline above the fold in the Nevada paper boldly proclaimed the 41-1 vote.[127]

I was the only vote against AB 489. I could not vote against my oath of office to uphold and defend the Constitution and preserve equality before the law.

This was not an isolated event where members of the Legislature ignored their oath of office and went over the fence of the Constitution. They passed an amendment to SB230 in 2007 that changed one word, *June* to *May*. That one word made the existing deadline for submission of a citizen initiative unconstitutional and shortened the time for collecting signatures. Ironically, this ploy was an amendment attached to a bill I requested, intended to make the petitioning process easier.

To challenge a law in court there must be an injured party. Therefore, we had to wait for this case to ripen. When we were unable to collect the necessary signatures by the new deadline date, our attorney filed against the unconstitutional law. It was a black-and-white violation with no room for the opposition to fight back. The Nevada Supreme Court decided in our favor and removed the law from the statutes.[128] If we had not sustained an injury by being unable to collect all of our signatures by the new deadline, we would not have had standing (the right to be bring a lawsuit) in court to challenge the law. The right to petition the government for redress of grievance would have taken a blow.

The Legislature, in many instances, understands that most people will not challenge an unconstitutional law because of the court costs or because they do not have standing by sustaining an injury caused by the law. It is another way to go over the Constitutional fence.

Election Fraud

Manipulating or defrauding voters has become almost accepted practice in recent elections. The infamous hanging chads of 2000 gave way to the A.C.O.R.N. scandals of 2008. Voters are a fragile group, at best. The accepted statistic is that fifty percent of those who are eligible to vote actually register. Of those who register, only fifty percent will cast a ballot. In other words, only about twenty-five percent of the people usually vote. This is largely because voters are cynical about the value of their vote and are disenchanted with the integrity of those running for election. When would-be voters are aware of deliberate voting fraud that robs them of their vote, they throw up their hands in disgust and refuse to participate.

In 2006, I went to court to defend Nevadans' right to vote. The voting machines calculate votes accurately to ninety-eight percent. Any candidate who loses or wins a race by less than a two percent margin is in a statistical tie. There is no way to prove the accuracy of the vote. Even though Nevada has a printed, paper ballot in the machine, it is merely a voter audit and not the official ballot. Once again, there is no way to challenge a law unless there is an injury.

In the 2006 Congressional primary, I lost the election by 421 votes. This was half a percent of the votes cast. "Hmmm... it looks like you are on the losing end of a statistical tie," a voting machine expert told me. "There really is not anyway to know who won that race for certain, especially with the irregularities at the polls."

I had sustained the injury. The polling place irregularities reported in the newspapers scandalized the electorate. I received dozens of phone calls with complaints from people who were turned away at polls that did not open on time, who were denied their right to vote because machines were not ready, or who had experienced machinery malfunctions while they were voting.

"If you drop the lawsuit over the election, I'll make sure you get any seat you want," a Senator promised me.

"If you drop the lawsuit, we'll make sure that the county registrar loses his job," another state power operative promised.

"If you do not drop the lawsuit, we'll make sure that you are finished in politics in this state. You will be branded as a sore loser and a sour grapes candidate," a party official threatened.

To each I responded: "There's a principle of greater value than my political career. If we do not protect our right to vote, we'll lose our freedom." Each one gave me the pat answer, "Sometimes you have to sacrifice your principles for the greater good." (Meaning, do not rock the boat or upset the system we have set up here.)

I could not compromise my principles. I went to court for three reasons:

1) To make the paper ballot the official ballot;
2) To demand a new ballot in Washoe County for the irregular voting process that included polls not opening until 10 a.m. instead of 8 a.m.;
3) Because people were refused the right to vote when a) voting machines were not operational, b) paper ballots jammed in the voting machines, and c) paper ballots did not print and these voters were uncertain whether their vote was recorded.

In one instance, a polling place was moved during the night before voting, perhaps by a janitor, but not by an official from the Registrar's Office.

The Registrar admitted to the Judge that there was no way to verify that even the Judge's vote registered in the machine and counted in the election! The Judge dismissed the case saying that he had no jurisdiction. I had no money for a higher court appeal. In court, the opposing attorney charged me with "sour grapes" and being a sore loser, a charge that the press gladly picked up.

Did Harry Reid Steal Nevada?

When anomalies continue unchallenged and unchecked, they "calcify" as part of the system and become harder to detect. In Nevada's 2010 U.S. Senate general election between Senate Majority Leader Harry Reid and me, several factual irregularities occurred as covered by a blogger:

> **First, there is the fact that Sharron Angle was ahead – and gaining steam – in all major polls** before the election, and that comparable polling data accurately predicted race outcomes in analogous races.[129]

Paul Joseph Watson of Prison Planet further explains, at Dark Politricks' blog:

"Four separate Rasmussen polls prior to the election had Angle ahead. Two weeks before Super Tuesday, she held a 50% to 47% lead over Reid. One week prior to voting, on October 26, her lead was extended to four points, with Angle at 49% and Reid at 45%."

"To have a nine point swing, from Angle enjoying a four point lead just a week before the election, to Reid winning the seat by a clear five points, is highly suspicious…Nine points is not within the margin of error for polls, especially those conducted by Rasmussen, which is considered to be one of if not the most credible polling agency."[130]

Then there were reports[131] **of voting machines that were automatically checking Harry Reid's name,** the same voting machines that were serviced by pro-Harry Reid, pro-Democrat Service Employees International Union[132] members. These voting machines have received undeserved (or deserved, depending on one's perspective) support from Harry Reid,[133] even though they are the same "100 percent unverifiable, error-prone, hackable, illegally-certified, electronic voting systems the state forces all voters to use at the polling place." The voting machine issues were observed in Clark County[134], "where three quarters of Nevada's residents live, and where Senate Majority Leader Harry Reid's son Rory is a county commissioner."

Then, as reported in *The Washington Examiner*[135], there were casinos, like Harrah's and MGM[136] (remember this, my friends, next time you are in Nevada), **who engaged in extraordinary measures** to get their employees to vote, as instructed by a Harry Reid staffer: who "told Harrah's it needed to 'put a headlock' on its supervisors 'to get them to follow through.'" Further, "This plea was distributed to senior executives throughout the company by a Harrah's vice president, Marybel Batjer. Batjer demanded that those executives 'do whatever we need to do to get the supervisors to know that there is NOTHING more important than to get employees out to vote. Waking up to a defeat of Harry Reid Nov 3rd will be devastating for our industry's future.'"

"Harrah's did just that, getting headcounts and insisting that supervisors explain why their employees had not yet voted. They also coordinated with employee unions to get buses and shuttles to take the employees to the polls.

"This was not a situation where a corporation was simply encouraging its employees to go to the polls and vote for their candidate of choice—Harrah's was telling its employees how important it was to elect Reid, setting up a whole system to coerce its employees to vote, even making records of who had not voted.

"Both Harrah's and the unions spend money, in terms of supervisor and employee resources on company time, and the cost of shuttles, etc., not merely in a nonpartisan way to get out the vote, but to facilitate votes for Reid."

It was reported[137] that the casino voting effort was done in conjunction with Culinary Local 226, a heavy Reid supporter that represents about 60,000 casino workers. Sharron Angle lost by 40,669 votes.[138]

Finally, there is the illegal immigrant issue. From an alert[139] issued by Americans for Legal Immigration PAC:

"The reports and indications also suggest the presence of non-citizen voters comprised of legal and illegal immigrants voting in elections. It is a felony for any non-citizen to vote in a US election and while the scale of involvement is unknown, it could be very substantial in some areas including North Carolina, Nevada, Colorado, and Washington State. In many of these areas, Democratic candidates campaigned and appealed to illegal aliens, and deployed illegals to bring out similar voters.

The Democratic 'Get Out The Vote' (GOTV) mechanisms have no interest or ability to discern voters who are American citizens versus non-citizens."[140]

Forensic evidence may be a smoking gun, but without actual disenfranchised voters in sufficient numbers, the outcome of an election remains unchanged. The corruption of the polling place allows the winner to march over the fence of the Constitution.[141]

Trespassers

Perhaps the most controversial violation of the constitutional fence comes at a point most dear to the majority of Americans. The Constitution invites humankind to enjoy freedom guaranteed by the Rule of Law and welcomes immigrants from around the world to pursue the privilege of the American Dream...*legally*. However, coming into the United States over the fences of our physical borders violates our laws. Illegal invasion is just one of the ways the fence of the Constitution is breached. For politically correct purposes, it is often called the "immigration of undocumented workers." Of course, it is illegal to cross the border without a visa, a green card, or a passport. It is illegal to take a job with illegally obtained or forged documents. In short, all of this is *illegal*; it is against federal law.

In 2004, the number of illegal aliens caught by the Border Patrol just at the Mexican border was $1.1 million. According to a 2009 national newspaper article, the number of illegal aliens from Mexico was the lowest in ten years, an indication that the economic slump is discouraging those who come north in search of jobs.[142] The estimated number of illegal aliens spans twelve to twenty million.

Illegal drugs and the illegal activity that accompanies them has led to a civil war in Mexico and raised violent crime rates in the United States. We all hear or read these stories, but it is becoming so widespread that we find the names of our relatives and friends among the victims. Ted and I received the early morning call to pray for an uncle abducted by the drug cartel from his law enforcement job in Jalpa, Mexico. His captors released him four days later, beaten but alive.[143] While walking to school one morning, a Las Vegas high school chemistry teacher was beaten, robbed, and killed with the gang member's car when he tried to run away.[144] We are frightened for ourselves and our children as Liberal Progressives refuse to allow police to question the citizenship of the rapist, thief, or murderer.

Illegals make up the largest group of the "uninsured" for healthcare, are about equal in number to the nation's unemployed, and cost hundreds of billions of dollars in welfare, law enforcement, healthcare, education, and other services. In other words, unemployment, the deficit, and the "healthcare crisis" would be reduced significantly if trespassers were not allowed to live above the law.

I had my own personal experience with trespassers.

"You have the burden of proof," the officer said to me matter-of-factly as he talked to me through a safety glass window of his patrol car.

"They're breaking the law! I did not rent the mobile home to them! They broke in and started living in my mobile home." I emphasized that it was "my mobile home" by passing him the deed to the land and the mobile home through the partial opening at the top of the window.

Without looking, the officer passed it back. "I'm sorry, ma'am, but you'll have to evict them. As long as they are in possession of the mobile home, you must prove that they do not have a right to live here. That means you must go to Justice Court and file an eviction. You must also pay the officer to serve the papers. Then they have thirty days to answer. If they do not answer, you must file another paper telling them that they will be physically removed from the property. At that point, we will come out again and make them leave. When that happens you must have a locksmith change the lock, so that they cannot return to the property." The officer had stated the procedure slowly (and clearly not for the first time in the course of his work).

The intruders, whoever they were, broke a window to get into the mobile home and hooked up the utilities. They just started living there without my permission or knowledge. They were trespassers. As long as they were in "in possession" of the mobile home, I had to prove that they did not have a right to live there.

"I will check out these cars for you." The officer motioned with his hand toward five vehicles in various states of operation. Two had no wheels, one had no engine, and another was an antique. The last one looked like it might be drivable. The officer ran the Vehicle Identification Number. "That one," he pointed to the drivable vehicle, "is stolen." I envisioned these interlopers in handcuffs in the back of his car on their way to prison for grand theft auto.

"We'll have it towed to the impound yard, but because there was no one in the car, I cannot prove that they stole it. Someone could have left it here, but I'll go knock on the door and see if they will tell me that it is their car." The officer continued and then proceeded to the door of *my* mobile home. He knocked several times, and even though we saw the curtains flutter, no one answered. The tow truck arrived, hauled off the car, and I went to file my Eviction Notice at Justice Court. Sixty days later, after the water company removed the meter they had illegally tapped into, the trespassers left.

The issue of undocumented workers is the same as this undocumented tenant. They are trespassers who not only break into our country over our borders, take whatever they want, cost all of us money, and demand legal privileges and protections, but also often commit other crimes, like stealing cars and importing and selling drugs while they are here. Their scofflaw attitude renders our Constitution impotent at best, robs us of our security and taxes, devalues our citizenship, and creates a foreign special interest group that influences and shapes our laws.

Immigrants Willing to Assimilate

Like most Americans, I can trace my roots to a foreign nation. My maternal grandmother's family immigrated through Castle Island in 1874 from Russian Poland. They were Swiss German Mennonites fleeing the conscription of their sons into the Czar's army. They had preserved their identity, their language, their religion, and their culture as red turkey wheat farmers in each European nation where they went to escape religious persecution. They did not immediately assimilate when they settled in Pretty Prairie, Kansas.

My grandmother was born in Pretty Prairie, Kansas, to a naturalized couple who had both come to America as eight-year-old children. Yet, my grandmother did not speak English ("American" she would say) until she went to third grade in an American school. Her father moved his family from the German community of Pretty Prairie to Castleton, Kansas, and immersed them in the English language and culture. Why? Simple. They were Americans who must have the earning opportunities that the English language and culture provide.

My grandmother was not put in an English as a Second Language (ESL) class with other German speaking students, nor did her family get free care from the local doctor when her little sister cut off the end of her finger in the windmill, or when encephalitis and scarlet fever claimed two of her preschool-aged siblings. Her father did not receive a farm subsidy when his crops were lost during the Dust Bowl. There was no such thing as a free school lunch or breakfast program.

My grandmother was expected to learn English and the culture of her country. Through immersion in English, by the end of her fourth grade year, she was able to recite more than twenty epic poems (she called them readings) from memory in both German and English. She could recite them until her death at age ninety-five. Her eighth grade English vocabulary was so accomplished that she was able to beat me, a college graduate, regularly in a game of Scrabble. She quit school out of necessity to care for her consumptive mother and her younger siblings.

While my mother's family embraced, loved, and respected the language and culture of their new home, the United States, they also proudly preserved and respected their heritage and origins from abroad. To embrace one does not require complete denial of the other. Our country, the Melting Pot, is rich in diversities brought here and preserved by legal immigrants and their families. It is one of the things that makes America so great. Nowhere is the value of this better illustrated than in the story of my mother's cousin, Jess. Even long after my grandmother's family immigrated to America, their descendants (including Jess) proudly preserved their Swiss German roots.

During the Second World War, nearly all the men in my family went to war. Jess, was wounded in Germany during a battle that sent his unit running from the slaughter, forcing them to leave the wounded behind. Jess rolled under a hedge to keep from being run over by the retreating jeeps and tanks. The Germans followed behind the Allies, with orders to take no prisoners. They bayoneted the wounded soldiers in those hedges. Just before the bayonet was thrust in Jess' chest, he shouted in German, "Don't kill me!"

Shocked to hear not just the German language, but a dialect of low German spoken in the interior of their country, the German soldiers stopped the killing and took the remaining GI's to a prison camp for interrogation, hoping to get information from their discovered "spy."

The language my grandmother called "slop bucket Dutch," a language she would speak only to relatives because she said it would show her ignorance to use it in other places, had saved the lives of Jess and his comrades as they were fighting for liberty and all the precepts of freedom that the Constitution of the United States defines.

The Constitution is the contract between and among Americans. It is the contract with every immigrant. It is the contract that attracts the tired, the poor, and the huddled masses yearning to be free.[145] The contract ensures freedom and security, as it protects citizens from abuses that would steal freedom and security.

This U.S. Constitution is worth dying for, and that has not changed since 1776. Today there is a foreign invasion of the United States underway that is being aided and abetted by those allowing the invaders to go over the fence at our borders, and consequently, over the fence that the Constitution provides to protect citizen rights.

"He who does not enter by the door, but climbs up some other way, the same is a thief and a robber."[146] The Constitution guarantees our freedom and security. It is incumbent upon each generation to defend the door to that freedom and preserve the security of the people who are citizens here. It is incomprehensible that our own government would set aside the Constitution and grant amnesty for the illegal people who come criminally to the United States. The first time they jump the fence, it is a misdemeanor, a small infraction. To diminish the crime because the punishment seems insignificant does not diminish the damage to the Rule of Law. This is tantamount to allowing robbers to ignore our laws and steal our rights and property.

The Constitution and Illegal Aliens

Abuses of our Constitution endanger our rights and our national security. The rights guaranteed by the Declaration of Independence and our Constitution are the inheritance of United States citizens. Citizenship is a privilege of those naturally born in the United States or who have become citizens through naturalization.

All persons born or naturalized in the United States and subject to the jurisdiction thereof are citizens of the United States.[147]

This sentence embodies the birthright of millions of Americans. The Supreme Court has never directly addressed the ambiguities of the phrase "subject to the jurisdiction thereof." It might exclude children of parents who are foreign nationals. Automatic citizenship is now granted to anyone born in the United States, even the children of tourists.[148] On its face, these interpretations of the Constitution are, at best, imaginative, but more likely it is just pandering to special interests.

One Tucson, Arizona, hospital markets its "citizenship for sale" delivery room to international mothers-to-be by touting U.S. citizenship for their newborns. The center does not mention citizenship in its "birth packages." It is an understood value-added. We get to pay for the foreigners' delivery and then welfare for their children, which many families use to live on. This is so outrageous that one has to agree with Charles Dickens, "'If the law supposes that,' said Mr. Bumble, squeezing his hat emphatically in both hands, 'the law is an ass, an idiot.'"[149]

My hero, Dr. John Eastman, argues that so-called "anchor babies," children born on United States soil to parents who are not citizens, according to the Constitution are not citizens. Dr. Eastman contends a clause of the U.S. Constitution has been misinterpreted and misused for more than a century to allow false claims to U.S. citizenship. He asserts that the 1866 Civil Rights Act (a statutory forerunner of the Fourteenth Amendment) citizenship eligibility statement, "All persons born in the United States, and not subject to any foreign power," is far more explicit in defining accurately eligibility requirements for U.S. citizenship than the more ambiguous Fourteenth Amendment clause, "subject to the jurisdiction thereof."[150]

This leaves little doubt in Eastman's mind that Congress understood a clear distinction between "basic territorial jurisdiction," such as traffic laws, and "complete jurisdiction," which encompasses a person's allegiance to a nation. These fence-jumpers want the benefits of our free market society and the American Dream, but they are still under the "complete jurisdiction" of a foreign nation. This criminal entry and foreign allegiance compromises our national security and our Rule of Law. It also places a heavy economic burden on our social programs, education, healthcare, and employment.

Arizona and Oklahoma have reduced the number of illegal aliens significantly. Under the laws of these states, employers can lose their business licenses if they hire undocumented workers. Reid and Obama not only directed the federal government to sue Arizona over its 2010 Immigration Law (SB 1070), but they also allowed eleven foreign countries to join in that lawsuit in an attempt to effect directly American *domestic* law. That's just nuts!

In Arizona, the Maricopa County Sheriff has set up a hotline for citizens to report on employers who hire illegal aliens. Many deputies are given arrest authority by Customs and Border Protection to enforce federal immigration law. As a result, in the course of a traffic stop, illegal immigrants without a driver's license could ultimately face deportation. These factors, combined with a slowing economy, are forcing many illegal immigrant workers to consider leaving Arizona.[151]

Ronald Reagan said we must "humanely regain control of our borders and thereby preserve the value of one of the most sacred possessions of our people: American citizenship." Article II Section 3 of the U.S. Constitution clearly charges the President to "take care that the Laws be faithfully executed."[152] Ronald Reagan's humane solution to preserving our sacred citizenship was to give amnesty to those who came over the Constitution fence. I loved Ronald Reagan, but he was wrong about amnesty. [153] The 1986 Immigration Reform and Control Act only accomplished a short reprieve from the flood of illegal aliens crossing U.S. borders. Although the law incorporated more taxpayer dollars for border control and employer punishments, politicians had no desire to enforce the new laws. Extensive document fraud escalated, and the number of amnesty seekers surpassed all expectations. Not enforcing the law rewards criminal activity and emboldens the criminals to commit more crimes.

Fence-jumping also leads to massive income tax fraud. The most distressing aspect of Earned Income Tax Credit (EITC) stems from unlawful immigrants tapping into the program on a widespread scale. While they pay little or nothing in taxes, they receive hundreds of thousands in bogus returns. That same scam multiplies all over the country. Illegal multiple returns, fake Social Security Numbers, or claims for non-existent children or spouses make up about one-third of the EITC returns. Illegal aliens receive the lion's share of those credits.[154] The politically correct atmosphere permits illegal aliens to file for the credit with an *Individual Taxpayer Identification Number* as opposed to a Social Security Number (for which they cannot qualify).[155] Workers without Social Security Numbers can be hired to build roads and bridges under the 2009 stimulus plan and receive tax credits of $500 for individuals and $1000 per couple.[156]

Failure to interpret existing laws with common sense and creating new laws to serve special interests have combined to grow the illegal immigrant problem in the U.S. to staggering proportions. Judicial activists allowing anchor babies rights to welfare, education, and healthcare are subverting our Rule of Law. These same judicial activists refuse to deport illegals, fine employers, or secure the borders. All of this adds up to an ever-growing illegal immigration problem in the U.S. that is costing our nation dearly on many levels.

Does Congress Have the Will to Implement the Solution?

There are solutions, but Congress must have the will to implement them. First, we must elect representatives who will hold judges to the strict interpretation of the Constitution. We the people, through the ballot box, must also hold judges to that high standard of constitutional law. If we ourselves aspire to be judges, we must embrace the constitutional restrictions on the judiciary and understand that judges are the tail of the three branches of government, not the head.

Second, we must hold our elected officials accountable for their promises. If they make a campaign pledge and break it, it is the duty of the electorate to go to the polls and throw them out of office, either at the next election or through the recall process. We must do this and not let those subverting our Constitution drift into history by lack of term limits or by dying in office, as has been the practice until now.

In 2008, I ran against the most powerful man in the Nevada State Senate. He promised not to raise taxes. In 2003, he had engineered the vote for the largest tax increase in the history of Nevada. Faced with an enraged electorate, he claimed he had a conservative epiphany and there would be no more tax increases under his watch. After securing the election with false promises, and after spending $500,000 to my $50,000, he broke that promise by voting for a series of large tax increases in a time of recession. In response to the voters' displeasure for his support of Harry Reid, his colleagues removed him from State Senate leadership. He retired from the Legislature midterm, too late to hold a special election for his replacement. County commissioners appointed a replacement he trained.

Third, the Constitution's privileges of citizenship and freedom have been the enticement for immigrants throughout the history of our country. Most of us can trace our roots to a foreign land our ancestors left bravely left seeking, sanctuary and opportunity of freedom and citizenship under the Constitution of the United States. There is a solution to this problem of illegal immigration: *enforce the law and uphold the Constitution.*

Slashing bureaucratic red tape in our immigration laws would grant accessible citizenship to all the *legal immigrants* that we can absorb. Legal means they have some acquaintance with our laws, culture, and language and intend to assimilate into our society, just as my grandparents did. Millions are welcomed each year through legal immigration into the freedom and opportunity America provides to each of its citizens.

We can secure our borders. We can do it by strengthening the enforcement of existing immigration laws. We can secure our boarders by empowering our law enforcement officers to check immigrant status, fining, and penalizing employers who hire illegal aliens, and by using such new tools as cameras, sensors, satellites, and drones to monitor the border. We must also implement the border fence law, and complete the fence. We need a real fence not just a virtual fence. "Fences make good neighbors" and keep us safe.

We should also give those who are here illegally the opportunity to correct their status on an individual case-by-case basis. Lady Liberty's invitation to the tired, the poor, and the huddled masses yearning to be free is an invitation to those that want to become legal citizens of the United States. Immigrants should enter legally through the golden door of the Constitution, not over the fence.

What the Founding Fathers Knew

The Constitution the Founding Fathers envisioned framed a government that while creating protected freedom did not grab life, liberty and the pursuit of happiness from its citizens. [157]

Scholars recognize that John Locke's philosophy involving natural laws, natural rights, and government by common consent informed the writings of Jefferson. The boundaries created by laws defend the citizen's life, liberty, and property. John Locke and Algernon Sidney blended the concepts into five basic doctrines:

1) Unalienable rights or freedoms come from a Creator.
2) Freedom can only be enjoyed by a virtuous people willing to self-govern.
3) Freedom leads to happiness.
4) Representative government is elected to pass laws that defend freedom.
5) Freedom is sustained by society submitting to those laws.[158]

Violating any of these principles places our liberty in jeopardy. Denial of the divine origin of liberty makes the judicial activist a god, and, allows any interpretation of law and the Constitution's validity. If there is no truth, no original intent, it is all up for grabs. Without representative government moderating people's passions and greed, no government can survive. Factions will destroy the unpopular, and tyranny will rob the nation of its wealth as people vote themselves ever-increasing benefits.

Without the Rule of Law and obedience to the law, "The strong will do as they will, and the weak as they must." Chaos, anarchy, and a society of all-against-all will be created. Without virtue, and without the willingness to put others' wants, needs, and society's interests as a whole ahead of our own, we will create a society red in tooth and claw. Moderation, hard work, and enjoying the fruits of one's own labor without making demands of others' property are principles that the Founders understood as the virtues that lead to happiness. In addition to liberty and virtue, the nation requires security.

George Washington wrote his Farewell Address of September 19, 1776, with the help of Alexander Hamilton and James Madison. In this address, he names reasons why we cannot allow anyone, for any reason, to go over the fence of the Constitution and jeopardize our security. The Constitution is the contract with government that defines liberty and supports peace, safety, and prosperity. Without common consent to this contract of liberty and justice for all, conflict and discord undermine personal and societal happiness and prosperity.[159]

Abraham Lincoln understood this and could not allow secession of the South to disrupt the unity of our nation. The fragmentation of the Union would destroy the national character forged by the Founding Fathers. Lincoln understood the value of national union to collective and individual happiness. He understood that in the American Republic, God created all men equal with unalienable rights to life, liberty, and the pursuit of happiness. All men were equal before the law. It was a law that could be trusted to protect the basic rights of every citizen and not change at the whim of any special interest trying to accumulate more power and money.

Citizenship entails involvement in the national character through a common language, understanding, history, and participation in the rights and privileges of an American. In order to do this, each citizen must be educated into our laws, customs, history, and language. We must encourage assimilation within our borders and deny the separatist notions of Americans hyphenated by ethnic, class, or religious divisions. No qualification of an American makes him any more or less an American. To preserve our national unity we must each as individuals strive to be a part of this great nation because we owe our patriotic identity to it.

Washington wrote:

> Respect for [this Government's] authority, compliance with its laws, acquiescence in its measures, are duties enjoined by the fundamental maxims of true liberty. . . . The very idea of the power and the right of people to establish government presupposes the duty of every individual to obey the established government. . . . All obstructions to the executions of the laws, all combinations and associations, under whatever plausible character, with the real design to direct, control, counteract, or awe the regular deliberation and action of the constituted authorities, are destructive of this fundamental principle and of fatal tendency.
>
> The right of people to establish government presupposes that each individual will obey the law. To allow some to be above the law, have special privileges or rights, or ignore and change the law at their discretion is destructive and fatal to the American Republic. We are all equal before God and the law.
>
> [M]orality is a necessary spring of popular government... Of all the dispositions and habits which lead to political prosperity, religion, and morality are indispensable supports. In vain would that man claim tribute to patriotism who should labor to subvert these great pillars of human happiness—these firmest props of the duties of men and citizens. Let it simply be asked where is the security for property, for reputation, for life, if the sense of religious obligation desert the oaths, which are the instruments of investigation in Courts of Justice? And, whatever may be conceded to the influence of refined education on the minds of peculiar structure, reason and experience both forbid us to expect that national morality can prevail in exclusion of religious principles.[160]

Washington knew that morality is not legislated but found within the integrity of the individual. It was his firm belief, and it is mine that we all answer to God. If we do not know that there is a God and we are not Him, then morality is relative. If morality is relative, then judges will overstep their legal bonds to impose their own morality on the people. Politicians will desert their oaths of office to uphold the Constitution for expedience and popularity. Officers of the law will be slandered with charges of racism, sexism, and a host of other "isms" and "phobias" by special interest agendas, the press, and other politicians that benefit by going over the fence of the Constitution. When we sacrifice principles for friendships, America ends up with good old boy politics. We have a Republic that has become the greatest and richest country ever to exist, with unmatched prosperity and freedoms for its citizens. To keep it, we need to keep faith with the Founding Fathers. This means that we must honor God and Country with equality before God and the law, avoid tyranny and faction by moderating our passions and self-interest, put the needs of others and the country first, and pursue virtues of hard work, moderation, and not covet our neighbor's property.

These are the principles that made us a great nation, and that will keep us so.

"Making noodles in my kitchen with my grandsons is a family tradition for generations of mothers and grandmothers before me."

Chapter Nine

CHARACTER IS NOT
POLITICALLY CORRECT

The nation cheered, enacted Civil Rights laws, but then marched past equality into reverse prejudice by claiming unearned credit due to gender, race, and ethnicity.

MY MOTHER-IN-LAW worked in a bank for thirty-five years. Over time, she advanced from teller to loan officer, but no further. Her steady income supported a family of four and helped two boys go to college. She helped her husband pay for barber school and eventually open his own shop. She trained men in the bank who eventually became her bosses. From time to time, she would sigh at the injustice and press on.

In the 1960's, the feminist movement declared they would end what the suffragettes of the early twentieth century started. They celebrated by burning their bras. I was eleven at the time and welcomed the movement. As I prepared for college, in pursuit of a glamorous career in fashion design, I found that all the affirmative action laws had failed to change the hearts of real people. Injustices remained.

My guidance counselor at Earl Wooster High School adjusted her graying hair, stood, and looked over her glasses at me. "I'm afraid you've wasted your time," she said. "I'm not going to give you the scholarship applications. After looking at your grades, you are obviously *not* a college student. Perhaps you should consider a trade school."

Crushed, I sat glued to the chair. I just could not go home and tell my mother that I was not going to college. My mother would have fifty questions. I could not leave the counselor's office without answers. "My grades? I have a solid 3.5 GPA, and I'll graduate thirty-second in a class of five hundred and eighteen!" My heart was pounding in my ears, but I said it anyway.

She pressed her hands on her desk and leaned toward me. Her brows furrowed with displeasure; her voice hissed. "I *told* you. You're *not* college material."

"But there's a Fleishman four-year, full scholarship to the School of Home Economics. I want to be a fashion designer. I *have* to go to college. Just let me fill out the paperwork and take the tests. Just let me try!" I insisted as tears threatened to spill down my cheeks.

"No." The word hit my chest with a thud. She crossed the room to the door and opened it.

"Come in, Kurt." She turned her back to me but I could feel her smiling at the young man waiting to see her. "I really want you to take a look at all the opportunities I've found for you at good schools," she told Kurt. She dismissed me without a word or even a backward glance, as though I did not exist.

Four years later in the spring of my senior year at the University of Nevada, Reno, my high school guidance counselor came to a tea at my sorority house. I could not resist. "It is good to see you again," I said. "I just wanted to let you know that in June I'll graduate with my bachelor's degree in Fine Arts." She smiled. Clearly, she did not remember our conversation four years earlier.

Nearly twenty years later, I was certain things had changed. I worked for two female Juvenile Probation Officers. I was a tutor for Juvenile Justice in Tonopah, Nevada. Every Saturday, I taught the summer water-ski program at Walker Lake near Hawthorne. I supervised the Juvenile Offender Community Service Program at the Tonopah Life Center, a family fitness center I co-founded.

As a newly elected member of the Nye County School Board of Trustees after defeating the incumbent, I gained respect as a fiscal and social conservative. Senior Citizens loved me because I taught an oil painting class at their Center on Thursday mornings. I was a hero to bored teenagers because I opened the gym and made an indoor pool, racquetball courts, a Jacuzzi, an aerobics room, and a weight room available for their use. I pitched the idea of the Tonopah Life Center (TLC) to the Nye County Commission, and they gave me a thirty-year lease at one dollar per year. Previously, the facility had been unused for over ten years. We charged a small fee to pay for the utilities and maintenance of the facility. I was a successful community organizer, not a community agitator.

When Kim, my supervisor and head of Juvenile Probation, suggested

I apply for the new Juvenile Probation Officer position, I was honored and certain I would get the job. I scored the highest score on the written test and ranked number one on my oral interview. Only one man and one interview stood in my way. When I left the Judge's office, I felt certain I had the job.

That certainty lasted until I saw Kim's face that afternoon at work. "I cannot believe it!" she screamed, accompanied by a blue streak of curse words. The petite young, blonde swore like a prison inmate. (Prison inmates could come up with original and descriptive language. I had learned this from volunteering in a prison ministry at Winnemucca Honor Camp before we moved to Tonopah.)

Kim threw the letter on her desk. "He picked Tim! 'We need a man for the boys!' That is all he said." She fumed and paced. "You should sue. All the facts are on your side. It is a clear case of gender discrimination."

Dorinda, Kim's assistant, walked in, and joined the rant. The women were beside themselves with the injustice. They started plotting measures on my behalf. I had told them I believed God had a purpose and plan for my life, and the plan involved doing good, and following God's wisdom. This was a test of my faith. Did I really believe there was a plan?

"I'm not going to sue," I heard myself say. "I know this looks bad, but it is a good thing." I believed that then, and know it to be true even now, after Harry Reid's re-election.

They were stunned. Their anger dissipated like virga, rain that dries between cloud and earth before it hits the ground. The boys loved Tim. Dorinda and Kim loved Tim. I loved Tim. He was the best person for the job, even though I was more qualified on paper.

Tim was a stable influence in the lives of children who lacked stability in their lives. He did good work. Not getting the job looked bad for me at the time, but was good for me over time.

Three years later my husband, Ted, and I left Tonopah due to a relocation with his career in the federal government.

My experience was not unique. The cultural norms that created the system my mother-in-law and I faced grew out of our American heritage. Men were breadwinners, and women were homemakers. The Second World War brought women into the workplace as men entered the military. With few exceptions, women were fully capable of doing a man's job. Many women returned to the home after the war as men reclaimed their role as the breadwinners. Nevertheless, society and culture had changed with the war, and so had the role women saw themselves playing. Not everyone was convinced of that changed role. Some women would earn respect; others would force it.

Playing the Gender Card in the Game of Politics

Change can be difficult and often comes slowly, whether to an individual or to a society. In 1970, shortly after the advent of the second wave of the feminist movement in the U.S., about twenty-five percent of mothers with children under the age of three worked outside the home. While thirty years later that figure had more than doubled to over fifty percent, even more remarkable is the fact that by 2000, over seventy-five percent of mothers with children three years of age and over had entered the workforce. While some of this change can certainly be attributed to top-down policy changes, which removed some barriers to women in the workplace, I would argue that the majority of this change has happened more organically out of the increased economic necessity for dual incomes within the family. Government cannot coerce true change. It can help foster an environment, which does not hinder natural change, but real change must happen of its own accord. In the same vein, government cannot coerce sustained job creation. It can get out of the way of private business (reduce regulations, tax cuts, etc.) and thereby help foster an environment that will not hinder natural job creation, but real and positive change in the area of job creation must happen of its own accord as well. (I address this more specifically elsewhere in this book.)

While change cannot be dictated nor demanded, neither can respect. True respect is earned.

Some women demand respect, like the U.S. Senator from California who rebuked a Brigadier General, by commanding him to use her title rather than the military term of "Ma'am" used for addressing a female superior.[161] The Senator gained no respect for herself, nor any other woman, with that remark. She sounded whiney and shrill. Conversely, she did not show respect to the general by referring to his hard-earned title of "Brigadier General."

The feminist demand for birthright-based affirmative action has diminished respect for women, not increased it. Playing the gender card in politics is more than just a demand for respect. The gender card takes our eye off the ball and shuts down the debate of issues on their own merits. The gender card is a self-serving and negative manipulation that does not bring any honor or credibility to the true advancement of women. Consider what happened in a New York Senate debate when Rick Santorum offered Hillary Clinton a courteous helping hand. Her rebuke and that of the Left-leaning media was a factor that cost him in the election. The discussion immediately went from qualifications to alleged (or manufactured) gender bias.

While there is no trump for the gender card, another woman can neutralize it. When two women debate issues, there is no gender card. Sarah Palin is frightening to the feminist liberal woman because she completely neutralizes the gender issue. A conservative woman meets the liberal woman on equal turf. The debate cannot be defused.

The Pathology of Liberals

The pathology of the Elite Left movement can all too often be characterized by its members who consider themselves victims to some form of ongoing societal injustice or persecution. These "victims" fall into adopting a worldview that unfortunately encourages non-recovery and enlarges the pathology to a near religious-like fervor. Recovery is difficult for those who find individual worth in being a victim. Recovery threatens this identity, trapping them in a web of denial and narcissism. They get lost in the trees and can no longer see the forest. Even more twisted is that feminism, black power, gay advocacy, and multiculturalism use their victimization to intentionally manipulate the collapse of the culture's traditional moral barriers and values, demanding their agendas dictate and dominate society.[162]

As part of the Elite Left, the feminist movement is bent on reducing respect for motherhood, marriage, and the decency of being a lady. One of my mother's favorite sayings was, "Be careful how you use the word *lady*; it does not apply to every woman." Just being female was not enough. Manners are the root of civility in a civil society. Joy Behar called me a b----- on national television. That remark spurred online giving to my campaign that exceeded $150,000 in one day. I sent Joy flowers and a thank you note. A shrill demand for redress of real or imagined slights is behavior not characteristic of a lady. To pretend that all women want to forsake the traditional God-given roles of homemaker and mother is patently absurd. Women who seek employment just want a fair shake in the workplace. As government takes an ever-increasing percentage of our paychecks, it takes two incomes to raise a family and fund a household. Most women need to work, but they need not stop being ladies.

Liberated Woman and a Feminist

My mother was the ultimate liberated woman and true feminist, and I learned from her example. I believe in the strength and power of women, and I believe these feminine attributes should be celebrated. The Left has done its best to define feminism in terms of a battle between men and women. I believe men and women are equal, but they are different. We would be well-served as a society to spend more time and energy celebrating these differences—these different strengths—and how these differences were "designed" and created to work together and are truly complementary. Too often, the Left's feminist movement has tried to marginalize femininity and equate it with weakness, or subservience to men. Nothing could be further from the truth or more counterproductive for the advancement of women.

When my mother graduated from Bluff City High School in Bluff City, Kansas, the heartland of America, she went to work for a year at a bank to make money to pay for her education at Kansas State University. She majored in Accounting and graduated in three years. Meanwhile, she worked as a waitress in a soda fountain. Her sisters entered nursing school to help with the war effort, but the school rejected my mother because she was two inches too short. She rushed to get through college so she could join the workforce and help with the war effort. The war ended just before she graduated.

With degree in hand, she headed west, alone, to take a job as an accountant for an airport in remote Lovelock, Nevada. All of her siblings were married and had started families. My mother had had proposals of marriage, and she eventually wanted a family, but she wanted to "see the world first."

My mother was twenty-four when she married my dad. She said she could not resist the man who was lean, tan, and ready to take a flying lesson. After an eight-month courtship, they married. I am not a native Nevadan; I was born nine months later in Klamath Falls, Oregon. Perhaps I can claim native status, since my conception was probably in Lovelock, Nevada, and I am the namesake of a little girl in Lovelock, Sharron Casey. Like her, I have a double "r" in my name.

My mother worked hard in the family business, the Atlas Motel in south Reno. She raised four children. She also worked for Abbot Supply as a bookkeeper. In everything she did, she was a lady. She never used crude or vulgar language. She did not tell off-color jokes. "Always be a lady. It takes no brains at all to say four-letter words. A good vocabulary and good grammar are the marks of a good mind," Mom told me.

She made me learn to walk in high heels with my feet pointed forward, shoulders back, and a book on my head. "Do not slouch," she would call to me. My mother wore three-inch heels to compensate for being short. She said people would take me more seriously if I gave the illusion of being tall. Posture and high heels were the keys to that end.

"Remember," my mother, said, "try to stand across from a person to talk to them and not beside them. You'll have the advantage of perspective. You do not want to be little and cute. Little and cute is fine for young girls."

My mother was right. Tall people are more accepted in society and have an edge in hiring, dating, even politics. A 2009 study in Australia reported that tall people make more money, some as much as $800 per inch more than their shorter counterparts.[163] Does that mean we need affirmative action for short people? A federal Department for the Vertically Challenged? Maybe we short people should bring a class action suit against the writer of the 1977 song "Short People." In 1978, legislation was introduced in the State of Maryland to make it illegal to play "Short People" on the radio; contrary to popular myth, it did not pass. My great uncle Roy was a midget. He was perfectly proportioned at fifty-three inches fully grown, and the family called him—well, of course—"Shorty."

Being a lady is more than external proprieties; it is fundamentally about character and personality. My mother told me, "People will be drawn to someone who is kind, patient, truthful, reliable, trustworthy, and has a sense of humor, especially about themselves."

I hated the lecture about how "beauty is only skin deep." I confess that sometimes, to irritate her, I would respond, "Yes, but ugly is all the way through."

My mother was right. The older I got, I observed that people craved leaders who set positive examples. Most Americans want the leadership that the nation's Founders demanded from each other—leaders with character.

Character Counts, but It Is Not Politically Correct

Martin Luther King, Jr. embraced character when he said, "I have a dream that my four little children will one day live in a nation where they will not be judged by the color of their skin but by the content of their character."[164] The nation cheered, enacted Civil Rights laws, but then marched past equality into reverse prejudice by claiming unearned credit due to gender, race, and ethnicity. Sorry, Dr. King, character and qualifications just are not politically correct.

Fifty-three percent of American voters elected a President, not on qualifications or experience—not even on the content of his demonstrated character. A news commentator said he "felt this thrill going up my leg…"[165] The national media promoted Obama on "feelings" and consistently gave him a "pass" on anything problematic.

The "fourth branch" of government, the mainstream media, abdicated their responsibility as information guardians of the Republic. Americans can no longer expect critical and unbiased analysis. Nor can the American public rely on clear-eyed examinations of government performance. "Reporters" have surrendered their legacy as honest journalists. The good news is that the age of Internet-distributed news has emerged. There is a new media source, less universally tied to liberalism, and more independent. The new free media is on the Web.

However, the media is not alone in flawed character. Career politicians are not the peoples' representatives that the Founders envisioned. The fast-tracked, push-it-through-and-do-not-read-the-bill approach is not in alignment with the Constitution of the United States of America. Our legislators do not even understand what they are voting on. Staffers and professional bureaucrats write the legislation. It is now all about hurry up, pass it, and give the government more control over we the people's money, freedoms, and lives.

Many cynical voters will not go to the polls because they do not see a clear choice. Corruption, ethical misconduct and moral failure are rampant in Washington, D.C. Americans are hungry for the clarion cry of freedom and national leaders who are people with character and unafraid of hard work, people who accept responsibility, and people who adhere to high ethical standards. We need politicians who look out for the people's interests first, not their own. America needs leaders willing to work in the light of day and accept responsibility when their programs and laws fail to succeed and make things worse.

As self-described victims, the Elite Left must blame others for their failures. They do not take responsibility. It is part of their pathology. That leaves us with two choices. One, we throw our hands up in despair and surrender to socialism. Two, we fight. Politics is a dirty business. If we Americans want to clean up government, more of us must be willing to risk running for office.

The Right Angle

In 1987, we moved to Tonopah. There was an open seat on the Nye County School Board. I wanted to run for political office. I had been a private school teacher. I had home schooled. I was a substitute teacher for over twenty-five years in the public schools, and I taught college-level art classes for five years. I understood education. Ted, my husband, said I should wait; our children were too young for me to take on a campaign and public office.

In 1988, my mother died suddenly of a massive coronary at age sixty-four. I do not believe I will ever fully recover from her death. I went to help my dad in Fallon and traveled often to Kansas to visit my mother's ninety-five-year-old mother. When Mom died, Grammie went into a nursing home, and her health began to fail. My husband was right (as he often is) that the timing was wrong for me to jump into politics. My children, my father, and my grandmother needed me. The Marines have their priorities right—God, Family, and Country.

In 1992, Ted said the time was right for me to run for the School Board. I thought he was crazy. It was no longer an open seat. I would be running against an incumbent. Once again, Ted was right.

My good friend, a Nye County Commissioner whose nickname was

"Holy Joe" because he led a scripture reading and prayer time before every commission meeting, said he would help me win. I started my door-to-door canvassing with a campaign piece printed on half a sheet of letter-sized paper. It said, "The Right Angle for School Board."

Nye County is geographically one of the largest counties in the United States. The closest towns are an hour's drive apart. I walked the streets of Pahrump, Tonopah, Beatty, Gabbs, Hadley, and Amargosa Valley. In Gabbs, a Great Dane bit me while I was walking door-to-door. Biting dogs are baptism by fire for any politician. The travel between towns, the dogs, and the sore feet are just part of campaigning. I won the election.

Dad said my mother would have been proud of me. My mother-in-law felt vindicated because I broke the "glass ceiling." On the School Board, I was part of a team that challenged the teachers' union, fired a teacher who cheated by telling students the answers to the achievement test, set up a disciplinary policy that stopped unruly student behavior, and helped build new schools without passing school bonds that would have meant a tax increase for the people.

In December 1995, we moved to Reno. Two weeks after we moved into our new house, some Washoe County School Board members asked me to challenge an entrenched incumbent for the School Board. I had not lived in Reno for twenty-five years. I had no name recognition. I did not think I could win, but I prayed. Ted agreed that I was supposed to run.

I did my best, but lost the election. It was another case where a short-term loss led to a long-term gain.

I decided to volunteer in the office of a State Senator I met on the campaign trail. At the end of the legislative session he said, "I think you should run for Assembly."

My reaction was, "You're crazy!" My Senator and my Assemblywoman were entrenched incumbents. A few months later, my Assemblywoman retired, and I had no more excuses, so I ran. I defeated two establishment candidates to win the seat. In fact, I won the next three elections, having gained respect as a strong candidate for my political campaign style.

The establishment uses a variety of manipulative and underhanded tactics to get their way. As a preemptive strike, sometimes they use overwhelming campaign war chests to intimidate and prevent would-be challengers from entering important races in the first place. When that does not work, they will employ even more elaborate schemes and will manipulate the system—legally, of course. And when *that* does not work, sometimes they will just go ahead and appoint whomever they want to a given office. Consider this, for example. In 2002, the establishment candidate outspent me four to one, leading the press to call me the "dark horse." The establishment then tried to give their candidate even more of an edge by giving him a geographic and incumbent advantage through reapportionment. Well, this time their attempts to gerrymander a campaign did not work; this dark horse crossed the finish line first. I won my seat against the odds.

But even then the establishment was not done manipulating the system. They are a wily bunch, stopping at nothing to get their way and take care of their own. After their candidate lost to me, they appointed him to the U.S. Attorney's Office for a few years. When he was terminated, his establishment mentor (a powerful Nevada State Senator) retired midterm, only fifteen days prior to the 2011 legislative session. This dubious timing "conveniently" left no time for a special election to take place, thwarting the voters' say in who would fill this vacancy. The establishment (retiring senior Senator's friends on the County Commission) hand-picked and appointed their choice. So whom did they pick? You guessed it…the man I had defeated in 2002.

Politics is tough business. However, I have learned that even those who disagree with me often respect me for my consistency; they always know where I stand on the issues. And while I do not typically initiate a fight, many of my colleagues, opponents, and constituents know that I do not back down if the fight comes to me.

American Common Sense Can Tear Down the Wall of Political Correctness

By my thinking, a true Renaissance woman is comfortable in her own skin, and earns, never demands, her position in the marketplace. She considers homemaking and child rearing not as slavery but as a sacred trust. She makes her relationships work. She protects her marriage as a sacred and God-ordained institution. She champions the value of every human life from conception to natural death. She is the Proverbs 31:25 woman. "Strength and dignity are her clothing, and she smiles at the future." She is the Left's worst nightmare. She is a woman like Michelle Bachman, Sarah Palin, and Sharron Angle.

A conservative woman can go toe-to-toe against the feminist Left's rants against home, family, motherhood, and traditional marriage without flinching. She is immune to the gender card, and the Left fears that immunity. The Left's only defense is vicious attacks on traditional women, marriage and motherhood, and on those who defend the unborn child. The feminist ideology demands that all women conform. If the woman does not work outside her home, she is a *parasite* or less *than fully human.*[166] The feminist Left created a new paradigm for women, especially those running for political office. When conservative women took the political stage, they challenged that paradigm. With challenge came pushback in the form of personal attacks. Kay Bailey Hutchinson calls it, "...desperately low tactics ...baseless attacks and charges aimed to discredit them as candidates by demeaning them as women. Gender-targeted slurs and attacks, such as those slung at Meg Whitman, Sharron Angle, Nikki Haley, and even Hillary Clinton in 2008, are indefensible...The political process should not punish women or hold them to different standards..."[167]

I worked as a waitress to put myself through college and joined a sorority in college, *Gamma Phi Beta*. Unlike the other sororities, we pledged everyone who wanted to join. We celebrated each other's gifts, talents, and intelligence. We destroyed the stereotype of exclusivity that characterized the *Greek* culture on campuses then.

I rejected the feminist Left siren song that shouted, "Burn your bra, live free, avoid the chains of marriage." I married Ted Angle in the summer of 1970, before our senior year in college. We have worked hard. We have two children and ten grandchildren. After four decades of marriage, we still love each other. It has not always been easy or blissful. Sometimes I get out my twelve-string guitar and Ted and I sing a wonderful song written by Don Francisco: "Love Is Not a Feeling, It's An Act of Your Will."[168]

Love *is* an act of will, be it love for spouse, children, parents, community, or country. In the twenty-first century political climate, love has eroded. Hoarding power and attacking opponents is a blood sport without honor or respect. No lie is too outrageous, no personal attack too mean, as long as it furthers political power. It is time to storm the fortresses of special interest power grabbing that are long ensconced inside the Beltway.

Good old American common sense and character can defeat the Elite

Left. The Progressives have embraced the false promise of equality through socialism and the redistribution of wealth. Progressives plan to redistribute *American citizens'* wealth to *their* privileged causes, supportive groups, and political allies. Progressives no longer see a line between right and wrong. Blurred in the tug between self-interests and situational ethics (which is no ethics at all), ultimately, this corruption of spirit only breeds more corruption in society.

By promoting class warfare, the Left aims to erect a wall of strife and distrust between different groups of Americans. Division is achieved by gender or race through hate crime legislation, set asides, and affirmative action. Americans must shout, "Tear down this wall!"[169]

SHARRON ANGLE

WORD OF LIGHT
CHRISTIAN ACADEMY
Winnemucca, NV
Kindergarten - Grade 12
Pastor Kraintz   Mrs. Angle
1984-1985

*"Choice in Education prompted me to teach in this one-room school
in Winnemucca and was the beginning of my political journey."*

Chapter Ten

EDUCATION: THE GOVERNMENT OPTION

The key is this: do not hesitate to act. Be proactive. Engage the battle. Become a warrior for our children. The future of the nation depends on it.

THE FRAMERS of the Constitution of the United States did not include any reference whatsoever to a national education system. The Framers saw this as a parental and local matter and as a strict individual right. There were mandatory requirements for particular degrees or professions during the Colonial era, but these were in privately controlled and privately funded schools.

This private school system, with an emphasis on reading so that people could read the Bible, produced a ninety-seven percent literacy rate. Most teachers studied in two-year "normal" schools, which were introduced in the early 1800's. This system remained unfettered by the intrusion of government until 1840.

Then along came the reformers. Horace Mann became the Secretary of Education in Massachusetts and created a statewide public education system with compulsory attendance based on the Prussian model of "common schools" that entitled everyone to education. After the Civil War, a coalition of black and white Republican legislators established free universal public education in the South.

In 1867, President Andrew Johnson created the first Department of Education, a non-cabinet level bureaucracy and renamed it the Bureau of Education in 1870, mainly charged with collecting statistics. People feared that it would exercise too much control over local schools... a fear realized a century later.

By 1870, all states had free public schools. In 1875 Speaker of the House, James G. Blaine, proposed an amendment to the U.S. Constitution to prohibit the use of state funds at "sectarian" schools. Blaine's proposed amendment was approved by the House, but failed by a narrow margin to gain Senate approval. Shortly thereafter, most states added similar "Blaine Amendments" to their respective state constitutions.

These first public schools were one-room schoolhouses where students read from *The McGuffey Reader* which was based on phonics and biblical values. Teachers administered corporal punishment for disciplinary infractions and were supported by parents and school boards alike. By 1910, most towns had added high schools, and by 1940, fifty percent of the nation's young people earned high school diplomas.

In the 1950's, the Bureau of Education became part of the Department of Health, Education, and Welfare, with more federal money pumped into the bureaucracy. In 1958, the first comprehensive federal education legislation passed as the *National Defense Education Act* (NDEA). It was, in part, a response to the launching of *Sputnik*, the Russian satellite, and was intended to train Americans to compete with the Soviet Union in the race for space.

In the 1960's, part of President Lyndon Johnson's War on Poverty included more funding for education for the poor at all educational levels. The 1970's saw an increased national emphasis on educating racial minorities, individuals with disabilities, women, and non-English speakers; correspondingly, this emphasis garnered significantly more tax dollars. Political correctness evolved from prohibiting discrimination based on race, sex, and disability through such mandates as co-educational physical education.

By the 1990's (and even earlier in big cities), political correctness extended to rewriting textbooks to emphasize minority histories and to de-emphasize dead white males, like the Founding Fathers. Textbooks focused increasingly on the problems of American history such as "racism, sexism, homophobia, and the rape of the environment." This came at the expense of America's traditional role as the champion of liberty, opportunity, and prosperity in the world.

Racism, sexism, homophobia, and other such negative and hateful treatment of any group by another is abhorrent, intolerable and the height of ignorance. Unfortunately, such treatments are a part of our national history (as they are in other countries), and they should be taught as such. However, they should not be taught at the exclusion—or outside of the context—of the far, far bigger, and positive history of our great nation as a champion of liberty, opportunity, and prosperity in the world. Further, we need to stop the ridiculous politically correct apologies for (and reduced teaching of) certain historical facts like our Founding Fathers being all white and being all men. Such things may be typical due to historical context; it does diminish their importance to our rich history. In addition to an increasing trend to throw more and more taxpayer money at education as a panacea for all of its problems (consistent with the trend to do the same for any vocal or perceived disadvantaged group with the belief that government money would solve their woes, too)modern education policy developed an ideological assault on the traditional family, religious values, and long-held American values. Public schools seem to be focusing more and more on the wrong things, have lost sight of what is truly important, and seem to forget why they exist in the first place. Started by churches and faith communities, public schools have now become a bastion of un-American and anti-Christian ideologues more interested in promoting their liberal agendas than in teaching our youth. As a result, public schools are now failing in their primary function to teach all children how to read or write.

The majority of compulsory education in the United States is public, or government provided, controlled, and funded. Poor student performance has engendered more and more government control from the top down by federal and state laws, and local regulation. Today, Americans must face an educational, moral, and ideological crisis created by an ineffective public education system awash in misused and misplaced taxpayer money.

My Dog in This Fight

As far back as I can remember, I have loved to draw. As I mentioned earlier, at one time I wanted to be a fashion designer. I majored in art and minored in home economics fashion construction at the University of Nevada, Reno. I was set and focused on my life's goal until life took an unexpected but happy turn. I met Ted Angle, fell in love, married him in the summer before our senior year in college, and gave up my goal to be a fashion designer. Ted is an outdoor guy. He loves to hunt, fish, and do most anything outdoors. His major was wildlife management with a minor in range management. I quickly redirected my college career to education. I could not be a fashion designer in the rural Nevada outback, but I could teach.

Ted took a temporary summer job with the Department of Interior's Bureau of Land Management in Ely, Nevada. Ted and I intended to return to Reno, after the summer. Ted planned to attend graduate school, and I was going to complete the student teaching block that I lacked when I graduated with a bachelor's degree. However, another happy right turn came in Ely. We became parents.

Over the next twenty-five years, we moved several times due to Ted's career. We went to Vale, Oregon. Then we relocated to Winnemucca, Nevada. Next, it was on to Tonopah, Nevada. Finally, we came full circle back to Reno where Ted had been born and where I had lived since my third birthday. Along the way and in various locations, I received on-the-job-training while working in various transpositions of the public education system.

The Reading Wars

While my public school education had a rocky start, my overall educational experience was positive. In first grade, I realized I could not read. I was a *dumb duck*, and I knew it! Mrs. Henderson divided her first grade class at Anderson School into three reading groups: *bright* bunnies, *average* kitties, and *dumb* ducks. Even though Mrs. Henderson never applied the adjectives of bright, average, or dumb, we all knew that being a duck was not cute; it was dumb. I struggled with the whole language concepts of Dick, Jane, Sally, Spot, and Puff. I could not grasp the sight-word memorization I was being taught. Instead of learning to sound out words, Mrs. Henderson expected my class to memorize whole words. In tears of desperation, I told my mother I did not want to go to school anymore. It was too hard.

After school every day for six weeks, my mother helped me decode the pages of my reading book using phonics. I learned to read and completely skipped being an *average* kitty. I went from *dumb* duck to *bright* bunny and never looked back. I could decode any book and did not have to rely on my memory or guessing at words. Six weeks of homeschooling set me on the road to successful learning. We did not call it homeschooling back then. My mother just called it good parenting.

With my mother's example before me, I learned to love to see the "aha" moments in students' eyes when they "get it." I have taught kindergartners and senior citizens. And I have taught numerous subjects along the way, from advanced algebra…to prerequisites for college art majors…to playing guitar…to how to be a precinct captain…to individual tutoring. I even taught juvenile offenders how to clean gym equipment. I've seen a lot in the world of teaching. No matter the age of the student, and no matter the subject, the thrill in teaching is the same for me; I just love being part of the learning process.

Frankly, most good teachers I have met teach for the same reason; they have a pure love for the challenge of reaching students and making the subject matter relatable to them. Good teachers also enjoy watching the excitement and thrill of accomplishment in their students' experiences.

The paid summer vacation, guaranteed tenured salary, or the thirty-hour workweeks are not the goal of the truly good teacher. Most teachers put in well over forty hours per week, many dedicating their "off-hours" to their students as well.

Over the years, education professionals have told me that I have a gift for teaching. The pieces of legislation I have sponsored that gave me the most satisfaction were education based. One law I sponsored is the Nevada Reading Excellence Act, which uses grant money from the Federal Reading Excellence Act to educate teachers on how to teach reading based on scientifically based reading research. In short, the Act trains and encourages teachers to teach phonics. The law was a crowning monument to my mother's investment and to the years that I spent teaching, finally jumping over the traditional schools' love affair with whole language. The law did not pass easily, and just because it is the law does not make it the practice. Teaching children to read by methods based on scientific reading research should have been a no-brainer, but it was one of the hardest fought pieces of legislation in my Nevada Assembly career.

A former staff member of Congress' Committee on Education and the Workforce testified at the hearing for my first Reading Excellence bill, AB292 in 1999, after he evaluated the state's reading curriculum. Although the textbooks mentioned phonics, the standards of the law signed by President Clinton in 1998 were not being met. Scientific research proved that whole language is inadequate. Learning to read requires systematic instruction in the alphabetic principle or phonics.[170]

If my bill passed, the State Board of Education and district school boards would have been required to provide Nevada kids with solid phonics-based courses of study in reading, or be charged with a misdemeanor under state law. The teachers' union opposed the bill because they thought that the misdemeanor penalties were too "punitive," and that some special-education students did not "do well" under phonics.

The amendment lost by a near party-line vote, twenty-six to fifteen, with only one Democrat breaking ranks. That vote reflected the union's campaign contribution investment, directly and through its affiliated PACs, of at least $260,000. That represented an average of $8,326 for each of the twenty-five legislators who received contributions.

In 2001, I sponsored the same bill without the penalties, AB 405. I managed to get the bill passed out of the education committee, but it was referred to the black hole of the Ways and Means Committee. My attaché (the formal title for my secretary) and I were lobbying the lobbyists to pressure the Ways and Means Chairman to release the bill because it had no negative fiscal impacts. To the contrary, it brought in unencumbered Federal grant money for reading. We had anyone who would listen hanging our handmade signs with a big screw burrowing into a schoolhouse and the words "Let AB 405 go" all over the third floor of the legislative building. At the last moment, AB 405 flew out of Ways and Means onto the floor where all rules were suspended, greased for passage, after some minor scuffling from the union die-hards. Our efforts had energized the entire community, both inside and outside the capitol building. Legislators in swing districts could not afford to take the union stand and still expect to win the next election. We won the "it is for the children" battle, but the war was not over, even for the Reading Excellence law.

With only four hours left in the session, the Senate began to put AB 405 through the legislative paces of committee hearings and passage. Time ran out just before the bill passed at 1:05 am. (The session formally ends at 12:00 a.m. standard time, since June is always daylight savings time in Nevada, we go one hour longer.) I marched to the Governor's Office where a renumbered AB 405 (SB 10) became one of the first bills passed unanimously out of the special session. My name was not on the final bill, but my fingerprints were all over it. A lot can be done if it does not matter who gets the credit. That was an important and positive lesson. However, I also learned that, in spite of all the fine teachers I knew, the teachers' union and the education establishment were more interested in pushing ideology, increasing union dues, and accumulating political power than in educating our children.

Reading failure was and still is a problem not only in Nevada, but also across America. As my friend, Herb likes to say when he teaches inmates at the county jail to read phonetically, "Learn to read so you can read to learn so you can learn to earn." While about five percent of our nation's children learn to read before entering school, twelve times that many—another sixty percent—find learning to read a formidable challenge.

While I struggled to get The Reading Excellence law passed, and a similar one that required scientifically based reading instruction for prison inmates, many adults would come to me privately and admit they were "functionally illiterate." It is easy to spot "basic" adult readers when they are forced to read aloud in public. Poor readers avoid reading aloud because their perceived intelligence and credibility are severely undermined by their poor performance.

The common excuses for the number of poor readers are poverty, immigration, television, or that English is a second language. Empirical research explains how and why students are badly short-changed: reading is a matter of skills learned, not intelligence. In most cases, if people cannot read, it is not because they are unable to learn how; it is because they have not been taught. Learning and using phonics fluently and accurately to read and spell words are the characteristics of a good reader.[171]

The situation is serious. The statistics are clear. The National Assessment of Educational Progress (NAEP) has been measuring basic achievement in reading and mathematics since the early 1970's. This Assessment is administered nationally to students at ages nine, thirteen, and seventeen. This standardized test measures and compares student performance in the three "R's:" reading, 'riting, and 'rithmetic. Sadly, even though "teaching to the test" has become the practice (which most my age consider cheating) it has not produced reading proficiency, which is the real goal, nor significantly higher test scores. In 2001, only twenty-five percent of college graduates rated "proficient" on federal reading surveys, making this generation less educated than their parents.[172]

Educational ideologues (championed by the National Education Association Union, which pushes for the status quo because any use of performance measurement of students threatens seniority and tenure and diminishes union dues) continue to fight the reading wars by arguing that ninety-nine percent of adults read at a basic level. "Basic" is a fourth grader reading at a first grade level, or, an adult with third grade literacy skills.

For over fifty years, the government schools have been teaching reading using "whole language." This has made reading a chore and all but impossible for many students. It is unfortunate for students that politically correct, ivory tower PhD's are unwilling to listen to alternatives, even when the science is solidly for phonics.

The inability to read well or enjoy reading is the primary cause for school failure and for the inability to go to college or succeed at work. High school dropouts and many graduates alike leave school without a love of reading, and without a basic ability to communicate or digest information.

Parents Need Real Choices

In my pre-legislative life I was first a wife and mother. I am fiercely protective of my children, and now my grandchildren. When my son, Vince, was five and "ready" to enter kindergarten, I sent him off to public (*i.e.*, government) school along with my daughter, who was a third grader at the top of her class. It was bittersweet watching my "baby" leave my constant care. I breathed a sigh of relief for the end of diapers and the advent of having time for myself, but I also felt a deep sadness for the end of a sweet innocence and dependence that would never come again.

In the middle of the year, Vince became sullen and unresponsive to the teacher. She said he was socially immature and needed to be "held back" in kindergarten. I believed her. Two years later Vince told me what really happened.

"The teacher said you needed to stay back so you would be able to learn," I explained to my seven-year-old when he blamed me for being a grade behind in school.

"That teacher was really dumb, and she was not a good teacher," he replied.

My younger brother, David, was bored with kindergarten because I had taught him to read, write, and do basic math before he started school. When David advanced to the first grade with the same teacher, leaving behind the sandbox and naps for the three "R's," the teacher became his favorite. Perhaps my recollection of David's kindergarten experience colored my response to Vince's teacher's diagnosis, and I should not have been so quick to accept it.

I pursued the conversation with my son, "Why do you think your teacher was dumb?"

"Well, she had us sit on the floor with our eyes closed. Then she said, 'Concentrate on your imaginary friend until you can hear him talk to you, and then ask him what his name is.' Well, mom," he said, "that is just dumb. I told her I would not do it because I had a friend who was not imaginary, and his name was Jesus. After that she was always mad at me."

The implications of Vince's revelation were shocking. His teacher was introducing a strange abstraction to kindergartners, and Vince had the audacity to not only refuse, but gave her one of the best testimonies of Christian faith I had ever heard. Vince's stand for his faith had cost him. The teacher judged him as "immature" and he had been "held back" a grade by the time I discovered the truth.

That second year in kindergarten started with Vince getting daily beatings from older children on the walk home from school. Why? My son was a "flunker." After the first two weeks, I drove him to-and-from school for the rest of the year. I also started to look for alternatives when my son woke up too "sick" to go to school each morning. Vince was a six-year-old dropout who felt like a failure and hated school. I had to do something.

I was a teacher, so the natural solution was to take Vince home, teach him myself, and get him caught up with his class so he could return to the public school. After all, that was what my mother had done for me as she advanced me from a *dumb duck* to a *bright bunny* with a course in phonics. I was ready to help my son the best way I knew how, based on my own personal successes in teaching. Then I hit a significant roadblock.

Our friends, the Wallace's, were also having difficulty getting their "round" children to fit into the "square" holes that represent the education mindset of the government school. They had decided to home school. After all, state law said that parents could home school their children. They took their two children out of the public school during the school year while Ted and I decided not to disrupt the year and waited to remove our two children until the end of the school year.

Very quickly, the Superintendent of Schools told Dave and Pat Wallace that if they did not put their children back in school, they would be charged with truancy and neglect, and their children would be put in a foster home. They hired an attorney. Incredulous, Ted and I helped Dave and Pat raise funds to pay for the impending court battle. Their attorney issued a Temporary Restraining Order against the school district pending the case decision. The Order allowed the children to stay home, but also placed the greater legal burden of proof on the Wallace's. This was my first experience with an activist judge.

In court, the Judge decided that, although the law simply said parents could home school their children, he interpreted it to apply to families that lived more than fifty miles from the nearest school, which in reality was a completely different law than the one the Wallace's were using to defend their right to home school. The Judge's interpretation of the law grew to fit his ideology. The Judge divined in the shadow of the penumbra of the law that clearly its intent referred only to those families living on ranches where busing long distances made public school impractical; only such families' children could be home schooled. His decision assumed that public schools were the only legitimate educational choice, though he proposed stipulations that must be in place should a public school district decide to allow home schooling to those living within a fifty-mile radius of a public school.

That court decision denied the Wallace family the right to home school and put the Wallace children back in public school. The Wallace's initially appealed their case all the way to the Nevada Supreme Court, but because they could not afford the legal and court fees, they were forced to withdraw the matter. We were all furious and more determined than ever to fight for the right of parents to direct the education of their own children. To this end, we found a group of parents in Nevada and in the nation who were fighting for home school laws. We requested and wrote a bill to change the Nevada law; lobbyists started working, and the battle began. Since Nevada's Legislature meets every two years, we had a two-year gap from the time of our Bill Draft Request until it would become law, and there was no guarantee that the Legislature would pass our law. Our family needed an immediate fix in the interim.

Our next best alternative was a private parochial school exempt from the state's curriculum and regulation. The Wallace's pastor said, "You can use our fellowship hall at the church for your school."

The Word of Light Church opened the Word of Light Christian

Academy in the fall of that same year. We had fourteen students in K-12 on the self-paced Alpha-Omega curriculum. I was the lead teacher. My friend Pat Wallace was the school secretary-treasurer. Two mothers volunteered as aides, and the pastor was the principal. The second year we had twenty-four students in our one room school. We taught four kindergartners to read and graduated two seniors.

When the 1983 legislature was in session, over five hundred people from across the state and nation attended a hearing on our new home school bill. The Chairman gave us thirty minutes in a room that seated fifty. It took the first thirty minutes of the hearing to move us to a larger hearing room.

Two hours into the committee hearing, the Chairman said, "If you are going to say something that has already been said, or if several of you have the same testimony, please just let one person speak for the others." It was intimidating, and some of those wanting to testify started to comply.

A cowboy from Elko unwound his long legs from the theater style chair and stood. "I drove five hours today to speak to you, and I will have my say. The rest of these folks have something to say, and they will say it." He sat down and the testimony continued for two more hours with some repetition and without anyone speaking for a group.

The Chairman took a committee member vote, and our bill passed out of the Assembly Education Committee unanimously. He adjourned the meeting.

As he swept past me, he said not so much to me as to himself, "If I had known this was such a big deal, I would have thrown it in my drawer, and it would never have seen the light of day."

I turned to my cowboy friend. "Can he do that? Just kill it without a hearing?"

"Yeah. He could have refused to take a vote and just stuffed it in his drawer after the hearing. We were lucky they took a vote and we're on our way." The cowboy picked up his hat, as I stood incredulous. I knew then that someday I wanted to be a part of taking government back for the people from the special interests.

Regrettably, the new home school bill died in committee in the Senate because the State Board of Education came forward and testified that they were writing regulations to govern home schools as prescribed in existing law. Unbeknownst to us, after the judge's ruling in November 1982, the

State Board of Education had immediately begun to write regulations that exactly mirrored the judge's opinion in the Wallace case and saddled Nevada families with multiple regulations and onerous government oversight for the next twenty-five years. Any parent wanting to home school was now required to "ask permission" of government bureaucrats by submitting extensive paperwork to the school district each year and submit their children to the public system for testing yearly beginning in the first grade. Home school curriculum had to be approved by the state. Under the new regulations, I was required to pay a certified supervisory teacher to come into our home to help with our home school progress. I had to submit daily lesson plans. Despite of all these requirements, at least we could home school our children!

After two years of hard work (by both my children and me) I put my children back into the public school. Vince graduated as class salutatorian, earned a Bachelor's degree in education, a Master's degree in Land Use Planning, and today teaches middle school history.

I am proud of my children, and I am glad I fought for an alternative that met their individual needs for educational success.

Over the ensuing years, many home school parents worked tirelessly to whittle away at some of the burdensome regulations the State Board of Education adopted in 1983, and then added more to in 1985. A little over twenty-five years after the Wallace case, Nevada home school parents traded those over burdensome regulations for the super deluxe *Home School Freedom Law*. In 2007, I requested SB404 and lobbied the Legislature for its unanimous passage. Once again, home school parents banded together to write a law that is now the model for other states, thereby enabling parents to direct the education of their children without oppressive government regulation or oversight.

Drugs versus Discipline

The Columbine shooting tragedy rocked my legislative world. I wrote a resolution in remembrance of that day, which a Democrat legislator I once mistakenly called a friend promptly stole. Again, much can be done if one does not care who gets the credit.

A more important and related piece of legislation warned against the over-medication of children. There is some credible evidence that these school shootings have a common thread. That thread is psychotropic drugs designed to treat the over-diagnosed Attention Deficit Disorder (ADD) and Attention Deficit Hyperactivity Disorder (ADHD).

I submitted a bill that would prohibit teachers from recommending these drugs or offering a diagnosis of these disorders. I saw this as an area that should be between the patient and the doctor, not a decision made under pressure from frustrated educators with untrained eyes. For the Committee testimony, we had each legislator take the following test.

Check the qualities that apply to you:

1) Easily distracted, miss details, forget things, and frequently switch from one activity to another
2) Have difficulty focusing on one thing
3) Become bored with a task after only a few minutes
4) Have difficulty focusing attention on organizing and completing a task
5) Have trouble completing assignments, losing things needed to complete tasks
6) Do not seem to listen when spoken to
7) Daydream
8) Fidget and squirm in their seats
9) Talk nonstop
10) Have trouble sitting still
11) Constantly in motion
12) Have difficulty doing quiet tasks or activities.
13) Impatient
14) Blurt out inappropriate comments

Most legislators gave answers consistent with those who are (mis) diagnosed as having hyperactive disorder. The mother of eleven-year-old Chris, my legislative intern (the youngest intern in Nevada history, but very capable in spite of his youth), told the Committee that in preschool at age two-and-a-half, it was suggested that Chris was hyperactive and that he should be tested and put on medication. His pediatrician confirmed he was merely a bright, exceptional child. While Chris was in a Montessori school, his mother was told again that he had ADHD, and would need medication or would have to find another school. Chris read at a very early age and was capable of working at a higher level than other kindergarten and first grade classmates. Instead of meeting Chris' needs, educators tried to diagnose him with ADHD. Repeated visits to doctors and psychologists proved he was very intelligent. Refusing to medicate Chris, his mother removed him from the school system and home schooled him.

The system is simply not adaptable to the very gifted or the very challenged. Many gifted children are bored with the mediocrity of a classroom that aims at the majority or the lowest common denominator. The challenged child, who has missed too much school, changed schools, or just has difficulty learning at the prescribed pace, becomes discouraged. Though present in body, they drop out in mind. Both categories of students can pose severe discipline problems and be disruptive to a classroom. The current system's simple solution of choice is to sedate them, and the best way to do that is to medicate.

When the hyperactivity drug bill failed for the second time, I went with members of a national women legislators federation, along with two top Hollywood actresses, to my Nevada Senator's office in Washington, D.C. Together, we convinced him to introduce the bill at the federal level. For this bill, "star power" helped. Legislators, like many people, like to meet and make time to listen to celebrities.

Ironically, I have drawn criticism in every campaign since 2006 because of the religious preferences of those stars with whom I partnered to promote this specific legislation. The root of this specific line of manufactured criticism began several years prior in 2001, when one young reporter (turned state Senator) wrote a story sensationalizing and deeply criticizing my interest in exploring a specific prisoner program's success that happened to be thinly tied to the founder of Scientology. (Interestingly, this former reporter has since apologized to me for his fabricated attack.)

As a state legislator, I was always interested in cutting government spending and inefficiencies. I learned of this prison program with a documented success record against drug addiction in some of the world's worst prisons. I saw in this program the potential to save millions in prison inmate recidivism costs and the potential to bring significant revenues to Nevada as the training center for other states implementing this program; not least of all, I saw in this program the potential to help some prisoners turn their lives around. I suggested that other legislators take a trip to see this program in action for themselves. Because this newspaper story vaguely connected the program to a vitamin therapy created by the late L.

Ron Hubbard (founder of Scientology), the trip was canceled, the program was not investigated any further, and no bill was drafted or introduced. Since that reporter's story broke, the late night radio crowd, press, and political opponents have tried to defame me, and have insulted a group of Americans (Scientologists) by disregarding their First Amendment right to religious belief free from persecution.

Because I am a Christian, many of my detractors have tried to marginalize me as some "dangerous" narrow-minded religious zealot. Some have falsely characterized my Christian convictions as getting in the way of me being an open-minded freethinker. Ironically (but conveniently for them at the time), these same detractors tried to twist facts—that I was willing to explore and potentially embrace some practical successes another faith, Scientology, had experienced in the area of treating drug addiction--to brand me as a Scientologist, and correspondingly to paint Scientologists in a negative light. So *who* is narrow-minded?

As a general rule, my Christian faith has very little in common with Scientology; that is no secret. But that is no reason for me or anybody, for that matter, not to be willing to explore viewpoints or frames of reference outside of our typical "comfort zones" in the interest of finding practical ways of helping our fellow citizens. The same should be applied to the political world. Although my conservative values typically have very little in common with Democrats (and vice versa), we should always be willing to explore each other's viewpoints, often outside of our respective comfort zones, in the interest of finding what is truly best for our country and fellow Americans, irrespective of political proclivity. Our debates and politics need to be far more principled and far less positional.

Reagan encouraged his cabinet to use successful business practices to build efficiency in government. He was interested in results regardless of the source. Reagan, the great coalition builder, coined the eighty percent precept. "The person who agrees with you eighty percent of the time is a friend and an ally – not a twenty percent traitor."[173]

The hyperactivity bill passed at the federal level and became federal law. Encouraged with this win, I reintroduced my bill at the Nevada State Legislature simply asking them to codify the federal law into state law (a technicality since federal law applies to the states).

The Chairman refused to schedule a vote on the bill after the testimony.

I had failed to get the legislation passed at the state level, but had succeeded at the national level.

On the Board

When we moved to Tonopah in 1987, a seat on the Nye County School Board opened. I wanted to run. I had been a teacher most of my adult life. I had a broad understanding of education from teaching in the public schools, private school, home school, college, and with senior citizens. I thought it was a good fit. It was a very clean campaign. My opponent and I did not debate or send direct mail. I walked door-to-door with a homemade campaign piece entitled "The Right Angle for School Board" and won the hearts and minds of the people, as well as the seat on the Board.

Board members confronted with problems have very little authority to resolve them. State legislators appropriate funding for school districts accompanied by mandated regulations. The parents complain. Our seven-member board acted as the mediator between lawmakers and complaining parents. We fired two teachers while I was on the Board. This was an incredible task because the union pledges to protect a teacher's job even if that teacher has proven to be unfit to teach.

One case involved a teacher who gave the answers to the achievement test to his students *while* they were taking the test. After the Board dismissed him, this same teacher went to Idaho to teach. No one in our school district ever received a call for references by the school that hired him.

Another case involved a teacher coach who had been molesting girls for years before being caught. The Board could not fire him until after his conviction. We put him on leave without pay.

Another coach caught having sex with a student in the back of a school bus resigned before we could fire him. The girl would not bring charges. The union defended them all, despite the outrageous circumstances.

Sitting on the School Board, I learned about the unintended consequences of legislative action by citizen legislators who listen to lobbyists and disregard those who must work with the laws they pass. I also got a close look at the ulterior motives of the biggest foe of good education in America, the teachers' union.

As the legislative liaison for the Nye County School Board, I went to the Legislature with explicit instructions to testify against class size reduction. Smaller classes sound good on paper, but when the number is rigid and there is no money to cover more classroom construction or more teachers, it can break a school district by taking dollars away from the real mission of education. There is only anecdotal evidence that these rigid class sizes have any impact on learning. Class size reduction usually results in there being a shortage of teachers, so under-trained or weak teachers enter the work force, and the effectiveness that *might* occur is lost. Another problem is that unless teachers change their method of teaching, they will have basically the same results in a small class as in a large. The envisioned on-on-one time doesn't occur as a matter of course. The hidden agenda of reducing class size is to hire more teachers and provide more union dues to the teachers' union, not provide better education to the student. Learning has to do mostly with a good teacher and students willing and able to learn.

When I testified against the class-size reduction bill, I met scowls and horrified surprise from some of the other school board members from around the state. Many retired educators serve on school boards and are invested in the union line. The union representatives spoke in favor of the bill in the supposed interest of the children, but the real motivation was hiring more teachers, thereby collecting more union dues. The double-edged sword of funding for unions while killing parental choice was exemplified by Senator Harry Reid's "yes" vote on May 15, 2001, that funded smaller classes with $2.4 billion in taxpayers' dollars for recruiting, hiring, and training one hundred thousand new teachers. The amendment killed a bill allowing parents with children at under-performing schools to use public funding for private tutors.

The union negotiator visited board meetings frequently at contract time. His line was always the same. Nye County should pay our teachers better because Eureka County, rich in gold mines, paid their teachers better. He gave a flowery speech one afternoon to the Board at our meeting in Amargosa. The union provided the insurance for the teachers, he said, so I asked the obvious question.

"Sir, I'm so glad to hear that you are providing the insurance benefits for our teachers and that you protect them from omissions and errors. Nye County is in a budget crunch. The county needs to build three more schools, and we have bonded to the maximum. So it is encouraging to know that we can drop our insurance coverage on the teachers because you've taken care of that."

He sprang to his feet sputtering, "No, Mrs. Angle! You can't do that. You are the primary provider." His meaning was that the union only protected the teacher from litigation after exhausting the school district insurance company's resources. Most teachers never hear this part of the story.

The truth was out. There is very little benefit provided by the union for its member that a rider on their homeowner's insurance could not do just as well, and for a lot less money. Every year teachers are coerced, badgered, or frightened into joining the union. Only a rare person can resist this extreme form of peer pressure. (Ironically, their dues may only entitle them to one and a half hours of the union lawyer's time should they have to defend their job.)

Teachers' Union Treachery

Make no mistake about it; the union funnels most of the teachers' dues to its political agenda. While claiming that their efforts are for the children, that is rarely the case. The unions are resistant to change, even in the face of incontrovertible facts based often on perceived potential losses to their own pocketbooks. Teachers' unions unite to block meaningful reform from coast-to-coast. Unions are committed to maintaining the status quo, wanting more money to hire more teachers, who are then likely to become dues-paying union members. Many reforms that foster cost-effective excellence in the private sector are consistently condemned by teachers' unions and fought with strong-arm tactics.

The well-developed national union has a reputation for stopping true school reform, even in small increments, with rhetoric rather than fact, which goes back for decades. The California teachers' union affiliate fought to keep school choice voter initiatives off the ballot in 1992, calling them "evil."[174] That same year in Washington, D.C., the union used members' threatened refusal to write college recommendations to coerce students and parents into supporting the union's fight against the transition of a half hour of prep period into teaching time each day.[175] When a national manufacturer offered private school scholarships to low income students, the union threatened a boycott of the company's product, and that company's vending machines were vandalized.[176] A Los Angeles superintendent recommended merit pay for teachers as a remedy in 2000, when two-thirds of the districts' public schools students failed. The union destroyed the measure, declaring it would be "a cold day in hell" before it passed.[177] A Detroit philanthropist offered to pay for fifteen charter schools in 2002. The union answered with a one-day teachers' strike squashing the $200 million deal.[178]

What can be Done?

Over the years I have spent in public service, the same question arises. "How can we disqualify the teachers' unions and remove their life crushing hold on education?" First, the public needs to become more aware of the real sources of the problems. The most egregious culprit is the National Education Association (NEA), which has been the biggest single obstacle to education reform in this country.

The NEA employs a larger number of political organizers than the Republican and Democratic National Committees *combined*. UniServ, the NEA's most expensive budget item, assists local teachers' unions with collective bargaining. UniServ is the delivery system for the union's political agenda through its network of "member-to-member" communication. To provide seamless state, local and national political activism, UniServ's network of local directors are employed by one of the 13,000 local NEA associations in every congressional district, but selection, training and funding—over seventy million dollars a year—comes essentially from the NEA.[179]

The directors facilitate candidate interviews and endorsements. The NEA "recommends" that its members canvass neighborhoods in a powerful get-out-the-vote effort. A glance at contribution and expense reports for state and local candidates will reveal layers of union affiliates that are almost invisible to government oversight, all of those layers give the maximum contributions.

One solution to teachers' union power grabbing is grassroots activism. The battle joins at the point of information. Voters must be informed of the "pay for power" that goes into candidate campaigns. A list of union contributions for each candidate should appear in voter guides. For conservative candidates the endorsement of the union should be the kiss of death. There should be a loud "no" vote on any candidate who takes this money.

Teachers need to know about professional associations and other alternatives to union membership, such as the Association of American Educators (http://www.aaeteachers.org/) or the Christian Educators Association International (http://www.ceai.org/) that offer equal or better benefits for less cost and with no attached political agenda. I have a friend who avoided the union for years by simply buying an errors and omissions policy rider on her homeowner's insurance. The cost is a fraction of the annual union dues, and it comes without the political strings.

Parents need to apply pressure to their children's schools through attendance at board meetings and parent-teacher meetings to make sure that union political notices are never placed in teachers' school mailboxes or sent home with the students. They should object to union meetings held on school property without charge or during school hours. They should support their teachers' right to work without union membership.

Another solution is legislative activism that dismantles the bureaucracy and puts education back into local control. The cabinet level Department of Education was created by law during the administration of President Jimmy Carter in 1980, and as such, was separated from the Department of Health, Education, and Welfare. This Department of Education should be frozen and then defunded with the ultimate goal of eliminating it as a cabinet post. The authority for education resides constitutionally in the individual states. This is not an original thought with me. Remember in 1870, the people feared that a Department of Education would exercise too much control over local schools. In 1996, dismantling the Department of Education was part of the Republican Platform and has been a campaign promise made by Presidential candidates since Ronald Reagan.

Finally, the states need more choice in education legislation that frees parents to determine the best direction for their children's education. Choices can include charter schools, private schools, parochial schools, online schools, and home schools, as well as movement from school to school regardless of zoning within the government school district to meet the needs of the child. With choice comes competition. Competition produces a better outcome and lower costs.

The steps to solving the problems of education are bold strokes. Changes in the education system provoke hard-fought battles. It will take all of us working together to succeed. All Americans must contribute by going to meetings, by insisting on putting the education of children before increased union dues, by breaking with sight-say reading, political correctness, sedating children, and other educational atrocities that fill our schools. Some Americans will help by refusing to join the union or fighting to decrease union influence, some by running for office without ties to the teachers' union, and some by removing their children from public government schools, opting instead for private, charter, or home schooling.

The key is this: do not hesitate to act. Be proactive. Engage the battle. Become a warrior for our children. The future of the nation depends on each generation.

"I have been singing in church since Jesus came into my heart in 1976."

Chapter Eleven

CLINGING TO OUR GUNS AND RELIGION

I think it is fair to say that our nation's Founders clung to their guns and religion. Conservatives of today are reflections of our Forefathers in lockstep with the mainstream of America at its inception.

BARACK OBAMA CHARACTERIZED the values of voters who are not Progressive urban supporters of *the one*. In an outrageous bigoted statement, he said, "And it is not surprising then they get bitter, they cling to guns or religion or antipathy to people who are not like them or anti-immigrant sentiment or anti-trade sentiment as a way to explain their frustrations."[180]

Obama tarred his opponents with the worst motives *he* could imagine: Christian faith, constitutionalism, support of individual liberty, and freedom from government. He projected his own antipathy and bigotry on "people who are not like" him. Politicians and media personalities who avidly promote government control over all areas of American life also disseminate this slander. Liberal Democrats are intent on usurping the people's independence from government. The Progressive revolution of Reid-Obama-Pelosi aims to promote dependence on the government, control by the ruling class, and an end to the American liberty and independence enshrined in the first two amendments of the Bill of Rights. Free speech, religion, and guns are the tools that defend a free people. From the First and Second Amendments of the Constitution come the strength, rights, and power to stand up against a powerful and tyrannical government. Of the single-issues driving most voters to the polls, those championing gun rights and the right to life are the largest and most fervent.

Using a divide-and-conquer tactic, the Leftist Progressive political elite separate conservatives into two categories: *fiscal* conservatives and *social* conservatives. They marginalize social conservatives as Rightwing religious fanatics, described as backward, paranoid, twitchy-eyed conspirators. Fiscal conservatives are derided as the "greedy rich."

Yet, there is no doubt that this country would not exist if it were not for the men and women of faith and the hard-working entrepreneurs who created a society and economy that is the envy of the world. When political bigots routinely vilify people of faith, these slanderers reveal their own bias, their own greed, and their own lust for power. The Elite Left embody that which they ascribe to their opponents.

Why We Cling to Our Guns

Americans cling to our guns and religion because the Founders understood that these were unique foundations of the freedom and liberty articulated in the United States Constitution. When we read the Constitution that guarantees those rights, we should adhere to Jefferson's admonition:

> On every question of construction (of the Constitution) let us carry ourselves back to the time when the Constitution was adopted, recollect the spirit manifested in the debates, and instead of trying what meaning may be squeezed out of the text, or invented against it, conform to the probable one in which it was passed.[181]

Beginning with the Amendment deemed most controversial, we read:

> A well-regulated Militia, being necessary to the security of a Free State, the right of the people to keep and bear Arms, shall not be infringed.[182]

The right to keep and bear arms guarantees all other rights. In his address to the first session of Congress, George Washington called this right the teeth of liberty.

> Firearms stand next in importance to the Constitution itself. They are the people's liberty teeth keystone... the rifle and the pistol are equally indispensable... more than 99 percent of them by their silence indicate that they are in safe and sane hands. The very atmosphere of firearms everywhere restrains

evil interference. When firearms go, all goes, we need them every hour.[183]

Thomas Jefferson (author of the Declaration of Independence, member of the Continental Congress, Governor of Virginia, Minister to France, Secretary of State, Vice President, President) was adamant about the right to keep and bear arms. His words destroy every argument from today's Progressive Left that would justify confiscating our firearms.

George Mason defined "militia" as the individual citizens. He asked, "[W]ho are the militia, if they be not the people of this country...? I ask; who are the militia? They consist of the whole people, except a few public officers."[184] Concerning the Second Amendment, the Founders were clear that the right to keep and bear arms is an individual right, not one restricted to the military or National Guard.

> A militia, when properly formed, are in fact the people themselves . . . and include all men capable of bearing arms. . . To preserve liberty it is essential that the whole body of people always possess arms... The mind that aims at a select militia, must be influenced by a truly anti-republican principle... whereas, to preserve liberty, it is essential that the whole body of the people always possess arms, and be taught alike, especially when young, how to use them.[185]

I believe every free man has the right to arm himself for his own domestic protection. It is not just my opinion that crime is lower in those states with laws permitting citizens to carry concealed weapons. Crime is higher, and more vicious, in cities with gun control laws. These are facts, supported by statistics. Those states with freer gun laws also have more fiscal freedom. In states where the citizenry is armed, anti-crime programs cost less. Study after study proves the slogan, "If guns are outlawed, only outlaws will have guns." Restrictions upon the registration and licensing of weapons do not deter crime. Instead, restrictive laws infringe upon our right to keep and bear arms. These laws can easily become incremental steps toward confiscation. Criminals will not register or license their firearms.

Jefferson has the answers to today's opposition who bring up age-old arguments:

> Laws that forbid the carrying of arms...disarm only those

who are neither inclined nor determined to commit crimes…
Such laws make things worse for the assaulted and better for
the assailants; they serve rather to encourage than to prevent
homicides, for an unarmed man may be attacked with greater
confidence than an armed man. [186]

To allay the fears of those who are afraid that the right to bear arms
would be abused, Jefferson wrote,

> The few cases wherein these things [proposed Bill of Rights]
> may do evil, cannot be weighed against the multitude where
> the want of them will do evil…I hope therefore a bill of
> rights will be formed to guard the people against the federal
> government…*James Madison*[187]
>
> The strongest reason for the people to retain the right to
> keep and bear arms is, as a last resort, to protect themselves
> against tyranny in government. *Thomas Jefferson*[188]

Just in case the Left would try to put Jefferson alone as the suspicious
"your government can not be trusted" conspiracy theorist, look at what
some other founders had to say:

- The Constitution preserves "the advantage of being armed
  which Americans possess over the people of almost every other
  nation…[where] the governments are afraid to trust the people
  with arms." *James Madison*[189]
- "[A]rms discourage and keep the invader and plunderer in
  awe, and preserve order in the world as well as property…
  Horrid mischief would ensue were the law-abiding deprived
  of the use of them." *Thomas Paine*[190]"
- What, sir, is the use of militia? It is to prevent the establishment
  of a standing army, the bane of liberty. Whenever Government
  means to invade the rights and liberties of the people, they
  always attempt to destroy the militia, in order to raise a
  standing army upon its ruins." *Elbridge Gerry*[191]
- "No free government was ever founded or ever preserved its
  liberty, without uniting the characters of the citizen and soldier
  in those destined for the defense of the state…Such are a well-
  regulated militia, composed of the freeholders, citizen and

husbandman, who take up arms to preserve their property, as individuals, and their rights as freemen." *Charleston State Gazette*[192]

The Second Amendment includes the right to own, use, and carry weapons of military pattern. The Founders intended to guarantee a citizenry able to defend itself from tyranny and invasion. This would require that free citizens have access to weapons that will give them that protection. An excerpt from the Pennsylvania Gazette on February 20, 1788, verbalizes this intent:

> The powers of the sword, say the minority of Pennsylvania, is in the hands of Congress. My friends and countrymen, it is not so, for the powers of the sword are in the hands of the yeomanry of America from sixteen to sixty. The militia of these free commonwealths entitled and accustomed to their arms, when compared with any possible army, must be tremendous and irresistible. Who are the militia? Are they not ourselves? Is it feared then, that we shall turn our arms each man against his own bosom? Congress has no right to disarm the militia. Their swords, and every other terrible implement of the soldier, are the birth-right of an American.... The unlimited power of the sword is not in the hands of either the federal or the state governments, but where I trust in God, it will ever remain, in the hands of the people.[193]

Is there a correlation between gun control and government intrusion through bank bailouts, corporate takeovers, stimulus failures, and government intrusion on healthcare with the disrespect expressed for the electorate by placing those who disagree with government policies on Obama's "snitch on your neighbor" list, or Homeland Secretary Janet Napolitano's domestic terrorist lists? Well, of course, there is. Simply put, it is a continuation of the government's power grab.

Pushing gun control is the government's way of testing the water temperature where the collective frog of the American populace sits in a pot over a flame. How long before we jump out of the proverbial boiling pot? Tyranny does not come from our military. Tyranny comes from coercive government rules and penalties, burdensome mandates, takings, taxation and abuses of government power, the independent administration of czars and the judicial bench. The TEA Party phenomenon represents the awakening of the people. The water is too hot, and the frog's legs are coiling. This silent majority of Americans has been patient to a fault with the trend toward an increasingly tyrannical government that is taking away our rights, one at a time. The constitutional model of government as a servant to the people has turned upside down. Now public schools teach government dependence.

When I was a legislator, the Assembly had to instruct schools specifically to teach the Constitution, the Bill of Rights, and the Declaration of Independence. The Left could not defeat this legislation outright, as they have with regard to teaching the Bible. Instead, with regard to our founding documents, the Left attempted to bury them under a mound of other papers that have little to do with our basic freedoms, and more to do with political correctness. Our audacity in asserting that freedom must be taught in school was met with surprise on the Right, who assumed that it was being taught, and with offense on the Left that conservatives dared demand it be taught.

The Left's spokesman, Barack Obama, finds the Constitution that does not allow the Supreme Court to "break free" from "essential constraints" offensive. He has stated that it teaches "negative liberties." In other words, it teaches what the government may *not* do, rather than "positive liberties," or what the government has the right to do.[194]

For example, the government is not a cornucopia of blessing to give us everything we want by taking from those the government thinks have too much.[195]

The Progressives use any available crisis to vilify opponents with incendiary rhetoric and accusation. The tragic shooting of an Arizona Congresswoman and slaying of bystanders in 2011 brought a despicable, politically motivated, ferocious attack from the Left against Sarah Palin and me personally and those associated with the grassroots TEA Party movement collectively.[196] The Leftwing media and politicians exploited the grief of a community and shock of the nation to further a political agenda aimed directly at the freedom of speech and the right to bear arms. The fact that an isolated apolitical, clinically disturbed, confessed, premeditated murder suspect was in custody due to many eyewitness accounts did not hinder liberal blame throwing. The Leftists twisted a phrase out of context, basing their argument solely on my use of a comment first coined by Dr.

Eastman referring to the Founder's *Second Amendment remedies* intent to deter tyrannical government. Using this reference was purely for historical context when I was talking to a radio host in 2009 about the importance of the Second Amendment. I was absolutely not suggesting or advocating violence. Once again, the Left and the liberal media were not missing an "opportunity" to exploit "a crisis" to promote their agendas, no matter the level of falsehood they peddle as truth. This one example of using words out of context in the aftermath of such a horrible national tragedy shows they have no bounds and that nothing is off-limits to them. Further, they clearly create and apply certain "standards" only when it is convenient for them. Consider, in comparison, that President Obama's inflammatory campaign rhetoric that his Latino supporters should "punish" their "enemies"[197] and a Republican win would incite "hand-to-hand combat"[198] are common political fare for the Democrats and unchallenged, accepted speech by the press.[199]

We must retain our right to keep our firearms. Thousands of gun laws and dozens of programs and policies treat the citizen as a nuisance (or worse) who interferes with the work of government bureaucrats.

Freedom lovers embrace the Second Amendment because it is a constitutional right that guarantees all the other rights.

Why We Cling to Our Religion

"...[T]hey cling to guns and religion," was Obama's charge as if it were a novelty in American life, but religious faith has been a part of American life since the discovery of the continent by Christopher Columbus who believed the world was a round globe because he read it in the Scriptures.[200] It was an integral part of our Colonial era. At the 1787 Constitutional Convention in Philadelphia, Benjamin Franklin (assumed to be one of the least religious of the Founding Fathers) said, "God governs in the affairs of men. And if a sparrow cannot fall to the ground without His notice, is it probable that an empire can rise without His aid? ... Without His concurring aid, we shall succeed in this political building no better than the builders of Babel."[201]

Franklin also said that he believed the writing of the Constitution was "influenced, guided, and governed by that omnipotent, omnipresent, and beneficent Ruler, in Whom all inferior spirits live, and move, and have their being."[202] The First Amendment is not ambiguous. Recently the legal system, aided by a Left-leaning press, has tried to spin the basic rights guaranteed by this Amendment.

> Congress shall make no law respecting an establishment of religion, or prohibiting the free exercise thereof; or abridging the freedom of speech, or of the press; or the right of the people peaceably to assemble, and to petition the government for a redress of grievances.[203]

Our Founders were men of faith, and many were "men of the cloth." In fact, twenty-four of the fifty-six signers of the Declaration of Independence were Christian pastors, and the rest were members of their congregations. The night before the Battle of Lexington, the local militia leader, Sam Adams, and John Hancock asked Reverend Jonas Clark if his congregation was prepared to fight. Reflecting on his sermons on the rights of the colonists, he answered, "I have trained them for this very hour!" After the Battles of Lexington and Concord the same morning, Reverend William Emerson, carrying his musket and dressed in his ministerial frock, met with his parishioners." Let us stand our ground; if we die, let us die here." While exhorting an eighteen-year-old, "Stand your ground Harry! Your cause is just and God will bless you." Known as the "Soldier Parson," an Elizabethtown, New Jersey minister, after running out of musket wadding, passed out hymnals by Isaac Watts shouting the battle-cry, "Now put Watts into them, boys!"[204]

The Supreme Court of the United States unanimously ruled that, "This is a religious people...From the discovery of this continent to the present hour, there is a single voice making this affirmation." [205] The most frequently cited source during the founding was the Bible. The first act of Congress in 1774 was to open with prayer and read four chapters from the Bible. During that time, members of Congress regularly attended church together and appropriated money for missionaries and religious instruction.

In 1777, Bibles in the English language were only available in England. During the Revolutionary War, Congress, facing a national shortage of "Bibles for our schools, and families, and for the public worship of God in our churches," declared that "The use of the Bible is so universal and its importance so great" that they "desired to have a Bible printed under their care and by their encouragement." Congress ordered twenty thousand Bibles imported from "Holland, Scotland, or elsewhere" and brought "into the different ports of the States of the Union."[206] In 1782, Congress approved the first English language Bible to be printed in America with the inscription "the United States in Congress assembled...recommend this edition of the Bible to the inhabitants of the United States" as "a neat edition of the Holy Scriptures for the use of schools."

This is only a sampling of the faith of the Founding Fathers. Their dogged commitment to the liberty described in the Bible motivated them to dedicate their lives, their fortunes, and their sacred honors. They were patriots, but first they were rebels against a government out-of-touch with the people it governed. It was their faith that made them declare their dependence on God four times in the Declaration of Independence. The British government considered these freedom fighters to be religious, Rightwing conspirators.

Lest we think this is an anomaly of the past, consider the constant affirmation of faith throughout American history. In 1853, the United States Senate declared that the Founding Fathers "had no fear or jealousy of religion itself, nor did they wish to see us an irreligious people...they did not intend to spread over all the public authorities and the whole public action of the nation the dead and revolting spectacle of atheistical apathy." In 1854, the House of Representatives declared, "It [religion] must be considered as the foundation, on which the whole structure rests... Christianity, in its general principles, is the great conservative element on which we must rely for the purity and permanence of free institutions."

Congress added "In God We Trust" to our coins in 1864. Congress put "In God We Trust" on all currency and made it the official national motto in 1956. In 1870, Christmas was declared a federal holiday. From 1904 to 1954, the federal government printed *The Life and Morals of Jesus of Nazareth* for members of Congress.

President Franklin Delano Roosevelt led the nation in a six-minute prayer on D-Day, June 6, 1944, declaring, "If we will not prepare to give all that we have and all that we are to preserve Christian civilization in our land, we shall go to destruction." In 1954, by law Congress added "One Nation under God" to the Pledge of Allegiance. President Dwight D. Eisenhower said, "Without God there could be no American form of government, or an American way of life. Recognition of the Supreme Being is the first, the most basic, expression of Americanism." President John F. Kennedy declared that, "The rights of man come not from the generosity of the state but from the hand of God."

People of faith are not out of step with the mainstream in this country; they are the Main Street of this country. I think it is fair to say that our nation's Founders clung to their guns and religion. Conservatives of today are reflections of our Forefathers in lockstep with the mainstream of America at its inception.

There is danger in forgetting the founding ideals and accepting the notion, popular among secularists today, that politics and faith do not mix. Church leaders today do not mention freedom like the pastors of the eighteenth century.

If the people "who cling to their religion" once more have the courage of their convictions, there will be political implications as there were during our nation's founding. The reason Obama and the Left negatively caricature people of faith was explained by Alexis de Tocqueville. "When a people's religion is destroyed...then not only will they let their freedom be taken from them, but often they actually hand it over themselves."[207]

Conversely, if the church awakens, pastors will decry from their pulpits the same truths that inspired freedom in 1776, and they will not be silenced by the fear of losing their 501(c)(3) income tax exemption should they cross the manipulated line of separation of church and state. Strong theological conviction would have political implications now, as in the past. I am a Christian, as were almost all of our Founding Fathers. That should not be misinterpreted to say that I think our government should be operated by a "state religion." Religious tolerance is a hallmark of Americans. There is no room in our constitutional culture for those bent on bringing harm, or death, to those who do not share their faith like those trying to govern nations with radical Islam. We must cling to our religion and should not apologize for (or shy away from) being a nation of faithful people... far from it. Our First Amendment guarantees us freedom of religion, not freedom from it.

What Else Must We Consider?

The entire concept of social conservatism wraps around these two amendments of the Constitution: the right to bear arms and the free exercise of religion. When government controls and dictates to a society what they will believe and how to use their income and savings, then that government has seized freedoms. That is why the Founders emphasized "negative" freedom and severely limited government's power and rights. As government grows, freedoms diminish. Not only does government confiscate the nation's wealth, paying themselves and their allies handsomely to administer these funds, they also determine the basis of redistribution of these funds to each of us. They dictate our obeisance. This is how tyrannical government strips away our money and freedoms. Taxpayers object to having their money confiscated to promote issues in opposition to their most sacred beliefs.

Just as a tyrannical Progressive government can take away our income, so it can insist on what is proper for us to believe, and not to believe. Political correctness, hate crime legislation, affirmative action, destruction of religious monuments, and banning the Bible from government schools are all attempts to criminalize thought and speech, especially religious thought and speech. The right of conscience is clearly a part of religious freedom. A person's beliefs are both personal and sacred, a matter between himself and God. The Constitution guaranteed a free exercise of religion, but religion is a potential power base beyond and apart from the government. Progressives cannot tolerate the declaration of a power higher than government whose precepts may inform governmental decisions.

The Right to Life

"I won't be here tomorrow. I'm pregnant, and my mom says she'll kick me out if I do not get an abortion, so I'm going to get the abortion tomorrow," said fifteen-year old Diana matter-of-factly as she dropped her schoolbooks on the table where I tutored her and five other juvenile offenders. Remanded to me by court order as part of their adjudicated sentence, these adolescents spent weekdays after school with me for tutoring to improve their grades in school and for community service cleaning duties at a local youth fitness center I had co-founded in Tonopah. Cleaning bathrooms, racquetball courts, the pool, and the weight room usually convinced most of these would-be criminals to stay on the straight and narrow path.

I was stunned but managed to ask calmly, "You don't seem very far along. Would your mom let you wait a little while? Do you have to do it tomorrow?"

"I guess I could wait. I only just found out, and I can do it any Tuesday." Diana responded without emotion, but the fear in her eyes searched me for a solution.

"Good. Do not do anything for three weeks, okay?" I had gained her trust, but I wanted a promise.

"Okay," she said. It was good enough for both of us, and we settled into her lessons.

It only took two weeks for me to connect Diana with Brenda and Rick. After the birth of their second child, Rick had had a vasectomy. Then the horror of every parent's life happened. The baby died. They tried to reverse the vasectomy without success and were rejected for adoption because the sterilization was voluntary. It seemed that their grief compounded without remedy, until Diana entered the scene.

Rick and Brenda arranged for an open adoption. Diana's mother "kicked her out" of her house, but Brenda and Rick took her into their home. They paid for the doctor visits, the delivery, and the adoption. They raised Diana and her baby, Kenzie, as part of their family, giving Diana opportunities, even after high school graduation, to visit her little girl in a loving home with wonderful parents.

Thirteen years later, as a Nevada state legislator, I spoke to a 4-H group from Tonopah. After the speech, one of the teens approached me. "I'm Kenzie, and I know what you did. Thank you for my life." I hugged that little girl with overwhelming joy and gratitude to God in my heart. Kenzie and others like her are the reason I am pro-life and why I will err on the side of life.

The "right to life" is an unalienable right in the Declaration of Independence. Abortion and infanticide are nearly as old as civilization. The Founders took steps to eliminate it within the free society. The right to life applies to all people, regardless of their age, gender, or place of occupancy. Life is a right endowed upon each individual that should not be taken away either as a whim, or as a matter of expediency, when another individual is inconvenienced.

In the spring of 2009, Gallup found for the first time that a majority of Americans, fifty-one percent, identified themselves as pro-life, while forty-two percent said they were pro-choice. Upon deeper examination, we see that this has been a trend for the pro-life movement for some time. A series of polls over the last decade showed that most Americans take one of three pro-life positions: (1) abortion to save the life of the mother, (2) abortion in cases of rape and incest or, (3) no abortions at all. When asked about specific abortion methods and abortions at different periods of the pregnancy, many who identify themselves as pro-choice would prohibit ninety-five percent of all abortions.

These statistics confirm the social conservative values held by the majority. Obama's radical abortion positions—including support for the Freedom of Choice Act, public funding of abortion in America and abroad, and a willingness to force doctors to violate their consciences—together with Obama romancing Planned Parenthood and other abortion groups, are all actually pushing many Americans to be more pro-life. Obama implemented radical abortion policies and packed the courts and his Administration with abortion advocates, all with the support of alleged "pro-life" Harry Reid, who admits he could support a health care plan funding abortion. The Susan B. Anthony List exposed Reid's record. "Senate Majority Leader Harry Reid says he's pro-life but he voted to use U.S. tax dollars to fund overseas abortions. He also voted to deny health care to unborn children of low income women."[208]

As Ronald Reagan put it, there is no right to abortion in the Constitution.

"Make no mistake, abortion on demand is not a right granted by the Constitution. No serious scholar, including one disposed to agree with the Court's result, has argued that the framers of the Constitution intended to create such a right.

We cannot survive as a free nation when some men decide that others are not fit to live and should be abandoned to abortion or infanticide. My Administration is dedicated to the preservation of America as a free land, and there is no cause more important for preserving that freedom than affirming the transcendent right to life of all human beings, the right without which no other rights have any meaning."[209]

Several abortion issues fall into gray areas for many voters, but are not gray for those who have studied abortion. These issues include partial-birth abortion, embryonic stem cell research, and government funding for private agencies that promote and provide abortion on demand. Through educational efforts, the pro-life movement graphically exposed partial-birth abortions as infanticide of a most barbaric nature. Even some of the most liberal proponents of a "woman's right to choose," could not stomach this choice.

The area of stem cell research is largely misunderstood. There are two branches of stem cell research: 1) the commonly accepted and highly effective stem cell research that encompasses adult stem cells and umbilical cord stem cells and 2) the suspicious *embryonic* stem cell research. Embryonic stem cell research requires the termination of human embryonic life (abortion) in order to harvest the stem cells. Studies show these stem cells often cause cancer and have no medical effectiveness. The proponents cite wonderful future cures that *could* be associated with this research. There is little to no evidence to substantiate those claims. They justify the *means* because of this alleged miracle cure *end*. Sound science cannot promote embryonic stem cell research, nor can private companies raise substantial funds to support the research. The abortion industry, based on selfish personal interest, deceives the public and steals public monies through unconstitutional taxpayer support.

This debate over embryonic stem cell research is an example of how Progressives use the abandonment of restraints of government and abandonment of religion to expand government powers and tyranny. Nowhere in the Constitution does it say that the government should fund embryonic stem cell research. A certain group of researchers and industries create imaginary promises or crises, contribute to politicians, and finally get the government to give them billions in exchange for a few million dollars of campaign contributions. Billions of taxpayer dollars grease these political decisions for special interests despite any fiscal, moral, or religious objections.

Finally, the abortion industry promotes its agenda by hiring powerful lobbyists. Various organizations funnel taxpayer dollars to fund ventures that provide abortions. Planned Parenthood is perhaps the most commonly known organization supporting the Left's abortion agenda. Planned Parenthood, under the guise of helping poor families, has expanded its family planning techniques from normal contraceptives to contraception by abortion.

There are responsible choices for women, such as abstinence, contraception, and adoption. Abortion is an irresponsible choice based on fear, narcissism, poverty, convenience, or the selfish notion that one life is more valuable than another life. One of the fundamental tenets motivating the Founding Fathers to create this great nation was what they described as the "unalienable" right to life...as granted by God, and not as a matter of convenience.

The right to life issue is probably most associated with abortion and the pre-born, but it encompasses all the issues related to human life. It establishes that people of color have a right to life and cannot be enslaved as inferior human beings. Right to life establishes that the disabled have that right and are not expendable as having an inferior quality of life. The right to life embraces the lives of the elderly and defends against a death panel decision that determines they have outlived their usefulness to society. When a value scale other than the sacredness of all life can be applied to any life, America is on the slippery slope to the slaughter of the innocent and inconvenient. In fact, the Planned Parenthood movement, born in the theory of eugenics, has already disproportionately aborted the poor, the minority, and the disabled.

Repeated polling proves that America is a pro-life nation and while Pro-Lifers are the Republican Party's most loyal voting block, many Pro-Lifers are, in fact, Democrats and Independents. Many Pro-Lifers have demonstrated they will not participate in elections when they feel their issue is being "sold-out" by a candidate. To win elections, conservatives must engage, not enrage, this voting block.

Defining Marriage

Protection of marriage is a provision of many state constitutions. The definition of marriage "between one man and one woman" is the traditional definition supported by the majority of Americans. Yet in recent years, out of a pragmatic attempt to recruit from a broader pool of workers, corporate America has been spending hundreds of millions annually in lobbying for same-sex marriage, applying same-sex affirmative action in the workplace, promoting the same-sex agenda, and implementing Progressive business procedures. The federal government has been a willing accomplice, demanding that taxpayers and all private businesses provide (pay for) these benefits, even if doing so infringes upon individuals' right of conscience, and thereby their freedoms.

Society has historically regarded marital love as a sacred expression of the bond between a man and a woman. Marriage stabilizes families, and society itself finds it a firm foundation for the future. The Judeo-Christian tradition defines marriage as a holy means by which husband and wife participate with God in the creation of new human life. For these reasons, among others, our society has always sought to protect this unique relationship. In part, the erosion of these values has given way to a celebration of forms of expression that most reject.[210]

Sodomy laws existed in some states until radical homosexual activists targeted them. The laws were not an intrusion into anyone's bedroom, as opponents suggested, although the very passage of such laws by states and communities expressed societal disapproval of such conduct. Law enforcement officials have testified that these laws were very effective tools for the prosecution of rape cases. The expunging of such laws by legislators, due to their fear of homosexual activist lobbying, have eroded citizen protection. The fears and the attacks levied by this lobby are real. The 2011 attack on a southern fast food restaurant chain was one such attempt to silence dissenting voices to the LGBT (Lesbian Gay Bisexual Transgender) agenda.

Traditional financially stable families are in the best interest of the country. In a 2008 Father's Day speech, even President Obama invoked traditional and natural family values, quoting the statistics on the importance of two parents, especially the involvement of fathers. He opined that the foundations of society are weaker because children without fathers tend to have behavioral challenges, are runaways, or become teen parents. These children have five times the probability of a life of poverty or crime, twenty times the likelihood of going to prison, and are nine times more apt to drop out of school.[211]

Going to War

A major purpose of our federal government is to protect freedom through national defense. World War II was the United States' last constitutional War. Alexis de Tocqueville said, "There are two things which a democratic people will always find very difficult—to begin a war and to end it."[212]

Perhaps that is why the wars since then, including the wars in which we are now engaged, have not been declared officially by Congress and are, therefore, not constitutional wars. By sending troops into "police actions," the legalities become muddied. Are detainees "prisoners of war" if there is no war? Are detainees enemy combatants or merely criminals? Are American troops soldiers or police officers? These ambiguities leave our citizens divided, other nations confused, allies unsure of our resolve, and provide an opportunity for our enemies to exploit these internal divisions.

When there is an attack on our country, our Constitution requires the common defense, yet Congress votes to deploy troops and can refuse to fund those troops. The Senate Majority Leader, Harry Reid, told Veteran's groups that he supports them. He pointed to his votes that call for aggressive action against our enemies, yet he refused to fund those efforts and verbally slammed the military declaring, "This war is lost,"[213] during the Iraq War.

We need politicians of courage and conscience. Political correctness will not give way to constitutional correctness, unless Americans elect politicians who object to sending young men and women to war without all the weapons available, including legal weapons, such as a declaration of war, and a determination to win. With the majority in Congress opposing the constitutional solution, the results have been manipulation of political influence, public confusion, defense industry opportunism, and undue risk to our brave military. This should offend the conscience of every American.

The forces of international Islamic terrorism are currently the greatest single threat to American liberties. It is their sworn oath to destroy free nations and set up Koranic theocracies by imposing Sharia law. They have made great gains in Western democracies like the United Kingdom and other countries of Europe. The United States must reject and resist this primitive menace. There is no co-existence with Islamic extremism, are exhibited by the terrorists' own declaration and demonstration on September 11, 2001.

The United States faces an enormous and complex predicament. There is no easy solution, but there *is* a solution. As General Petraeus said, "It's hard but not hopeless." First, the United States military must train indigenous forces and help them secure the borders that currently allow terrorists to move freely from Afghanistan to Pakistan (like Osama Bin Laden who was finally killed in Pakistan). We must allow our special operations military to hunt these terrorists as enemy combatants wherever they are. I had the privilege of flying a mission ahead of a convoy in Iraq in 2006. In theory, I was in the "cockpit" of an Unmanned Aerial Vehicle flying in Iraq, but of course I never left the control room at Creech Air Force Base, just north of Las Vegas, Nevada. The mission was to scout ahead looking for danger to our troops.

UAV drones of all types and surgical offshore missile launching will not win the war on terror. I see four options now that we are engaged in a war that is not necessarily about geographical lines but radical political goals.

The first option is to "cut and run." Just get out. A full immediate withdrawal would create a larger safe haven for Al Qaeda and embolden them to range further afield and wreak more terror and destruction. Those who favor this course say that the American presence amounts to unwanted occupation of the host nation by adding to instability which in turn fuels more insurgency. Typical host nations, such as Iraq, Afghanistan, Pakistan, and Somalia, all welcome help from the United States and its allies, but when there is talk of abandonment, the governments begin to look for compromises with the terrorists just to survive. Any indecision or lack of resolve invites weakness by host governments.

An enemy's aura of invincibility helps keep some terrorist organizations from taking actions. This is the essence of peace through strength of which President Reagan spoke often. Conversely, perceived weakness or lack of resolve encourages adventurism by organizations of insignificant strength or unpopular support. In the 1970's after our defeat in Vietnam, communist groups were on the march around the globe from Nicaragua to Iran, taking advantage of the war fatigue and disgust prevalent in the United States. Subsequently in the 1990's after the U.S. retreated from Lebanon and Somalia, Osama Bin Laden judged the U.S. as weak, and attacked with impunity. He set about to exploit the weakness he saw. September 11, 2001, was a direct consequence. On October 2, 2009, FBI Director Robert Mueller testified in a hearing on Capitol Hill that the Al Qaeda-linked group al-Shabaab "would send American recruits back to the U.S. to launch attacks." Al-Shabaab had pledged allegiance to Osama Bin Laden and had training camps well established within Somalia with eleven hundred foreign fighters. In September of 2009, Omar Hammami of Daphne, Alabama, was identified as the American mouthpiece for al-Shabaab. In October of 2008, the FBI identified a Minneapolis man, Shirwa Ahmed, as the first known American suicide bomber. He trained in one of the Somali camps. Authorities believe there were nearly two dozen other Americans in this group.[214]

The second option is to scale back by leaving a reduced U.S. force to train indigenous troops and utilizing Special Forces to perform limited missions, such as hunting the most wanted extremist leaders and disrupting enemy control and command. Military analysts predict that reducing the U.S. role to that of only training and counterterrorism would embolden the Taliban and Al Qaeda, thus permitting the enemy to assert themselves as winners, and would bring increased risk to remaining allied troops and diplomats.[215]

The third option is to continue emphasizing training and growth of indigenous forces while maintaining a strong NATO force as trip wires against escalating conflict. The U.S. would supply necessary equipment and seek diplomatic resolution with the enemy organizations.

Finally, the forth option is to send more combat troops to overwhelm the enemies and help struggling nations to regain effective control of their countries. Winning would mean creating the peaceful conditions necessary for a local government to achieve effective control without the further need of foreign troops.

Without classified information, we must trust our military generals to make the right decision. In the future, putting the issue of war (and not police action) clearly in constitutional context protects our own national security. The United States must never again abandon our military to a political tug-of-war. American foreign policy must ask and answer this question, "Does a potential conflict serve the just interests of the United States in securing our liberties as contemplated in the Constitution?" Our policy makers must answer correctly in order to maintain an effective, fully staffed, and credible volunteer military. May we never again see a conscription military pressed into an unconstitutional conflict.

Israel

"*Sha'alu Shalom Yerushalayim*—Pray for the peace of Jerusalem," commands the Psalmist continuing, "They shall prosper that love thee." Through its formation, wars, and family connections, Israel has come to hold a very special place in the hearts and minds of many Americans.

Through great political struggle for more than a hundred years, in 1948, the new, secular state of Israel was created and legitimized through the machinery of the United Nations and was endorsed especially by President Harry Truman on behalf of the United States of America. Supporting the security of the state of Israel, as well as the security of other established nations, is in the best interests of American national security. People who have struggled for independence (or against abuse like the people of Darfur, Zimbabwe or Rwanda) have a human right to a peaceful existence within the borders of land to which they have earned entitlement, whether through struggle or inheritance. Just like the United States, these nations are sovereign.

My friend, Mike, survived the holocaust and lived to fulfill his potential because of freedom. He wrote me this e-mail:

> I am a Lithuanian born Jew who lost his parents and three siblings by Nazi atrocities during World War II. A fourth sibling, ten years older than I was at that time, was killed by the Bolsheviks—my term for communists and Leftist terrorists. I, myself, spent three years and 8 months in the Kaunas Ghetto as well as Lager 10 of the Landsberg Kaufering Outer Camps of Dachau. I was liberated by the U.S. Army the night of May 1 and May 2, 1945 near a place called Bad Toelz, during a forced march when the SS was trying to keep us from being freed by the advancing US forces. I came to the US in September 1947, and joined the US Air Force in January 1948, soon after it became a separate military department. I served in the US Air Force during the Korean War and am thus considered a veteran of that war.[216]

Benjamin Netanyahu reminded the United Nations that the denial of the Holocaust is the denial of the value of humanity. That atrocity demanded the attention and action of the world, even though Neville Chamberlain tried to conciliate with the leader of an evil regime elected in a weakened, war-riddled nation. There is no compromise, no conciliation, and no consensus with evil.

Freedom of Conscience

Alexis de Tocqueville observed, "The Americans combine the notions of Christianity and of liberty so intimately in their minds, that it is impossible to make them conceive the one without the other. Christianity is the companion of liberty in all its conflicts——the cradle of its infancy, and the divine source of its claims."[217] The introduction of Marxist socialism into our government eroded this truth. De Tocqueville explains, "Democracy and socialism have nothing in common but one word, equality. But notice the difference: while democracy seeks equality in liberty, socialism seeks equality in restraint and servitude."[218] The redistribution of wealth is a socialist ideal that brings servitude and curtailing of freedom. Taxation has been the stealth vehicle to this end. "The American Republic will endure until the day Congress discovers that it can bribe the public with the public's money,"[219] said de Tocqueville. This will happen when governmental bribes guarantee benefits as rights and entitlements.

We must take back our right of conscience by electing representatives who understand the freedoms guaranteed in our Constitution. Some will accuse those running for office, who share the faith of our Founders, of being "too religious." The Constitution intended to govern a moral and religious people, and "is wholly inadequate for any other," Benjamin Franklin observed.[220] Some in his day accused Franklin of not being religious enough. Moral individuals will work to restore the constitutional structure of our Republic and shun the corruption that has infused our government. Moral absolutes, such as not lying or stealing, should inform a politician's actions. Creating crises, making up new rights, and then extracting confiscatory tax rates and deficits to buy patronage, line pockets or hire ever more bureaucrats were the very evils that the Constitution, religion, and a moral populace were promoted to forestall. It was, in fact, a sermon, "Sinners in the hands of an Angry God," that fanned the flames of revolution giving birth to this nation.

Let us raise together again the flags of the Founders, "Don't Tread on Me," "Give Me Liberty or Give Me Death," and "I Have Just Begun to Fight." The majority who agree that freedom is worth fighting for can prevail again. Socialism can and must be defeated at the ballot box. Benjamin Franklin said, "Yes, we must, indeed, all hang together, or most assuredly we shall all hang separately."[221]

"*The large generation of baby boomers beginning to retire, have the time, energy, life experiences, independence, and finally the common sense to lead the charge to take back our country for our children and grandchildren.*"

Chapter Twelve

THE RIGHT ANGLE FOR A NEW CONSERVATIVE MOVEMENT

The socialist Democrats are relentless and play hardball, while too many Republican legislators are playing with a mush pounder.

AS OF THE WRITING of this book, the conservative movement is gaining momentum, rocking this nation as it did in 1776. Americans have an opportunity to reset a course that our Founding Fathers would recognize. We can stand up against the growing tyranny in Washington and preserve our freedoms, our liberty, and our prosperity. As a bumper sticker proclaims, "I'll keep my freedom, my money, and my guns; you can keep THE CHANGE."

The critical question is, "Do we have the will to turn the right direction?" We can no longer use the "c" words for government: capitulation, consensus, and compromise. "Reaching across the aisle" has cost us our principles and much of our freedom.

Those words have always meant defeat for conservatives. We must be determined to take no prisoners in the political battle with the socialist Left.

Freedom is not guaranteed. It must be fought for and secured by each successive generation. My father's generation, called the "Greatest Generation," fought World War II. They knew who the enemy was. Japanese tyranny under Emperor Hirohito bombed Pearl Harbor, and German National Socialism under Hitler threatened to take over the West. Once engaged there was no doubt that America would fight to win and protect liberty. Those who did not, or could not, join the military worked that much harder in their civilian jobs at home to support the war effort abroad. The nation united to defend all that we stood for.

Most of our soldiers, sailors, pilots, and marines volunteered to serve. They all risked, and many sacrificed, their lives for freedom. When they returned home after V-E Day and V-J Day, they did not boast of their bravery, or willingly recount the excitement of battle. They returned quietly and humbly to their families and jobs, continuing to build the free market capitalist system, providing prosperity, liberty, and freedom.

I grew up during the Vietnam War, an undeclared war where our honorable heroes received a dishonorable welcome home. Student demonstrations and cowardly politicians turned the resolve of the country away from victory. The politicians refused to keep the promises of financial and military support to the South Vietnamese after our troops withdrew. They voted to cut and run. Millions died in the Communist blood baths in Vietnam, Cambodia, and Laos. Tens of thousands of Americans died for their freedom, their sacrifice discounted by retreat. The Vietnam War was perhaps the most embarrassing and dishonorable moment in our nation's history. The embarrassment and dishonor resulted from what took place at home and had nothing to do with the valor, bravery, and incalculable sacrifice of our soldiers and their families. The way our own were mistreated…I pray it never, ever happens again. Forty years later, many in the "boomer" generation are still trying to make sense of what seemed to be a senseless war with a senseless outcome.

Politics became a dirty word for most baby boomers. Many boomers opted for a more meaningful life that included "higher aspirations" than grappling with the corruption of Washington, D.C. Boomer political inaction, and reluctance to engage the fight for freedom allowed more corruption. Edmund Burke's challenge went unheeded as good men did nothing, and evil triumphed. For forty years, Democrats held Congress, spending trillions on a War on Poverty that only worsened poverty and destroyed poor families. Politicians of all stripes promised Social Security and Medicare to the elderly in a Ponzi scheme that is trillions of dollars in deficit now, and will not be available to most baby boomers, much less their children. The Left advocated appeasing the Soviet menace and supported or ignored our enemies abroad, all while they lined their own and their political allies' pockets with millions upon millions of dollars, regulating and taxing our economy nearly to death. Through decades of political neglect, Americans wandered. Although bright, conservative stars shone for a while, they were routinely dimmed by the relentless effort of the socialist Left to strip our nation of its constitution.

In 1976, Americans saw a swell of freedom begin to blow across our land.

Although Ronald Reagan lost the Republican nomination to Gerald Ford, Reagan ignited our imagination. Reagan's words reignited the Founder's vision once more in American hearts. After Reagan's election in 1980 and until 1988, America became the "Shining City on the Hill." In 1988, George Herbert Bush became the heir apparent, but we knew Reagan, and Bush was no Reagan. Seeing the moderate Republican establishment writing on the wall, for the first time Nevada boomers went *en masse* to the Nevada State Republican Convention to take back the party of Reagan and reestablish conservative principles. I sat in my county delegation and watched the fight as two hundred establishment delegates maneuvered to wrestle power from five hundred new voters that were against the "good old boy" agenda.

Conservatives (labeled "religious Rightwing fanatics" in the press and by the senior state Senator) wrote the Party platform and elected all the delegates and officers except one, the Treasurer's position, which turned out to be the fatal error of compromise with the old guard. The checks required two signatures. The ability to pay bills was completely thwarted when the old guard Treasurer refused to sign checks with the conservative Chairman. After the Treasurer pushed the party to near bankruptcy, the Chair resigned and the party went back to the old guard leadership. It was a hard lesson learned on both sides. The senior state Senator set up funding for candidates inside the Senate Caucus, removing it from the party where it had been. There was little reason for candidates to seek party approval since there was no money available to support them.

This continued until 2008, when the State Republican Convention witnessed another surge of interest. This time it came from a generation of computer savvy and constitutionally literate thirty-somethings. They were eager and naïve, but they let us battle-wise veterans show them the path to victory over the old guard. Once again, the new conservatives were labeled, this time as *Ron Paulers*. As before, this new conservative coalition was bested when the old guard did the unthinkable. When the votes were going decidedly against the establishment, the Chair of the Convention, at the prompting of the Party Chair and other establishment insiders, recessed the Convention and turned out the lights. Instead of reconvening the Convention, the Party Chairman appointed delegates and put the matter of the illegal convention to the decision of the Republican National Committee (RNC). The RNC issued a reprimand, and then, true to the by-laws of the RNC, the Nevada delegates were seated with equality of representation from both groups. When "lost" ballots from a round of voting conducted before the lights went out miraculously appeared over a year later, the votes proved that the new conservative surge won all the seats, while the old guard maneuvered a tie at the National Convention.

No matter the demagoguery or the political trickery, the movement for freedom remains strong. There is too much at stake. Too many have heard the call to liberty. It is not about religion, even though the religious are part of the movement. It is not about one man, even though many politicians have heard the call. It is not about one generation, because my father, my son, and I have all heard the cry, "take this country back." It is not about one state, even though I concentrate on my experience in Nevada. Every state has their corrupt Establishment where power rangers and politicians play both sides of the fence for personal gain. It is not about one issue. Even though America is primarily concerned with the economy, there are interested and invested voices from many quarters, such as the illegal immigration protesters, the Second Amendment enthusiasts, and the Pro-Life supporters. It is not about the legacy media's bias or the talk show's Right-leaning hosts. This is a movement across America that has created a big *freedom tent*, calling conservatives to work together, despite of our differences, against the common enemy, socialism. We do not want the government to run our lives, confiscate our firearms, over-tax our money, and abridge our freedoms. Too many before us have paid too high a price for us to surrender the freedoms patriots bought with American blood, sweat, and tears.

In 2006, I ran for U.S. Congress. That experience gave me the opportunity to meet many who had heard the call to the freedom fight. Four years later, there are even more who hear that call, as evidenced in the TEA Parties speaking in the voice of liberty that sprang up from the grassroots. These energized Americans span the population spectrum from seniors to young people, and include people from all races, faiths, and socioeconomic backgrounds.

It is time for all of us here at home to join the Keepers of the Flame, who serve in the Armed Forces. The large generation of baby boomers beginning to retire, have the time, energy, life experiences, independence, and finally the common sense to lead the charge to take back our country for our children and grandchildren. The real crisis is that America is on a path to slide into the European-like socialism promoted by Reid, Obama, and Pelosi. As such the United States would become a nation with a permanent underclass of twenty percent unemployed, government-rationed healthcare, euthanasia for the elderly, government-promoted and funded abortions, and attacks on religious freedom and free speech in the name of hate crimes. These will all be coupled with an ever-declining standard-of-living, dumbed-down public education, a diminishing population, and the continuing invasion of unassimilated, illegal aliens.

Are we tilting at windmills? Is the fight already lost? Have we waited too long? Did we fiddle while Rome burned? Is there still time to stop the rush to socialism? These questions haunt most Americans who feel the urgency now! I say it is not too late, but we must come together and act decisively…and immediately.

Congressional Republicans consolidated their various "plans" in 1994 in the *Contract with America.* Without an equally strong plan for the future, Republicans are vulnerable to the accusation of being the party of "No." Conservatives need inspiring leadership. The Leftists are experienced street fighters who show up with clubs and knives while conservatives show up for the fight dressed in tuxedos. The socialist Democrats are relentless and play hardball, while too many Republican legislators are playing with a mush pounder.

The Call for Liberty

The Right Angle for our generation of conservative freedom fighters rests on five principles of liberty in the Constitution. They are what I refer to as the "Call for Liberty:"

1) The Rule of Law: The Constitution guarantees that all men are created equal based on divine rule and the Rule of Law, a precept drawn from the ancient Greeks. The oath of office asserts that no one is exempt from the law established by the Rule of Law. The Constitution is the right Contract with America. For elected representatives, the oath of office to uphold and defend the Constitution must be ironclad. If a member knowingly violates this oath, there must be discipline through impeachment for the violation. All laws passed by Congress must apply equally to the

Congress. Passing a single subject rule for all legislation would provide transparency to the public.

2) Fiscal Responsibility: Elected officials have the legal and moral obligation to be accountable for the finances, government revenues, and Treasury because they belong to someone else. This principle describes both financial reform and tax cuts. It is a balanced budget where expenses match revenues. Our top priority should be paying off the debt. With the debt reduction as the top budget item, all other spending will focus on that objective.

Legislators must expose, reverse and drive a stake in the heart of the failed Keynesian economics of tax and spend. A good first step begins with auditing the Federal Reserve, demanding simplification of the tax code and conducting a comprehensive audit of Congress and the Executive departments for waste, fraud, and abuse. The deceptions behind 1) baseline budgeting for the federal budget, and 2) automatically expanding expenditures using formulas built into law, must be exposed. Instead, we must adopt a new budget structure which, as a starting point, is based on what was actually spent the previous year. We must also pass a balanced budget amendment to the U.S. Constitution and put an end to the massive irresponsible and immoral debt our federal government has been all too willing (and able) to charge cavalierly to future generations.

Limited taxation is necessary for government to perform and administer essential public needs. However, the key is to limit the size of government, and therefore, to limit the need for taxation. The best way to control an overbearing government is to control strictly the amount of taxes it imposes on the people. The first step is simplifying the tax code to a fairer, flatter tax system. Excusing almost half of the population from paying any taxes at all makes many people eager to vote themselves more and more benefits at no cost to themselves. This generation of conservatives must pledge to reduce taxes, beginning with the permanent repeal of the capital gains tax and the inheritance tax. Another step would be requiring a two-thirds vote of each house to pass a tax increase. Citizens should be better informed on their entire tax burden (both direct and indirect)—federal, state, local, higher prices of regulation, sales taxes, fees, what taxes their employer pays for them—all of it.

3) Limited Government: Economic prosperity is dependent on the free market. The principle of limited government restricts and prescribes by law the functions and powers of government. Lower taxes and less government regulation lead to more freedom and a prosperous economy. Kennedy and Reagan proved that this works. A business-friendly environment will help the United States to be more competitive in the world marketplace. Recognizing that government regulation can be a major impediment to productivity and to competition, legislators must rely more on market forces and less on government. It is time to support and defend right-to-work laws, pledge to require that union votes be by secret ballot, and assure that union dues are not spent for political purposes without the explicit written permission of the union member. There must be a permanent repeal of the Davis-Bacon Act.

Energy independence is vital to freedom and prosperity. Rapid increases in gas prices must be met with short-term efforts that bring immediate relief, while keeping an eye toward long-term energy policy changes that reduce America's dependence on Middle East oil. As a long-term policy, Americans must utilize more of our vast domestic energy supplies: drill here, drill now, save money. Legislators should repeal strangling and confining regulations on the expansion of nuclear power plants, and domestic drilling in areas such as Alaska National Wildlife Refuge (ANWR), and the gulf coast. We need to dispel the myth of man-caused global warming.

To correct our failing public education system, we must:

1. Create incentives that promote competitive excellence;
2. Approve the rights of parents to choose public, private, or at-home education;
3. Eliminate spending on failed programs; and
4. Pledge to put education into local control rather than federal control.

Downsizing and then eliminating funding for the Department of Education is also a step toward recovery. Parents of public school students must have the right to opt into any instruction rather than having to opt out of instruction that they feel is inappropriate.

Medicare/Medicaid and Social Security must be reformed by repealing *Obamacare* and assuring that payments are made on time to doctors and hospitals and at full market value. Emergency rooms can no longer serve as primary care centers for the uninsured. The small number of uninsured working poor should have government-provided catastrophic coverage. Mandates for costly, elective services must be removed. Citizens must be allowed to purchase basic health insurance policies across state lines with the ability to add those benefits that are specific to each person. There must be caps on non-economic damages in all tort actions to eliminate the costly practice of defensive medicine. We must support associational healthcare and tort reform that will lower the cost of healthcare to businesses and individuals and thereby allow for larger pools that would spread the risk of those with pre-existing conditions. We must create personal health savings account options with tax credits for those dollars saved and spent on healthcare.

4) National Sovereignty: *National sovereignty demands supreme, absolute, and uncontrollable power over regulated internal affairs without foreign interference.* Legislators should demand constitutional declarations of war before committing troops or funding, but the United States must not abandon our current commitments in the Middle East or embolden terrorists and put ourselves at risk at home. For the stability of our future at home, we can accept no outcome other than speedy victory. We should not support or compromise with socialist tyrants like Castro, Chavez, or Ahmadinejad. The War on Terror is the central national security challenge of our time. We must have a military force with superior strength and readiness to deter all threats to our national security, and deter all threats to the safety and freedom of our citizens. Our military must be equipped with the best weapons and intelligence possible. Placement of our troops under any foreign command, including the United Nations or foreign capitals must be strictly opposed.

Fiscal stability depends on secure borders and enforced

immigration laws. Every day, thousands of people cross our borders illegally and undetected. Legislators must promote a much heavier physical deterrent presence on our borders, including military assistance to help the Border Patrol do its job. Amnesty proposals in any form that send a subversive signal that breaking the law is acceptable in this country must be opposed. The Help America Vote Act (HAVA) must be amended to require official photo identification for voting throughout our country. Our legal immigration laws must reflect immigration each year that is consistent with the ability to assimilate into American society without creating ghettos of poverty and crime. America is a nation of immigrants. Immigrants must be ready and willing to become citizens, learn English, develop marketable skills, or learn skills that will enhance their own and our nation's prosperity. New American citizens must be dedicated to liberty, prosperity, and the American way of life.

5) Personal Responsibility: Individual accountability and resourcefulness separate the adult from the child. Maturity is the hallmark of the fully integrated, fully functioning human being. Responsibility goes hand-in-hand with success, achievement, motivation, happiness, and self-actualization. Individuals must realize that no one is coming to the rescue. At the same time, there is very little that you cannot do or have after you accept the notion, "If it's to be, it's up to me!" Reaching goals requires self-discipline and persistence. We must stop making excuses and assigning blame to poverty, lack of parental guidance, or simply society as a whole for people's dysfunction and antisocial behavior, thus discouraging any responsibility for one's actions. Necessity is the mother of invention and in the case of economic solutions, the mother of innovation.

Legislators should adopt reasonable limits on punitive damages and reform product liability laws, commonly called "Tort Reform." Government employees, at any level, should not be allowed to serve in any elected capacity. Participation in legislating and policy making by groups that have everything to gain from being part of that process encourages waste, fraud, and abuse.

The system can no longer be a cash cow for other government

programs. The government looted twenty-five trillion dollars from the Social Security system, while adding welfare programs to a system intended to provide a supplemental pension for retirement. If politicians do nothing about Social Security and Medicare, America's children and grandchildren will not see a dime from them, and they will inherit an unmanageable financial burden. The inevitable crash will require great changes. Those now depending, or soon to be dependent, on Social Security must be protected.

When Newt Gingrich introduced the *Contract with America* six weeks before the 1994 Congressional Election, it was signed by all but two Republican members of the House and by all of the Party's non-incumbent Republican congressional candidates. The Contract offered specific legislation and detailed a precise plan. It included key conservative principles of limited government, lower taxes, support for entrepreneurs, as well as tort and welfare reforms. Republicans gained a majority of seats in the 104th Congress. The contract was the *Magna Carta* for that conservative movement victory. We sent an army of neophytes to clean up the legislative cesspool, but when they had stayed awhile, they decided it was a hot tub. This time we must send those seasoned and battle-ready to stand on principles…those who will not compromise those very principles for the "greater good" (whatever that means).

Like the *Contract with America* in 1994, the five principles in the *Call to Liberty* are the application of a clear constitutional path to good governance that can be easily understood by every American citizen. The Constitution is the *Right Angle* to counter the soft-core socialism that is ruining America.

The new coalition of conservatives understands the issues. We know what is at stake and what needs to be done. We have the *right* wind of the Founding Fathers at our back. We have the right to take OUR country back to right constitutional principles, led by the right people. The *Right Angle* for this generation of conservatives is more than Right versus Left. It is right versus wrong. Now is the time to do the right thing.

Please join me.

"I'm sitting in a race car that goes from zero to three
hundred miles an hour in four seconds."

Epilogue

WHAT'S NEXT?

We came through an intense primary winning against all odds, only to be cast immediately, and nearly penniless, into a general election that ramped-up like a racecar from zero to three hundred miles an hour in four seconds.

I WAS FEELING MISERABLE a few days after the November 2010 general election, thinking about Harry Reid serving another six-year term in the U.S. Senate as I read the blog post asserting as fact that division and incompetence within our campaign was to blame for our loss.[222] (It was the first of many slanders by opportunists claiming to be insiders and hoping to make some easy money or a name for themselves with little regard for truth.) Then the phone rang. It was Jeri.

"Sharron, you have to say something! You have to defend us! Who has betrayed you?" Her voice came in short bursts. She was clearly exhausted. We were all exhausted after nearly two years of campaigning. The schedules were grueling, the scrutiny intense, and the criticism unfair and biased. The fatigue of constant attacks had left us all wondering if there was someone inside the campaign sent to sabotage us.

We came through an intense primary win against all odds to be cast immediately, and nearly penniless, into a general election that ramped up like a racecar, from zero to three hundred miles an hour in 4 seconds. ("The 'G' forces are so extreme that you have to tie your chin down to hold your head up to steer," my friend Bill had explained to me as I sat inside his racecar at his rod and piston factory in Carson City.)

The blog said an anonymous "they" were assigning blame within the campaign for the loss (whoever "they" were). Often I would ask, "Who are those guys?" feeling more like Butch Cassidy than the $14-million candidate that by now had my picture above the fold in many newspapers almost on a daily basis.

"The Left knows you have power, and they are trying to push you out on the fringe so you can't have an impact in the future," my press secretary said as we talked about the article. "You put together a team, a force to be reckoned with, that nearly defeated the most powerful man in the Senate. Harry Reid has been working on this campaign for the last five years. You put it together in less than two years, coming from literally nothing and out of nowhere to put him behind four points on the day of the election."

The Primary Team

Each member of our team had used all their God-given potential and had made sacrifices along the way in bringing their unique talents to the campaign. Campaign Manager, Terry, a cool head from the beginning, was the brains behind the policy development and messaging for my speeches. He encouraged me to speak to the issues from my heart.

"You don't need a teleprompter or to write on your hands. Just tell the truth. People want real representation they can trust." It was good advice, and from that beginning conversation in February of 2009, he helped me put together the team.

Jerry came on as Press Secretary. Jerry knew Nevada and had a good relationship with the local press. He understood media markets and technology. Jerry and I had a long working relationship history and I trusted him with my life.

Will had joined me in 2005 as an intern. He was a political science student with wisdom beyond his years. He took charge of the website and all social media. He understood my stands on the issues and my political record.

Alan, a retired engineer with an eye for details and a stubborn dedication to following the law, served as Treasurer. A conservative, he questioned every dime that was spent and had all the i's dotted and t's crossed before the checks were written.

Paul and Bob came on as Southern Nevada coordinators, and Steve took the reins of the rest of the state. They set up the calendar and scheduling plus transportation, we all called "Driving Miss Daisy."

As we worked together over the next fourteen months, I discovered the hidden talents of each one. The campaign expanded as we added volunteers and vendors. The army grew in zeal and conviction, and it was contagious. We drew people who had never been involved in politics but realized that they needed to become active. They put shoe leather to the challenge that freedom came at the cost of constant vigilance. They knew the Constitution was a contract of liberty. Many of them, like Terry, a heroic Vietnam Veteran, knew what it meant to defend the Constitution with their lives. They also brought a healthy cynicism about all things originating in Washington, D.C. Nevadans are used to an over-intrusive and regulating federal government. They were ready to elect someone who embraced their Tenth Amendment values of independence.

That was the magic of "41 to Angle." A badge of honor I wore for standing alone (There are forty-two members in the Nevada State Assembly.) and voting on principle against unconstitutional laws, poor public policy, and tax and fee increases so many times that my reputation was legendary among my friends and my enemies.

"All we need for a good campaign is a good candidate, a good message, a good plan, and some money," Terry said. We had everything but the money. At every event, at every meet and greet, on every talk show I made the following plea, "Harry Reid has twenty-five million dollars; I need a million people with twenty-five dollars." Phyllis was in charge of the "lick and stickers," volunteers that gathered every Wednesday in my Northwest Reno home to send direct mail with the same message. It was slow at first, but people across the nation responded.

We hired a company to nationalize our direct mail. We engaged an escrow company to work with Alan, who was skeptical at first because they had a Washington, D.C. address. I called donors in Massachusetts, New Jersey, New York, Florida, and Texas, and was touched by their humbling response, "We believe in you. We are praying for you."

I set up a national prayer team.

We worked the plan all over the state. We had no buses, no entourage, no banners, or four-color printed mailings. Kathi joined the team in Las Vegas, bringing terrific skills of organization and team-building from her experience in marketing. She coordinated and focused numerous volunteers' talents and life experience in small business and the corporate world. Everyone brought themselves, their families, and their personal resources to the campaign.

God Shows Up

We had the resources, but we needed a miracle! I woke April 5th, the morning before our weekly team conference call, with a great urgency on my heart to speak to *Him*. I learned a long time ago that I know only two things for sure. There is a God, and I am not Him.

I prayed, and God showed up! In a series of events that followed, the campaign accelerated to win the primary election.

That same afternoon Jerry called, "Mark Levin wants you on his show April 16th." To my great surprise and honor, during that interview Mark Levin endorsed me. Jerry told me later that it was the first time since he had known me that I was at a loss for words during an interview.

On Friday, April 9th, Larry at Gun Owners of America called me. "Sharron, I'm going to be on Reno talk radio talking about Harry Reid's awful record on the Second Amendment in about an hour. The show host doesn't know we're going to endorse you on the show, but I wanted you to know."

Monday, April 12th a friend at the Tea Party Express called. "I begged them to let me call you and tell you," she was breathless. "We want you to come to Washington, D.C., April 15th so we can endorse you, but you can't tell anyone," she continued. I was stunned. I knew this was big, and I was ready to go. The news leaked out but not from our campaign.

I toured with the Tea Party Express bus across Nevada. When the crowds got bigger, more candidates demanded the spotlight, and I had to take my place in line. The biggest Nevada TEA Party event attracted a crowd of over thirty-thousand enthusiastic patriots. I rode into Searchlight, Nevada, Harry Reid's hometown, on the back of a Harley Davidson Road King with Leo, CT and the bikers. We knew it was our only way through the six-mile traffic jam. I was glad for the leathers I wore when the cold wind blasted us with sand because the event was held in the gravel pit. I stood in the back of a crowd behind a rope as they escorted Sarah Palin in to speak. I worked the crowd and waited for my chance to speak two hours later.

April 13th a call came from my friend Paul. "Sharron, Phyllis is going to endorse you." The Eagle Forum endorsement solidified the social conservatives.

On April 14th, someone who works closely with the Club for Growth called. "We've been talking about you, and it looks promising." The Club for Growth endorsed immediately after the TEA Party Express.

All those endorsements in the same two-week period were the miracle we needed.

Adding to the Team

The polls rocketed me to second place. A week before the primary, we all came together in my kitchen and watched the drama play out. On primary election night we had a party in Reno and then in Las Vegas. When we arrived at Las Vegas McCarran Airport, I was winning at forty percent. I was overwhelmed. My team was overwhelmed.

The night of the primary win, we did not bask on our laurels. Terry called the team together, and we began to put into practice our plan to win the general election against Harry Reid. After all, that was the reason for running. The people had confidence in us, and we had the momentum to raise funds.

"We have to go to Washington, D.C. to get their help," Terry said. "We're going to need professionals to take on the Reid machine." I knew Terry was worried about bringing the D.C. folks into the campaign because of the distrust in our base of Washington, D.C. insiders. I also knew that he was worried about his own abilities. He had led men in battle in Vietnam; he had been the CFO for private businesses; he had served in public office; and he had worked on campaigns as well as in field operations for a Senator. None of us, even those in D.C., had ever run a multimillion-dollar campaign like this one.

Terry is a fearless competitor and told me, "Once you've seen the 'beast' you have no fear." He was referring to his brushes with death in Vietnam, but I knew what he meant. After my son was born in April of 1976, I had a pain in my side that at first I thought was a pulled muscle from doing cartwheels with my three-and-half year old daughter. When the pain increased, I started going to doctors. Each one assured me that there was nothing physically wrong. By December, the pain was so intense that I tied my right arm to my side with a brace my brother had used for his broken collarbone. When I was no longer able to feel the difference between hot and cold or sharp and dull in my legs, my mother-in-law insisted I see a neurologist.

Those were the days before referrals and insurance provider lists. After a twenty-minute examination, the doctor told me he was going to do surgery, and he immediately admitted me to the hospital. He did not have a diagnosis, but he said there was something seriously wrong and I should "get my affairs in order." By the end of a series of tests, he knew that I had no spinal fluid below a point between my shoulder blades. He listed me as a paraplegic and scheduled an exploratory surgery. The prognosis was a fifty-percent chance of living through the surgery and a twenty-percent chance of ever walking again. Ted and I talked about how he would raise our children alone, that I wanted him to remarry, and because of my new faith in Jesus, I was not afraid to die. During the surgery, the doctor removed a benign tumor from my spinal cord hidden inside my spinal column where none of the medical technology of the day was able to detect it. Eight days later, I walked out of the hospital as the staff wept, calling me a miracle. The surgeon said I would never lift over twenty-five pounds, but a decade later, I won three NASA (Natural Athletes Strength Association) statewide weight-lifting trophies in bench, squat and dead lift. I still work-out three to five times a week.

I was born to a time of medical advancement that saved my life. Longer life is a gift of value to be used for God, my family, and my country. I value every moment of every day, and I try not to waste any. I had seen my own mortality, and now I am fearless, just as Terry said.

Our first stop was a fundraiser in New York City, and I was on national television with Sean Hannity. It catapulted me into instant celebrity. I was dismayed by the reaction of the press and the worldwide fascination with me. Jerry was getting over a hundred calls a day from the press asking for interviews. It was like drinking water from a fire hose. I was constantly aware that we had only a short time to convince the electorate to vote for me and I was impatient over the loss of valuable time.

Yet much of the press focus was not on issues but "buzz." Some came to make their name on the national scene by trying to capture the footage that would launch their careers onto the national stage. I spent a day with one reporter who got a call near the end of the interview. He exclaimed, "I've made it big. I just got a call from CNN and MSNBC. They want all my footage."

Others were embarrassed that a primary winner phenomena had caught them by surprise. Even after the 2010 election, they were determined to be first with the story, regardless of the fact that it was pure conjecture.

Some ideologically driven press personnel clearly supported Harry Reid and promoted the Progressive Left agenda. A rare few were professionally interested in reporting news, not sensationalism. I respected them and still do.

My first encounter with the press in D.C. was outside a Republican Senate lunch. In my packed schedule for the day, no one from the press had made an appointment, yet nearly fifty media people crowded to take pictures and shout questions as I left the luncheon. I smiled, waved, declined to interview because of my schedule and got into the third floor elevator. Reporters raced one another down the stairs, and as I exited on the first floor, equipment flew across the floor in front of me. They rushed me as I entered a waiting vehicle. The story that day was "Angle Runs from the Press." From that moment when some abandoned professionalism for the sensational spin on a very large stage, other opportunists later made deliberate attempts to capture me leaving events.

Our focus had to be, and was always, on winning the Senate seat and removing Harry Reid as Senate Majority Leader. Celebrity would not overcome major hurdles. Harry Reid said he had been campaigning for the past five years. Harry had access to more money than I did, and claimed that he had a war chest of twenty-five million dollars. Harry had friendly press who sometimes acted like they were filming a Hollywood political propaganda documentary. Harry was on television and radio in commercials, blasting away at me from the day after the primary. Harry had a seasoned team in place. Harry had spies. Harry had the machine. The race would be close. Were there enough people in Nevada on our side?

We expanded the team to thirty. We hired six from other states with networks in Washington, D.C. We set up a campaign office in Reno and three offices in Las Vegas and depended on Republican county offices in the other fifteen counties to help with the get out the vote efforts (GOTV). Several dynamic young people and life-experienced veterans joined the team as fundraisers. Some were communicators and responders to the cynical, liberal media, while others helped connect us to their friends and resources across the country. It took us a month to accelerate from a staff of seven and a budget of $1.5 million, to over thirty employees and a nearly $30 million venture, more than any other Senate campaign in the country. At first, the press and some local Republicans criticized the team, but when the money flowed, the commercials went up, and pollsters put us on top, that criticism stopped.

Hidden Challenges

I first became aware there was such a thing as 'campaign spies' when, during the primary, a young woman with a camera (Sue Lowden called her "the Reid tracker") captured Sue in a candid moment that developed into "chickens for check-ups." From there, press and the Left wing television shows grabbed these sound bites and distorted them to distract the voters from the issues, acting more like paparazzi than professional journalists.

The same thing happened in our campaign in the primary when a specific $10,500 request that went to over two-hundred prayer warriors appeared as part of an article claiming that my campaign was "desperate." The publication of the contribution request actually backfired against the press and helped our campaign! God answered our needs and our prayer, and I thanked the reporter for having the courage to publish my request in the largest newspaper in Nevada. However, the second time that a portion of my prayer request was twisted on a national blog, Jerry became concerned. I discontinued the prayer chain knowing God would impress hearts with our needs without our having to ask. From that moment, we realized that every single word I uttered and every communication inside or from the campaign was going to be closely scrutinized and potentially twisted and used against us.

We were undeterred, and God continued to be a strong presence throughout the campaign. Reports hailed me as the fourteen million dollar woman for fundraising efforts in the third quarter. The people had heard my pleas on talk radio, and ninety-four percent of that money came from donations of less than one hundred dollars. People were giving of their substance, not their excess. People from all over the nation were engaged in the race.

"You seem to be made out of Reagan's Teflon," a volunteer commented as the verbal assaults from Harry Reid and the press bombarded us. The poll numbers put us routinely in the winner's circle.

Perhaps the most surprising victory for me was the October 14 debate. My coach told me, "Just deliver the opener and closer, and try to get four good jabs in as sound bites for the press."

"Man up, Harry Reid," was born.

I learned the hard way that it is not against Nevada law for a person to tape a meeting conversation without another's knowledge and then to release such tapes publicly. A meeting that I attended at the request of another person, which was described to me as being a private meeting—and which I *believed* was a private conversation—was secretly taped and then given to the press. A negative press frenzy ensued but ironically, people called our office and said, "It's good to know that Sharron says the same things in private that she says in public."

It was well known that my major primary election opponent had been the Washington, D.C. favorite, but after I won the primary, I had the support of national, as well as Nevada, Republicans. Some of the Nevada Republicans who rallied to my support tried to persuade those involved with "Republicans for Reid" to change course and join our cause. In some cases, these pleas were successful, and we were largely able to unify our party.

In other cases, there was not only a fear of Reid retribution, but there was also a desire for "rewards" that Harry Reid—or any incumbent—can provide to supporters. Just after Reid won the election, the editor and publisher of the largest Las Vegas newspaper were released after twenty-nine year careers. Coincidentally they had courageously, and publicly supported me.

On the "pay back your friends" side of the ledger, during the lame duck congressional session in November-December 2010, Reid pushed Internet gaming legislation for the casinos, the DREAM act for illegal aliens, the repeal of Don't Ask Don't Tell for the gay-lesbian community, and an Omnibus Bill full of earmarks as paybacks for favors during the campaign.

The Truth about the General Election

"Just because it is factual doesn't make it truth," a woman warned a class she was teaching on being careful when talking to the press. "For instance, we have a woman on the payroll that is seen frequently with known criminals and has been in jail recently. She has fresh needle marks on her arms and she has been bringing a white substance across state lines. What do you think we should do with her?"

The group agreed based on the facts, fire the woman and tell her to get help.

"You reacted to the 'spin'," she said. The class was puzzled. "Here is the truth. In my job, I frequently go to the jail to counsel known criminals. I have a rare blood type so I give blood once a month, explaining the needle punctures. I like fresh whole milk so I go to a friend's farm in California to get it." She smiled. "You see I told you the facts but it wasn't the truth."

In campaign postmortems, every pundit and consultant has a theory about what went wrong. Every reporter has some facts. There are even those claiming to be inside the campaign, selling the "real" story for financial enrichment and celebrity. The numbers show what went right. I defeated Reid by 19,677 or eight percent in the counties outside of Clark County.[223] Las Vegas is in Clark County, a county that did not know me before this election and a county where the most mischief was reported.

Election night I called Harry Reid to congratulate him on his victory. We talked a little about the campaign, and I told him I would be praying for him to represent the Constitution and the desires of Nevada and the country. It lasted about three or four minutes, and there was no animosity.

Our exhausted, disappointed, and sometimes complaining team had done their best. We fired no one and assigned no blame. The campaign offices were closed, signs were removed, equipment was sold, and the debt was paid. Did we make mistakes? I am sure we did. Do we have regrets? As the song goes, "too few to mention." Could someone else have defeated Harry Reid? The deck is stacked against any primary winner challenging an incumbent opponent with starting advantage, a multi-million dollar war chest, no primary election race, negative tactics, and get-out-the-vote machinery. In the last seventy years, only one Senate Majority leader has been defeated, and that happened only after the successful challenger ran back-to-back Senate races in the state.

What's next for me? Only God knows.

We do know that the solutions for our nation are as simple as cut back on the spending, pay back the debt and take our country back to constitutional principles. And I know that my decades-long efforts to bring the voice of the people back to government did not end with the general election in 2010.

We enjoyed some amazing victories: winning the primary, energizing tens of thousands of citizens not only in Nevada but also across the nation, and setting records with fundraising and grassroots support. I could not be prouder of the efforts we made and the successes we had.

Of course, losing the general election was disappointing and painful.

After all my scars from my previous political fights when standing on principle as a state legislator and bumping up against the establishment, I did not think it was possible to be surprised at the power of certain forces in Nevada who are determined to stop the changes we so badly need in our state and our country.

There were so many unforeseen challenges in trying to bring down the most powerful Senator in America. Nothing was more startling than to realize that in the Nevada Senate race, there was an active, well-organized, well-funded, and concerted effort between and among the Reid campaign, the Democratic Party, the labor unions *and* some casino owners and managers to ensure a Reid victory. On Election Day, my campaign attorney filed a complaint with the U.S. Department of Justice when we learned through a whistleblower of the collusion and the scheme that was in place to harass and intimidate low-level casino workers to vote for Harry Reid. We can only hope that the Department of Justice will investigate and do its job and if laws were broken, that those responsible are held accountable.

Like Reagan and Lincoln after their losses, I have chosen to focus on the great accomplishments we achieved, looking *forward* to the *next* opportunities. We must never grow tired or weary of doing our duty as citizens. Those who are taking our country down the road to destruction are hoping we will stop trying, that we will decide we can never win and that we will just go home and watch television.

Our response must be this: yes, we have been through a skirmish but we can't quit...and we *won't* quit! We must not grow tired of doing the right thing. Americans are resilient and full of "can do" optimism. We can make a difference. We can change the direction of this country if we never, never, never give up.

In my concession speech—from my heart not from notes or a teleprompter—I reminded those in the room, as well as a nation of supporters, of our victories and our thankfulness to God. We have awakened a silent majority, and we must not go back to sleep. We will not go back to sleep.

Tomorrow is another day for us to reclaim our country, and if we approach that task from the *right* angle, with God's help, we *will* succeed.

End Notes

Introduction by Lee Carey

1. John L. Smith *Angle Possesses Conservative Cred* Las Vegas Review Journal November 10, 2009

Foreword

2. Anjeanette Damon *Sen. Reid speaks about his son, re-election campaign* Reno Gazette Journal August 30, 2009,
3. Alan Gomez *Schumer: Tea Party GOP's proposed cuts are 'extreme'* USA TODAY/Washington 3/30/11

Chapter One—Above the Fold

4. Proverbs 27:6 Good News Bible Today's English Version

Chapter Two—Reagan Remains Relevant

5. Speech by Ronald Reagan 1975 *Let Them Go Their Way* Conservative Political Action Second Annual Conference, 3/1/75
6. Ibid.
7. Reno Gazette Journal Editorial Board interview 1/16/08 featured in the Huffington Post
8. See note 5 above.
9. The Daily Iowan *Hillary Clinton Barack Obama campaign ad* December 21, 2007
10. See note 5 above.
11. See note 5 above.
12. Las Vegas Review-Journal, *NORM: Reid says he was Obama whisperer,* June 7, 2009
13. See note 5 above.
14. Peter Roff, *California Rejects Higher Taxes—Obama, Reid and Pelosi Should Take Note* Thomas Jefferson Street blog May 20, 2009
15. See note 5 above.

16. See note 5 above.
17. See note 5 above.
18. Brandon Hall, *Prominent Nevadans Launch "Republicans For Reid"* press release for Harry Reid Las Vegas Gleaner June 3, 2009
19. Steve Tretrault, *GOP rides Reid on rail line funding in stimulus bill* Stephens Washington Bureau Las Vegas Review-Journal February12, 2009
20. J. Patrick Coolican, *Sig Rogich, influential in the GOP, endorses Reid* Las Vegas Sun February 26, 2009
21. Francis McCabe, *High-speed Rail Projects: Reid's switch draws fi re Maglev supporter says Senator sought favor with Rogich* Las Vegas Review-Journal February 28, 2009
22. http://en.wikipedia.org/wiki/ Political_scandals_of_the_United_States
23. See note 5 above.

Chapter Three—Pay Bucks for Power The Politics of Corruption

24. John Adams *Address to the Military October 11, 1798*
25. Michelle Malkin *The Democrat culture of corruption* Creators Syndicate Copyright 2008
26. Jonah Goldberg *Democrats wallow in a 'culture of corruption'Meet the new political bosses, worse than the old political bosses.* Los Angeles Times May 05, 2009
27. Ed Morrissey *Harry Reid And The Culture Of Corruption* Sphere It October 11, 2006, (See-total DC politician–ignorant, corrupt, and licentious.)
28. George Washington,October 27, 1789,letter to the Residents of Boston,
29. Thomas Jefferson 1787, letter to William S. Smith
30. 8newsnow.com posted January 11, 2011,*Sharron Angle Releases Statement on Arizona Shooting*
31. Samuel AdamsOctober 4, 1790,Letter to John Adams
32. Thomas Jefferson 1791 Opinion on National Bank
33. Thomas Jefferson, prospectus for his translation of Destutt de Tracy's *Treatise on Political Economy*
34. Thomas Jefferson 1820, to Albert Gallatin
35. James Madison, Federalist No. 57
36. Laurence J. Kotlikoff *The Case for the 'FairTax'* The Wall Street Journal March 7, 2005,

37. *The Sixteenth Amendment* to the U.S. Constitution ratified February 3, 1913

38. Frank Chodorov *The Income Tax:Root of all Evil* Introduction by J. Bracken Lee Governor of Utah The Devin-Adair Company New York, 1954 Online edition © 2002 The Ludwig von Mises Institute

39. John Linder *The Fair Tax Book* by Neal Boorst and Congressman John Linder pg. xi of the forward

40. Laurence J. Kotlikoff *Averting America's Bankruptcy with a New New Deal* by Laurence J. Kotlikoff Professor of Economics, Boston University Published in *The Economists' Voice* February 2006 Revised, March 13, 2007

41. See note 36 above.

42. Ken Dilanian *Obama, Clinton Helped Contributors Secure Special Tax Breaks* Thursday, February 28, 2008

43. David Freddoso *Trial lawyers' gun for their own loophole* Washington Examiner August 17, 2009:

Chapter Four—Small Business the Lifeblood of America

44. James Truslow Adam *Epic of America* 1931

45. WordNet (r) 2.1 (2005)

46. Jan Helfield *YouTube Paying income tax in America is Voluntary* Harry Reid in an interview with Jan Helfield April 1, 2008 http://www.youtube.com/watch?v=R7mRSI8yWwg

47. *Is Federal Income Tax Constitutional? Tax Protesters Say Government Cannot Collect Income Tax* June 18, 2007 WMUR 9 New Hampshire http://www.wmur.com/news/13523407/detail.html

48. *Ibid.*

49. From The Office of Public Affairs April 15, 2002 PO-2088 Treasury Releases *First in Series of Tax Simplification Proposals First Release Proposes Single Definition of Child*

50. Mark Twain 1866

51. Daniel Henninger *Obama's America: Too Fat to Fail The U.S. gets Old Economy on dialysis.* The Wall Street Journal June 4, 2009

52. Michael Buettner *GM is dropping Petersburg dealer* The Progress-Index July 2, 2009

53. Jamie LaReau *GM offers dealers up to $1 million to wind down stores* Automotive News June 3, 2009

54. Paragraph 9 (f) *GM Dealer sales and Service Agreement/ Participation Agreement* June1, 2009 found on web at http://

images.thetruthaboutcars.com/2009/06/original-gm-participation-agreement.pdf

55. Ross Edwards *GM Offers Closing Dealers Up to $1 Million* Thursday, Jun 04 2009 12:50

56. *GM trying to strong-arm Florida dealers, McCollum says* http://tampabay.bizjournals.com/tamp...html?

57. See note 52 above.

58. Roy Spencer *Climate Confusion: How Global Warming Hysteria Leads to Bad Science, Pandering Politicians and Misguided Policies that Hurt the Poor*

59. Richard Fleischer *Soylent Green* 1973 science fiction film directed by Richard Fleischer. Staring Charlton Heston, A futuristic look at the projected consequences of pollution, overpopulation, depleted resources, poverty, dying oceans, and a hot climate due to the greenhouse effect. Soylent Green is a processed food produced from the corpses of euthanasia volunteers. Based on *Make Room! Make Room!* the 1966 science fiction novel by Harry Harrison

60. Ronald Reagan 1992 at his last Republican National Convention

61. See note 51 above.

62. Ronald Reagan March 1983 proclamation on Small Business Week

63. Ronald Reagan June 1983 speech

64. Ronald Reagan speech to the joint session of the Alabama state legislature in March 1982

65. Ronald Reagan April 1982 speech before the U.S. Chamber of Commerce

66. Deuteronomy 12:23 *Spirit Filled life Bible New King James Version* General Editor Jack W. Hayford, Litt.D. 1991

Chapter Five—Who is Ruining the Economy?

67. Rose D. Friedman, Milton Friedman *Two Lucky People: Memoirs* . University of Chicago Press. 1998 p.605)

68. David L. Weimer *The political economy of property rights* , published in The Political Economy of Property Rights, Cambridge University Press,1997, p.8-9

69. Saul D. Alinsky *Rules for Radicals* New York Vintage 1971

70. Murray N. Rothbard *The Case Against the Fed* Ludwig von Mises Institute, 1994, p. 42

71. George F. Smith *Auditing the Fed will Audit the State* Mises Daily Posted on 7/1/2009 12:00:00 AM

72. *China 'worried' about U.S. Treasury holdings Premier Wen: U.S. must honor its words and ensure safety of China's assets* MSNBC Associated Press updated 11:29 a.m. PT, Fri., March. 13, 2009

73. Tania Branigan *"China is Worried about its US Assets, Says Premier,"* Guardian, March 13, 2009

74. First Inaugural Address of Ronald Reagan Tuesday, January 20, 1981

75. Ronald Reagan *Remarks to Representatives of the Future Farmers of America* July 28, 1988

76. Ronald Reagan *Address to the Nation on Federal Tax Reduction Legislation* July 27, 1981

Chapter Six—Universal Healthcare for Everyone but Harry, Barry, and Nancy

77. T.J.Ott Personal account of injury sustained in the battle of Makin Island November 19, 1943

78. *Of NICE and Men* The Wall street Journal Opinion A14 Tuesday July 7, 2009

79. *ABC News Townhall Special*, June 25, 2009

80. Betsy McCaughey *Obama's Health Rationer-in-Chief* The Wall Street Journal August 27, 2009

81. The second paragraph of the Declaration of Independence

82. Rep. John Campbell*A Right to Health Care?* Orange County Register July 12, 2009

83. Gerald Ford Address to Congress, August 12, 1974. The quote attributed to Thomas Jefferson and Davey Crockett

84. Govind Persad, Alan Wertheimer, Ezekiel J Emanuel *Principles for allocation of scarce medical interventions* The Lancet January 31,2009

85. Ezekiel J. Emanuel *Where Civic Republicanism and Deliberative Democracy Meet* Source: The Hastings Center Report, Vol. 26, No. 6, In Search of the Good Society: The Work of Daniel Callahan (Nov.—Dec., 1996), pp. 12-14 Published by: The Hastings Center Stable URL: http://www.jstor.org/stable/3528746

86. Susan Harding *Letter noting assisted suicide raises questions for Barbara Wagner* Story Published: Jul 30, 2008 at 6:30 PM PDT KATU Web Staff http://www.katu.com/news/26119539.html

87. 111TH CONGRESS 1ST SESSION H. R. 3200 To provide affordable, quality health care for all Americans and reduce the growth in health care spending, and for other purposes. IN THE

HOUSE OF REPRESENTATIVES JULY 14, 2009 http://frwebgate.access.gpo.gov/cgi-bin/getdoc.cgi?dbname=111_cong_bills&docid=f:h3200ih.pdf

88. Congressman Ed Royce *Public Option Will Kill Off Competition* Op-ed: Investor's Business Daily, July 13,2009 http://www.royce.house.gov/News/DocumentSingle.aspx?DocumentID=136969

89. F. A. Hayek, *The Constitution of Liberty,* University of Chicago Press1960

90. Washington Post, December 21, 2006, *Federal Subsidies Turn Farms Into Big Business"*

91. Douglas Belkin *Grassley Airs Doubts About Health Bill* The Wall Street Journal August 25, 2009

92. Jennifer Robison *Cost of Autism Care Mandate Debated* Las Vegas Review Journal October 7, 2010

93. Dioone Searcey and Jacob Goldstein *Health Care's Intangible Cost: Legal Liability* The Wall Street Journal September 3, 2009

Chapter Seven—Science Fiction Is Not Science

94. Montgomery, W.D. *Markets in Licenses and Efficient Pollution Control Programs* Journal of Economic Theory 5 (Dec 1972):395-418

95. The Wall Street Journal REVIEW & OUTLOOK March 9, 2009 *Who Pays for Cap and Trade? Hint: They were promised a tax cut during the Obama campaign* page A18

96. Alexander Bolton *Reid sees global warming debate as a big headache* The Hill Posted: 05/01/09 02:22 PM [ET]

97. The Wall Street Journal June 6, 2009,*'Worse Than Fiction'* page A12

98. Energy Supply and Use, Global Climate Change Impacts the United States, United State Global Change Research Project, 2008)

99. Airman 1st Class Ryan Whitney *Nellis activates Nations largest PV Array* Nellis AFB Public Affairs 12/18/2007

100. Eric Rosenbloom *A Problem With Wind Power* www.aweo.org

101. The Associated Press, *Wind farm plan opposed Northern Nevada residents say tourism would be affected* Las Vegas Review-Journal February 21, 2009

102. *Electricity from: Geothermal Energy* 2000 Pace University, White Plains, New York

103. Kathleen Moore *World: Amid Food Crisis, Opposition To Biofuels Grows* April 17, 2008 Radio Free Europe Radio Liberty

104. Ibid.

105. William M. Welch *Some rethinking nuke opposition* , USA TODAY Updated 3/23/2007 11:36 AM

106. *US Nuclear Utilities question waste fees* July 10,2009 World Nuclear News

107. Leslie Paige *Pulling The Plug on Yucca Mountain—A New Mountain of Waste* February 26, 2010 Wastewatcher Citizens Against Government Waste

108. Pete Fowler*Reid jubilant with Majority Leader prospect* The Ely Times November 10, 2006

109. *Gibbons to Reid: "Put Up or Shut Up" About Yucca* KLAS Las Vegas August 2, 2009 23:35 PM PDT

110. Marlene Lang *Scientific American examines spent nuclear fuel Nuclear Fuel: A Trash Heap Deadly for 250,000 Years, or a Renewable Energy Source?* Tue, 02/24/2009 16:39

111. *Processing of Used Nuclear Fuel* World Nuclear Association information paper March 2009

112. Peter Baker and Dafna Linzer *Nuclear Energy Plan Would Use Spent Fuel* Washington Post Thursday, January 26, 2006; Page A01

113. *Mixed Oxide (MOX) Fuel* World Nuclear Association information paper March 2009

114. See note 110 above.

115. Alan Chamberlain *Affordable energy in question* Reno Gazette Journal May 24, 2009

Chapter Eight—Over the Constitutional Fence

116. Robert Frost *Mending Wall* North of Boston second collection of poetry 1914

117. State of Nevada Certificate of Election

118. The Seventh Day Nevada State Senate Daily Journal Monday July 1, 2003

119. Benjamin Franklin Constitutional Convention of 1787 final day of deliberation in the notes of Dr. James McHenry, Maryland convention delegate

120. Vin Suprynowicz VIN SUPRYNOWICZ: *'It's a personnel matter'* Las Vegas Review-Journal November 23, 2003

121. Dr. John Eastman Institute Appeals to U.S. Supreme Court in Nevada Taxpayer Case Posted October 20, 2004 http://www.claremont.org/projects/pageid.1820/default.asp

122. http://openjurist.org/541/us/957/angle-nevada-state-assembly-member-et-al-v-guinn-governor-of-nevada-et-al

123. Secretary of State letter qualifying Nevada Property Tax Restraint Initiative for the November 4, 2008 ballot.

124. The Wall Street Journal on August 5, 2008 *Extracurricular Politics*

125. Sandra Chereb *PETITIONS: Lawsuit opposes initiative rules Group says lawmakers' limits violate Constitution* The Associated Press Las Vegas Review-Journal September 19, 2008 http://www.lvrj.com/news/28644124.html

126. Bill Fiedrich Speech before the Nevada State Legislature February 17, 2005

127. Russell M. Rowe *Legislature Adopts Property Tax Relief, but is it Constitutional?* COMMUNIQUÉ Official Publication of the Clark County Bar Association August 2005 pg. 28 http://kummerkaempfer.org/04_News/communique/08_05_taxrelief_rowe.pdf

128. Chris Rizo *Nevada justices deal win to property tax initiative* Legal Newsline Thursday July 17, 2008 http://www.legalnewsline.com/news/214205-nevada-justices-deal-win-to-property-tax-initiative

129. Lexinom *Hard Data Supporting Fraudulent Activity in Nevada Election* Free Republic November 3, 2010

130. Paul Joseph Watson *Did Harry Reid Steal Nevada* Dark Politricks November 3, 2010

131. Mark Whittington *Ballot Machine Malfunctions Reported in Nevada, North Carolina* Associated Content October 26, 2010

132. Jim Hoft *Breaking: Suspect Voting Machines in Nevada are Serviced by SEIU* Right Network October 26, 2010

133. Brad Friedman *Hacking Harry Reid (or Sharron's Angle)* Truthout October 26, 2010

134. Mark Hemingway *Nevada Voting Machines Automatically Checking Harry Reid's name; Voting Machine Technicians are SEIU members* The Washington Examiner October 25,2010

135. Hans A. von Spakovsky *E-mail Shows Illegal Activity in Reid's Campaign* The Washington Examiner November 3, 2010

136. Elizabeth Crum *Harrah's Bosses Put Squeeze on Employees to Vote in Pro-Reid Effort* National Review Online November 2, 2010

137. Jeff German *GOP Alleged Harrah's 'intimidated' 'coerced' Employees into Voting; No Employee Complaints* Las Vegas Legal News November 3, 2010

138. Nevada Secretary of State website U.S. Senate Statewide Results
139. News Blaze *ALIPAC Issues Major Election Fraud Alert* November 6, 2010
140. Written by moveonreid November 9, 2010 at 11:10 pm http:// moveonreid.wordpress.com/2010/11/09/did-harry-reid-steal-nevada-the-evidence-and-how-you-can-help…
141. Warren Stewart Around the States *Nevada Congressional Candidate To Challenge Primary Election Results* VoteTrustUSA August 28, 2006http://www.votetrustusa.org/index.php?option=com_content&task=view&id=1713&Itemid=113http://www.standingforvoters.org/recent.html
142. Miriam Jordan *Illegal Immigration from Mexico Hits Lowest Level in Decade* The Wall Street Journal July 23,2009
143. Borderland Beat *Narco Banner in Zacatecas* January 17, 2011
144. Las Vegas Sun November 6, 2010, *Police identify 3 arrested in death of Eldorado High teacher*
145. Emma Lazarus *The New Colossus* Statue of Liberty National Monument Emma Lazarus' Poem
146. John 10:1 Good News Bible Today's English Version 1976
147. AMENDMENT XIV *Passed by Congress June 13, 1866. Ratified July 9, 1868.* Article I Section 1
148. Michael Sandler *Toward a More Perfect Definition of 'Citizen'* In Focus, February 13, 2006, CQ Staff Congressional Quarterly's Weekly pg.388
149. Charles Dickens *Oliver Twist* chapter 51
150. See note 148 above.
151. Vincent Gioia *Illegal Immigration: Arizona and Oklahoma Solutions* National Ledger February 22, 2008
152. Article 2 section 3 *The Constitution of the United States of America* September 17, 1787
153. Edwin Meese III *Reagan Would Not Repeat Amnesty Mistake* Human Events December 13, 2006
154. Frosty Woolridge *Fraud & Abuse: Earned Income Tax Credit By Unlawful Immigrants* NewsWithViews June 29, 20
155. Jim Cunningham *Will illegal immigrants take the stimulus jobs?*, by San Francisco Examiner January 25, 2009 DC Corporate Ethics Examiner
156. Julie Hirschfeld Davis *Stimulus aids illegal immigrants* Hill Republican January 29 12:02 Associated Press

157. Rush Limbaugh *The Role of Government is to Secure Our Liberty, Not to Seize It* June 26, 2009 radio show transcript

158. J. David Gowdy *The Roots of Our Constitutional Liberty* by J. David Gowdy, President The Washington, Jefferson & Madison Institute Copyright © 1997: Institute for American Liberty

159. Ibid.

160. George Washington *Farewell Address* September 19, 1796

Chapter Nine—Character is Not Politically Correct

161. *Boxer, the U.S. Senator, Chides Brigadier General for Calling Her 'Ma'am': The feisty California lawmaker reminds an Army brigadier general of her title after he has the apparent gall to call her "ma'am."* FOXNews.com Thursday, June 18, 2009

162. Tammy Bruce *The Death of Right and Wrong* Three Rivers Press 2003

163. Mike Brody *Study: Tall People Earn More Money* Sunday, 12 Jul 2009, 1:38 PM EDT My Fox Atlanta Fox 5 television

164. Martin Luther King, Jr. *"I Have a Dream"* delivered 28 August 1963, at the Lincoln Memorial, Washington, D.C.

165. Chris Matthews February 13, 2008—During MSNBC's live coverage of Tuesday's presidential primary elections

166. David Gelernter, *Drawing Life, Surviving the Unabomber*, Free Press, 1997, p. 95

167. Senator Kay Bailey Hutchinson *Stop Insulting Female Candidates and Start Playing Fair* March 15,2011 I know all about transgressor

168. Don Francisco *Love is Not a Feeling*

169. President Reagan speech at the Berlin *Wall*, Brandenburg Gate

Chapter Ten—Education: The Government Option

170. MINUTES OF THE ASSEMBLY Committee on Education Seventieth Session March 29, 1999 AB 294 sponsored by Assemblywoman Angle Testimony of Robert W. Sweet, Jr., the author of the National Reading Excellence Act,

171. Deborah Carson *So Why Cannot Nevada Johnny Read?* January/ February 2000 Nevada Policy Research Institute Nevada Journal

172. *USA Today* Editorial July 9, 2008, *Our view on literacy: If you can read this ...you can understand why Reading First deserves to live...*

173. Ronald Reagan quoted on KCBS radio in 1972 by Reagan's gubernatorial chief of staff.

174. Troy Senik *Who Killed California?* author of California at the Crossroads: 100 Ideas for the Golden State.

175. James Bovard *Teachers Unions: Are the Schools Run for Them?* Shakedown (Viking, 1995) and Lost Rights: The Destruction of American Liberty St. Martin's, 1994.

176. Daniel J. Cassidy Kids Deserve Choice of Better Schools Monday, May 19, 2008 (Originally published in the Newark Star-Ledger, *7/4/99)*

177. See note 174 above

178. Lisa Snell *Teacher Unions Crush Philanthropy and Volunteerism Michigan rejects $200 million* December 1, 2003 Reason Foundation

179. George A. Clowes *Teacher Union Accused of Tax Evasion NEA tells IRS it spends nothing on political activity* Published In: School Reform News November 2003 Publication date: 11/01/2003 Publisher: The Heartland Institute

Chapter Eleven—Clinging to our Guns and Religion

180. Barack Obama Fundraiser April 6, 2008

181. *The Complete Jefferson* 12 Jun 1823 (p.32)

182. The Second Amendment to the United States Constitution

183. Thomas Jefferson (Author of Declaration of Independence, member Continental Congress, Governor of Virginia, Minister to France, Secretary of State, Vice President, 3rd President)

184. George Mason, delegate to the U.S. Constitutional Convention

185. Richard H. Lee, Additional Letters from the Federal Farmer 53, 1788 p. 32

186. Jefferson's Commonplace Book, 1774-1776, quoting from On Crimes and Punishment by criminologist Cesare Beccaria, 1764

187. letter to Madison 31 July 1788, The Papers of James Madison, Hobson & Rutland, p.11:212

188. Thomas Jefferson Papers p. 334, 1950

189. The Federalist, No. 46, James Madison

190. Thoughts On Defensive War, 1775, Thomas Paine

191. Debate, U.S. House of Representatives, August 17, 1789, Elbridge Gerry

192. State Gazette (Charleston), September 8, 1788

193. Pennsylvania Gazette on February 20, 1788

194. David J. Shestokas *The Obama WBEZ Interview: Breaking Free from the Constitution* Re: WEBZ interview January 18, 2001

195. John Longenecker *How the Repeal of All Gun Laws Will Free America* (Part 2) Sunday, 23 August 2009 00:00

196. Geraldo Rivera *Sheriff Blames Shooting on Political Vitriol from Likes of Sharron Angle* Fox video World News January 11, 2011

197. John McCormack *Obama to Latinos: "Punish" Your "Enemies" In The Voting Booth* October 25,2010 Weekly Standard

198. Michael A. Memoli *GOP Takeover in Congress Would Mean Hand-to-hand Combat Obama Warns* , Tribune Washington Bureau October 7, 2010 Los Angeles Times

199. Jim Hoft *Did Barack Obama Cause the Shootings Yesterday in Tucson* RightNet Media Gateway Pundit January 9, 2011

200. Isaiah 40:22 "It is he that sitteth upon the circle of the earth, and the inhabitants thereof are as grasshoppers; that stretcheth out the heavens as a curtain, and spreadeth them out as a tent to dwell in:"

201. Benjamin Franklin 1787 Constitutional Convention in Philadelphia,

202. Ibid.

203. The First Amendment to the United States Constitution

204. Dan Shippey & Michael Burns *Praise the Lord & Pass the Ammunition* The Breed's Hill Gazette May 2009

205. U.S. Supreme Court *Church of the Holy Trinity v. United States, 143 U.S. 457 (1892)* Argued and submitted January 7, 1892 Decided February 29, 1892 143 U.S. 457 Page 143 U. S. 465 P. 6059, Congressional Record, 48th Cong.

206. The Bible in America Museum 9/11/1777 Houston Baptist University October –December 2003 Vol. 1, Issue 1

207. Alexis de Tocqueville *Democracy in America: Volume II* Chapter 5 1841

208. Steven Ertelt *Pro-Life Group to Continue Ads Targeting Harry Reid Over Abortion, Health Care* LifeNews.com Editor September 21, 2009

209. Ronald Reagan *Abortion and the Conscience of the Nation* 1984

210. *Ronald Reagan, July 12, 1984*

211. President Barack Obama Father's Day speech at Apostolic Church of God June 15, 2008 in Chicago, Illinois.

212. Alexis de Tocqueville *Democracy in America, Volume 2* pg. 333

213. Joel Roberts *Senator Reid On Iraq: "This War Is Lost" Democratic*

Majority Leader Says Troop Buildup Is Not Working Washington, April 20, 2007 CBSNews.com

214. Catherine Herridge *FBI Director: Al Qaeda-Linked Somali Group Planning Attacks on U.S.* FOXNews.com Friday, October 2, 2009

215. Robert Burns *Obama weighing strategies for War* AP Sunday News-Leader

216. Mike Oliver *Excerpt from an e-mail letter to Sarah Palen* October 7, 2009 used with permission from Mike Oliver

217. Alexis de Tocqueville *Democracy in America, Volume 2*

218. Ibid.

219. Ibid.

220. Benjamin Franklin at the signing of the Declaration of Independence July 4, 1776

221. Benjamin Franklin at the Aug. 2 signing of the Declaration in Philadelphia, responding to John Hancock

Epilogue—What's Next?

222. Shira Toeplitz *Angle Campaign Sank Candidate* Politico November 21, 2010

223. Nevada Secretary of State http://www.nvsos.gov/soselectionpages/results/2010STatewideGeneral/ElectionSummary.aspx